CONTENTS

LIST OF ILLUSTRATIONS

LIST OF TABLES

OFFICE WORK CAN BE DANGEROUS TO YOUR HEALTH

CHAPTER 1

OVERVIEW

It is safer and healthier to work in an office than it is to dig in a coal mine or to labor in a steel mill. The air is cleaner and the work less strenuous. The noise is less deafening and the temperature more bearable. But the merit of the comparison ends there, for simply being safer and cleaner than a coal mine doesn't make the office clean or safe.

According to the U.S. Occupational Safety and Health Administration (OSHA), more than 40,000 disabling injuries and 200 safety-related deaths occur in offices each year. Out of the 2,200,000 office workers employed in California, one of the states that has analyzed such data, 12,263 reported a disabling work injury or illness during the first six months of 1978. The 1978 California statistics represented a dramatic increase both in the number of injuries and in the injury rate since 1959, the last time similar data were analyzed. While the number of workers increased by 167 percent, the number of accidents rose by 349 percent. The injuries ranged from strains and sprains to dislocations and hernias; there were even four amputations. And it is important to keep in mind that all these figures are underestimates because so many accidents and injuries go unreported. Does this mean the generally accepted view that offices are "safe" may be incorrect? We think so.

Of course, we do not want to go from one extreme and incorrect perspective on the office to another. The injury rate and the severity of injuries are significantly greater among blue-collar workers than among their office-worker counterparts. Data gathered in 1975–76 from about 80,000 households by the Health Interview Survey, a large health research project run by the U.S. federal government, show a blue-collar injury rate four times greater than the white-collar rate. Among women interviewed, the injury rate was 10.4 per 100 blue-collar workers and 4.7 per 100 office workers. With so many people working in offices, however, even a lower accident rate may take a greater health toll. In fact, there were twice as many accidents among white-collar women as among blue-collar in this survey. Sheer numbers make the difference: more than two-thirds of all paid women workers are employed in offices. When we consider the spiraling numbers of people who spend their working days in an office, it is obvious that the impact on the public's health of even minor office health hazards can be immense.

We can only draw one conclusion: the appearance of safety in the office is deceptive, and yet we are not writing this book primarily about safety. The unbolted partition, the wobbly chair, and the open file drawer are dangers it is necessary to correct, but they are relatively obvious once you know how to look for them. Health hazards from indoor air pollution or poorly designed equipment are different. They tend to be more subtle and are often controversial, even among experts. Your job in itself can be a health hazard if it makes you feel tired, fragmented, and unfulfilled. These health hazards have rarely been studied or even taken into account as office work has become the predominant occupation in North America.

Office work is a wide-ranging term. In today's offices are people whose product is creating or writing, such as engineers, designers, advertising executives, and writers. There are also people who work chiefly with other people, such as social workers. And then there are the large number of office workers who handle only data or other people's words all day, typing, transcribing, or filing. Table 1 shows both the number of people employed in these categories and the Department of Labor's projections regarding their numbers in the next decade.

All this work is associated with its own particular set of stresses and of satisfactions, for the nature of the job affects health and well-being.

TABLE 1. JOBS PEOPLE DO IN THE OFFICE

Listed here are some of the wide variety of occupations held by people who worked in offices in 1978 and a projection made by the U.S. Department of Labor for the year 1990. The 1990 figures were obtained by averaging the Bureau of Labor Statistics' high and low projections for the next decade.

	1978	1990
	(NUMBERS ARE IN THOUSANDS)	
Computer programmers	204	367
Computer systems analysts	185	398
Economists	27	42
Psychologists	78	109
Commercial artists	100	129
Public relations specialists	81	105
Writers, editors, reporters, correspondents	197	287
Accountants, auditors, assessors, appraisers	1,332	1,150
Architects	66	109
Caseworkers	236	344
Employment interviewers	51	91
Lawyers, law clerks, paralegal personnel	438	668
Librarians	130	140
Personnel and labor relations specialists	169	211
Tax examiners, auditors, and preparers	79	111
Travel agents	45	72
Underwriters	70	91
Clerical workers, including adjustment clerks, bank tellers, bookkeepers, cashiers, claims adjusters, claims examiners, clerical supervisors, collectors, credit clerks, welfare eligibility workers, file clerks, general office workers, medical insurance clerks, mail clerks	17,820	23,062
Office machine operators, including billing machine, duplicating machine, and keypunch operators, computer equipment operators	842	1,172

TABLE 1. (cont.)

	1978	1990
	(NUMBERS ARE IN THOUSANDS)	
Clerks, including postal, procurement, payroll, and personnel	1,013	1,245
Receptionists	369	522
Secretaries, stenographers, typists	3,574	4,531
Switchboard operators, receptionists	219	287
Telephone operators	312	395
Ticket agents	49	52

SOURCE: Excerpted from Max L. Carey, "Occupational Employment Growth Through 1990," *Monthly Labor Review,* August 1981, pp. 42–45. Statistics are based on the 1978 Occupational Employment Statistics Survey, conducted every three years by the U.S. Department of Labor, Bureau of Labor Statistics.

However, despite the great occupational differences between an engineer and a data clerk, there are overwhelming similarities in today's office environment. Problems such as poor lighting, poor air quality, poorly designed furniture and equipment, and even long hours at the video display terminal are faced by all office workers in rapidly growing numbers.

The U.S. Department of Labor reports that more than 52 million people worked in offices in 1978 and projects a minimum office population of 65 million and possibly 69 million by 1990. In other words, the majority of all working adults and the vast majority of employed women in the United States will spend at least one-third of their adult lives in an office.

What Is Occupational Disease?

There are many potential hazards to the body and the spirit in the office environment, but when you put them all together you don't come up with a disease called "office-itis," nor is it likely that an easily definable disease analogous to measles or mumps will ever be diagnosed. One reason is that most of the occupational hazards in the office don't make you sick enough fast enough. Unlike work where there is exposure to high concentrations of identifiable poisons, such as lead in a smelter, most office work does not produce a rapid, *acute* onset of symptoms. Rather, the office may house many comparatively modest hazards at relatively low levels. Each hazard may have a slow, subtle, effect, and symptoms may not become noticeable for a long period of time. Furthermore, many ailments may not readily be recognized as job-related because they are commonly occurring ones, such as a backache or an allergy. The slow, insidious onset of symptoms is characteristic of the way in which *chronic* diseases develop.

Another hallmark of chronic disease is that it is often not related to any one factor but rather to an array of causes or "risk factors." Cancer, for example, is a chronic disease that accounts for about 20 percent of all the deaths in the United States and Canada. Cancer takes many years to develop. A cigarette smoker or a welder or an asbestos worker will not develop lung cancer immediately after being exposed to the cancer-causing agents (carcinogens) on the job or in tobacco smoke. Rather, it often requires at least twenty years, and perhaps concurrent exposure to other agents or conditions that "promote" the cancer, for the disease finally to manifest itself.

In general, only a few things are really clear about the causes of chronic diseases. These diseases are complex: many factors contribute to their development. No one understands as much about chronic diseases as many experts would like and often pretend to know. The scientific community has not yet been able to define the perfect diet, exercise regime, or other life-style factor that will guarantee safety from chronic disease development.

One way to understand the factors that can lead to chronic disease is to carry out studies on large numbers of people, usually over the course of several years, to see if particular diseases or disabilities are developing among them in unusual patterns. If we are interested in learning whether a certain group of workers are at greater risk for developing cancer, we would have to find a group with a long-term work history, trace their whereabouts, and determine if they are living or dead, and if they are dead, what they died of. Or we could begin a study today and follow people for at least twenty years and see what diseases they develop in the future. Large numbers are needed to obtain statistically meaningful results. Each year, for example, only about 40 out of every 100,000 men die of lung cancer, the most common form of cancer in males. If a study on hazards included only 1,000 men, then we would "expect" to see only 0.4 cases of lung cancer each year. Among 10,000 men, we would "expect" 4 cancer cases each year, according to the national cancer rates. Six cancer cases in 10,000 men would mean that our group had one and one-half times the cancer rate of the general population. "Losing" 1 of the 6 cases would virtually, and incorrectly, eliminate the excess risk for lung cancer observed in the study. The group studied must be large enough and the record keeping over many years detailed enough not to put the outcome of the study in jeopardy.

Needing to study large numbers of people is another problem in recognizing occupational disease. Most offices do not have enough people working in them for long enough periods to provide the basis for a meaningful study. The situation is frequently one where a small number of people develop complaints but at an insufficient rate to indicate what the problem is, or one where there is a rapid turnover. Add to this the fact that levels of pollutants and other hazards in the office are generally not extreme, so that the disease they cause would be slower in developing and hence take a long time to show up. Consequently, only careful, extensive study would "discover" the disease. This is especially true because the victim of the ailment and his or her doctor usually do not associate the health problem with the job. As a result, each case remains an isolated event. The history of occupational health is made up of instances where a group of workers have gotten together, compared notes on personal and family health problems, discovered similarities, and then agitated for a study or for a change in conditions. These were almost always accidental, fortuitous incidents. Most occupational diseases remain uncounted and unrecognized.

Perhaps the worst problem, as great as the scientific difficulties of studying occupational disease, is our apparent societal unwillingness to earnestly and intensively study occupational disease and distress in both white-collar and blue-collar work environments. One need only contrast the national dedication to space exploration or microtechnology development with the national effort given to understanding risk factors in the workplace and the general environment to see where the root of the problem lies. We don't know much about occupational diseases, because we have devoted so few resources to looking for them.

Even today, after the horrors of asbestos and radiation exposure have become apparent, doctors and nurses learn virtually nothing about occupational disease in their medical training. More hours are spent studying tropical diseases than are devoted to occupational disease, if it is taught at all. Few of us, as patients, will be able to recall ever being asked by any physician about the nature of our work to learn whether it might be related to whatever we were suffering from at the moment. The federal research budget is minuscule and training programs in colleges and universities pitifully small compared to other fields of science. And often, even when occupational diseases are studied, the focus is not wide enough. Much attention has been paid to "executive ulcers," and while we don't underestimate the stress many executives feel, it is interesting that the phrases "bookkeeper's backache" or "data-entry doldrums" have not entered the vocabulary or become part of any medical dictionary. The effects of office working conditions, of smoking and drinking habits, of interpersonal relationships between husbands and wives, parents and children, co-workers and people in general, on the incidence and severity of chronic diseases are virtually unexplored. This should be a high priority.

Where does this leave the office worker, and what hope is there of doing something about health hazards on the job? If many things can cause the same disease, then how will it be proved that a particular working condition was responsible for the disease in question? And if people who don't work in an office can also get the disease, then how do we sort out office-induced diseases from diseases of the general population? These questions are not simple to answer.

We have used cancer as an example to illustrate some of the principles and problems of understanding chronic diseases, but not all chronic disease is fatal or has to be. Some occupational hazards studied simply make you miserable and less able to function. If you sit and work all day in a chair that is uncomfortable and you develop a backache, you may not be able to tell for certain that the backache is related only to the chair and not also due to carrying a toddler around. But there is sufficient biological and medical evidence clearly pointing to the fact that a poorly designed chair is harmful. There is no reason to wait for the perfect study to establish the exact degree of the risk before you get a new chair.

What Are the Hazards?

We have already noted that relatively little is known about office hazards. One of the few studies of a large population of office workers, carried out by co-author Stellman and her colleagues at the Columbia University School of Public Health,* pinpoints the major health complaints that workers report.

An important finding of the Stellman-Columbia study is the major extent to which both the physical and the psychological environment contribute to or detract from worker health and well-being. This finding is important because most researchers have tended to investigate the psychological but not the physical aspects of white-collar jobs, while the psychological environment of most blue-collar workers has generally been neglected in favor of a focus on physical hazards.

Physical factors that were studied and found to relate to health symptoms and stress in a statistically meaningful way included noise, air quality, the extent of machine usage, the degree of privacy, the amount of space allotted to each individual, and the number of times an individual is required to move his or her workstation. Participants reported that they worked on desks that were too cluttered and had problems with lighting and temperature. In all the offices studied, noise and lack of privacy were the factors found to contribute most strongly to distress as measured in several different ways. Many participants worked in large open spaces where they could not speak or think without being distracted. They believed that such auditory distractions affected their ability to work as well as their satisfaction with their jobs. The majority of workers had little control over their work environments. In some offices, where the work required extensive use of video display terminals (VDTs) for day-long entering of data, there were significant complaints of arm, neck, wrist, and finger cramps.

In one office, employees expressed a great deal of dissatisfaction with air quality. When the extent of nose and throat irritation and of colds among these workers was compared with that among workers who did not report an indoor air quality problem, the workers who had com-

*We refer to this study as the Stellman–Columbia University Office Worker Health Study. Jeanne M. Stellman is the principal investigator. Collaborators in the ongoing project are Drs. Gloria Gordon and Barry R. Snow, and Susan Klitzman. The study has involved the extensive cooperation of unions and management throughout the United States and Canada. It has been partially supported by the Center for Work and Mental Health of the National Institute of Mental Health. Fuller details and copies of professional publications arising from the study are available from Dr. Stellman at the Women's Occupational Health Resource Center at the address listed in appendix B.

plained were found to have four times the risk for developing upper-respiratory-tract symptoms.

Indoor air quality has been found to be a major problem in other studies as well. Shortly after moving into a brand-new, hermetically sealed office building on Long Island in February 1979, employees of the Itel Corporation began complaining of headaches, light-headedness, nausea, and irritation of the eyes, nose, and throat. The situation became so bad over the ensuing months that over half the staff was transferred to rented trailers adjacent to the building. An epidemiologic investigation revealed that persons who had used photocopying equipment most frequently had the greatest number of symptoms. Further, individuals who used machines with liquid-process developers showed more symptoms than those using machines with dry-process developers. Extensive air sampling failed to identify any single compound in high enough concentrations to cause the problem. However, engineering evaluation, including airflow measurements, determined that the amount of fresh air being drawn into the building was less than 7.5 cubic feet per minute per person, just under one-half the level recommended by ASHRAE (the American Society of Heating, Refrigeration, and Air Conditioning Engineers). It was concluded that inadequate ventilation was causing the problem, and, in fact, improving the ventilation has cleared up the problem.

Several environmental hazards of the modern office are highlighted in this short research summary, most prominently poorly designed or installed equipment emitting noxious fumes and operating in a sealed building that is also inadequately ventilated. Offices around the world are similarly affected. But when researchers or investigators have carried out a survey, as in the example above, to search for the problems, they have rarely found anything specific to blame.

The psychological environment too is an important source of dissatisfaction and distress. Many researchers have found that the attitude of employers to workers, the amount of control people have over their work, being required to see a minimum numbers of clients a day, having to be courteous on the telephone even to rude customers, continuously facing deadlines, are an important part of how satisfied people will be with their jobs. Job satisfaction is highly correlated with stress. A dissatisfying job can be one that is overly demanding, requiring long hours of work, or it may be crushingly boring, like entering rows and columns of data for seven hours a day. The job may have insufficient compensation either in monetary terms or in terms of giving one a sense of accomplishment. Social recognition of the importance of a job is essential. Although the data-entry clerk is crucial to the running of the stock market, she enjoys no mention in the stock market report, nor is there a Friday night program on public television devoted to interviewing four Wall Street office workers. Our society does not consider clerical workers important. Lack of social recognition makes an inherently dissatisfying job even more so.

A key factor in how satisfying or dissatisfying your job is is whether or not you like doing it. It helps to like your work. The number of people who don't like their jobs is astounding. Two of the questions that were asked in the Stellman-Columbia study of office workers were whether, if they were given the choice, the study participants would take their same job again, and also whether they would recommend their job to a friend. Out of almost six hundred people interviewed in one location, none would unhesitatingly take the job again, nor would a single one of the workers recommend his or her job to a friend. That is quite a commentary on the nature of work in the office and is probably closely related to the many adverse effects of stress.

Important resources for reducing stress are a supervisor who is interested and supportive, an environment that fosters co-worker cooperation and mutual support, positive feedback about the work that you are doing, a good chance for promotion and recognition. Research has shown that even extremely demanding jobs, such as very routine or closely timed work, will have fewer stress effects if there are substantial supportive resources available.

The Columbia study found that the majority of workers had little control over their work environments, and that the levels of job dissatisfaction, anxiety, and symptoms of stress were similar to those previously observed by other researchers among men working on automobile assembly lines. Stress is clearly a major office hazard.

The hazards discussed thus far are at the core of a wider spectrum of office dangers discussed in this book. These comprise both man-made and natural hazards that range from poor keyboard design to the chemical threat and fire potential of synthetic materials, and from infestation of water and cooling systems by harmful micro-organisms to radon gas emissions from granite building blocks.

Money, Productivity, and Health

Saving money in physically running the office and increasing office-worker productivity are two of the main driving forces behind the health hazards we describe throughout this book. The open, landscaped office without walls appears to predominate the design of new offices, but as we shall discuss in chapter 7, it is not free from health and safety hazards. Noise is difficult to control. There can be ventilation and heating problems. People are almost always given less room to work, and there is obviously much less privacy. But the open office is cheaper because more people can be fit into the same work area, construction costs are lower, changing office arrangements is easier, and less supervision is needed since one supervisor can see more people. There is also a tax advantage, because the modular furniture and partitions that replace the walls are considered furniture and can be depreciated at a faster rate. Energy costs are cut by lowering the ventilation rates, thus increasing the levels of air pollution. Cheaper construction costs lead to buildings that are inadequately protected against fire.

Furniture is another example. Cheaper furniture will be less carefully designed and place more stress on the worker. (Unsupportive chairs can be bad for you, just like unsupportive co-workers and bosses.)

And finally, there is the redesign of work itself. On every level, steps taken to increase productivity might well save money, but at too great a cost if the net effect is to increase the alienation we all feel doing the work. Office automation such as the use of word processing may cut salary expenses by decreasing the number of clerical workers, but it also increases the stress on the remaining workers by introducing what is in essence piecework and possible machine timing of tasks. On a higher professional level, engineers can indeed work more rapidly and efficiently using computers to provide design analysis, but by the same token, the job has become more computer-dependent. Designs and calculations must be built around the available programs or "software" in the computer. Even on the level of computer programming there is escalating alienation. A common complaint among computer programmers, creative individuals accustomed to devising whole systems, is that their job has become one of writing only a small section of some large program without adequate knowledge of where their own work fits in. We believe automation of white-collar work and the resultant "automation anxieties" will be one of the major ethical, medical, and political issues of the coming decade.

For clerical workers in particular, the most sweeping change in working conditions in recent years has been the introduction of computer technology. The "office of the future," the "paperless office," the "automated office"—all are terms applied to the linking of person and computer for secretarial and editorial functions, for routine clerical tasks, and for other office work. As Karen Nussbaum, president of 9 to 5, the National Association of Working Women, notes: "Office automation has a dual nature, like Dr. Jekyll and Mr. Hyde, and video display terminals are the potion. The industry pictures the beneficent Dr. Jekyll, enriched work, an end to routine work, and so on. But the evidence points to the demon, Mr. Hyde: restructured jobs in which an employee repeats the same small task over and over, machines that monitor and pace the worker automatically and mercilessly, and a work environment that is leading to an epidemic of stress-related diseases."*

The health and safety of office workers is an important and much neglected area, perhaps equal in importance to the health hazards of all other work, not because of the relative severity of the dangers when compared to a coal mine, but because of the huge and ever-growing numbers of people who work in offices, and because health and safety problems that cause distress, discomfort, and less than crippling disabilities cannot simply be ignored. We should not require body counts or epidemics of cancer before we begin action. Keeping health and safety hazards of office workers far down on the priority list is ignoring a major source of occupational distress, because office work *is* work in North America. The time to deal with these problems is now.

*Keynote address, International Conference on Office Work and New Technology, Boston, Mass., October 1982.

CHAPTER 2

THE BIOLOGY
OF OFFICE
WORK

The human body is a flexible complex of organs, systems, and bio-chemical processes that enable us to function continuously and for the most part to interact safely with our environment. The adaptability of the body, its ability both to defend itself in various surroundings and to repair itself when damaged, is astounding. For example, when we cut ourselves, our blood automatically begins to clot, germ-fighting cells immediately rush to the scene of the injury to prevent infection, and the skin begins to mend itself. The liver can detoxify many chemicals that we inhale or swallow, and to a large extent the lungs can expel foreign dusts. Even the stomach can selectively keep some foreign substances from entering.

The muscles and bones, held together by ligaments and tendons, permit us to adopt a huge number of postures, and even if we break a bone or tear a ligament our body can usually heal itself. If our muscles are strained we can rest and feel better, and by routine exercise and training we can become able to take on larger and larger loads. We are equipped with an autonomic nervous system, which keeps us breathing, circulating blood, excreting, and transmitting nervous signals without our conscious attention.

A human being also has built-in biochemical and physiological mechanisms for dealing with physical and psychological stresses, both good and bad. These mechanisms basically allow us to cope with the demands made on us.

Yet despite all the power of the human system to adapt to its surroundings and to defend itself against environmental stresses, many of us develop chronic illnesses, suffer, and die, often at an age far below our life expectancy. The majority of us now die from preventable degenerative conditions like heart disease and cancer which have avoidable causes. Why?

Of course, no one yet knows the answer to this question, and there are undoubtedly many factors that play a causal role. One factor is that the environments we live and work in are not the environments in which the human race evolved. The body's ability to heal and protect itself is its natural "defense system." This defense system helps keep us alive from day to day even though we live in a world of germs, dirt, and other health hazards. The system took millions of years to evolve, and the ways that it developed depended on the environment that people lived in. For example, peoples who developed in hot, sunny climates have different skin pigmentation than peoples who evolved in colder, darker areas. But one thing all peoples have in common is that *none* have evolved to work in a noisy, dirty factory surrounded by toxic fumes or at temperatures that are too hot or too cold. The modern work environment constantly challenges the body's defenses. It keeps them working all the time, and unfortunately, it defeats them in many cases. Office work is no exception.

The Body and the Office

To understand the effects of occupational hazards, it helps to know how the body works, and what kinds of diseases the different organs and systems of the body can develop. The rest of this chapter will be devoted to a discussion of the parts of the body that are most frequently affected by office hazards and to the biological effects of stress.

BONES AND MUSCLES

The bones and muscles make up the musculoskeletal system. Its purpose is to hold the body up and together. The bones give us structure in much the same way that the steel framework supports a building. In between the bones are joints, which are smooth surfaces like ball bearings that allow the bones to move without friction. The bones are held together by ligaments, and the muscles are anchored firmly to the bones by tendons. When the muscles contract, the body can move and perform work.

Equipment, tools, furniture, and the design of jobs themselves all force the body to assume particular working postures. A poor working posture forces the body into an uncomfortable position, whereas a comfortable working posture is usually also the "right" position in relation to the anatomy of the body. A healthful posture is one that places a minimum stress load on the skeleton and muscles and prevents injuries that can and do occur in offices. In 1978 the state of California's analysis of work-related injuries and illnesses among office workers reported a significant and rising number of fractures, sprains, strains, dislocations, and contusions. In 1978 more than two-thirds of the claims filed were for musculoskeletal injuries, a rate of about 3.8 per 1,000 workers. If we extrapolate this disabling injury rate to the national office-worker population of 20 million, we estimate that at least 76,000 such injuries occur annually. This estimate is a conservative one, since it does not take into account injuries that are simply treated by family doctors and do not make their way into the workers' compensation system.

A wide range of musculoskeletal aches and pains are caused by video display terminal work as many people now perform it. A major research study investigating VDT-related health problems at a large insurance company found that 15 percent of the people reported regular neckaches, 14 percent suffered backaches, and 25 percent had shoulder and 19 percent had wrist pains. Another study showed that VDT operators in an airline reservations office experienced shoulder pain, lower-back pain, and leg pains at the rates of 54 percent, 32 percent, and 24 percent respectively, while 18 percent had neckaches and 6 percent had headaches and arm and wrist pains.

Each limb and muscle has a range of movement that is both the most efficient and the most comfortable in which to function. The arm operates most efficiently when it is bent at a right angle at the elbow. When the elbow is not bent at a right angle, the arm is strained. A typist who is forced to bend her elbows at an acute angle below the keyboard level because the chair is too low or the keyboard too high will suffer muscle strain and fatigue. Similarly, a switchboard operator who has to reach out continually with her arm extended will strain the muscles and tendons in arm and elbow, particularly if a twisting motion of the hand is also involved, as in plugging in connections.

When the wrist cannot be kept straight and on a level plane, the tendons are bent, which creates a stress on them. Grasping a small object while working with the wrist bent is especially stressful to the wrist. Typists, cashiers, mail handlers, packers, and other people who use their hands, arms, wrists, and fingers in quick, flexing, repetitive motions, often suffer from tendon symptoms that include pain, swelling, and difficulty in moving the affected limb. The affliction may be tendonitis, tenosynovitis, "tennis elbow," or de Quervain's disease. The term "tennis elbow" is actually a misnomer, since it is the tendons in the forearm that are affected, not the elbow joint itself. Quite often the poor design

FIGURE 1. *Positions That Strain the Body*
Working for long periods of time with elbows raised, wrists bent, and fingers performing repetitive movements can lead to muscle and joint fatigue, aches, and even injury. Standing on a stable footstool for filing or raising chair height can help prevent biomechanical injuries.

of the work will strain other areas and cause other symptoms, such as tense and painful neck muscles or inflammation of the shoulder.

Particularly bad for fingers are tasks that require taking too wide a grip on a handle while pushing down with one finger. If repeated too long, this can result in inflammation of the finger joints, or "trigger finger." The only finger that can withstand repeated flexing is the thumb. The muscles from the other fingers reach all the way up the forearm to the elbow region, while the thumb muscles are short and strong, leading only to the palm of the hand. Thus, whenever possible, thumb-operated buttons should be substituted for buttons activated by other fingers. Reducing the speed of the work is also necessary, and particularly important where it is difficult to redesign tools, equipment, or workplace layout.

A related ailment is caused by compression of or direct injury to the nerves of the hand. Such injuries usually involve the carpal tunnel. The carpal tunnel is the channel in the wrist through which pass the muscles that flex the fingers, the blood vessels, and the median nerve, which is the main nerve to the hand. When a job requires the wrist to be bent as shown in figure 2, particularly when this position is assumed while the hand or fingers are also in motion, the carpal tunnel is compressed. This inappropriate, stressful bending of the wrist is called ulnar deviation, and it can lead to tenosynovitis, a condition characterized by numbness in the palm, thumb, and index, middle, and ring fingers, all of which are supplied by the median nerve, which passes through the carpal tunnel. Mail handlers are particularly at risk for developing tenosynovitis.

Complete rest away from the job will often cure hand and wrist problems, but as soon as the worker goes back, they may flare up again. Physicians often perform surgery or prescribe treatment with anti-inflammatory drugs without analyzing the source of the injuries. These will probably also be ineffectual if the worker returns to the same job. The only reasonable way to deal with these ailments is to prevent them, which means redesigning jobs, workplaces, and equipment. This is particularly relevant to women, because most equipment is designed for a man's hand size and grip. Thus, equipment and tasks should be redesigned so that it is the tool that bends, not the wrist. Sometimes a measure as simple as changing the distance between the worker's chair and the workbench or table can improve the position of wrist or arm.

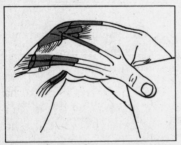

FIGURE 2. *Hand and Wrist Injuries in the Office*
Bending the wrist at an angle to the arm, particularly when
combined with repetitive hand or arm movements, compresses
the carpal tunnel, the channel in the wrist through which
pass the muscles, nerves, and blood vessels to the hand. This
can lead to tenosynovitis, a condition characterized by pain
or numbness in the hand and fingers. Jobs should be
redesigned to avoid this posture, and the rate of work should
be comfortable and not strenuous.

Another good preventive measure is alternating jobs so that the worker does not repeat the same stressful motions all day long.

Since the advent of the electric typewriter, typists are less likely to develop inflammation of the tendons and tenosynovitis. However, the poor design of the QWERTY keyboard remains a cause of fatigue and pain. The QWERTY keyboard, which was introduced by the Remington Arms Company in 1873, is the one used in almost all keyboard machines (QWERTY refers to the first six letters on the second row).

There is an unequal distribution of work between the hands and fingers when typing on the QWERTY board. The left hand is used 60 percent of the time, a disadvantage to the majority of typists, who are right-handed. Only about 30 percent of the typing is done on the central home-row keys, which are the most easily reached. Of the ten most commonly used letters in English—*a, e, h, i, l, n, o, r, s, t,*— only four are home-row keys.

As is true of so many other pieces of equipment and furniture, the QWERTY keyboard is probably a result both of lack of forethought and of consideration for the human being who must use the keyboard, and of the need for greater efficency. The original mechanical typewriters had type bars that moved forward to strike the paper. When commonly occurring letter pairs like *i* and *e* were struck, the bars would get caught. So the QWERTY keyboard was designed to increase efficiency by alternating the left and right hands for typing common letter combinations.

Alternatives to QWERTY have been designed and tested. One highly recommended keyboard design, based on biomechanical and work-efficiency principles, was first proposed by Dvorak in 1936. Dvorak's keyboard gives 56 percent of the keystrokes to the right hand and assigns the most strokes to the strongest fingers, the index, middle, and ring finger. Seventy percent of the typing is on the middle row. Between-row movement is reduced by 90 percent, as is the number of words typed exclusively by one hand. The Klockenberg keyboard separates the two halves of the keyboard, angles them back 15 degrees from the center, and tilts them downward. Research on the Klockenberg keyboard has shown that it reduces both wrist and shoulder deviations and that the frequency of aches, pains, and fatigue is thereby lowered significantly. Other suggestions for improving keyboard design include keeping the rise between the rows to a minimum, and keeping the whole keyboard as close to the work surface as possible, which would also reduce wrist deviation. Sloping the key surfaces forward improves the angle of finger strokes. All these features are also important for VDT units, where the QWERTY system is now being introduced on a mass scale.

Most experts have little hope that the QWERTY keyboard will be replaced. One reason is the potential cost of retraining the current generation of operators. The use of the QWERTY keyboard was formalized by the U.S.A. Standards Institute in 1968 and by the International Organization for Standardization in 1971, decisions that inadequately consider biomechanical stress and health. Alternative designs are shown in figure 3.

THE BACK

The back is made up of the spinal column and the ligaments and muscles that support it. The bones of the spine, the vertebrae, support the body. The joints between the twenty-four vertebrae allow the body to move. There is a spongy cushion, a disc, between each two bones; these discs act as pivots and shock absorbers in the spinal column. Ligaments bind

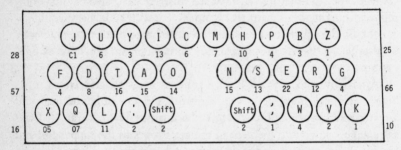

SUGGESTED TYPEWRITER KEYBOARD

A

KLOCKENBERG'S PROPOSAL FOR SEPARATION, ANGULATION AND
TILTING OF KEYBOARD HALVES.

B

FIGURE 3. Alternatives to the Standard Keyboard
A. The typewriter keys have been arranged so that the strongest fingers do the greatest amount of work. The letters are distributed so that the right and left hands each perform about 50 percent of the work load.
B. The Klockenberg keyboard has been designed with a separate keyboard for each hand. The halves have been angled and tilted to provide a more appropriate position for the hand, wrist, and arm.

the bones and disc together and also bind the winglike projections of the vertebrae. All these connections make the spinal column stable. The muscles of the back surround and are attached to the bones and their projections. When the muscles on one side of the body contract, the body can bend sideways. Contraction of the muscles in the front and back of the spine allow it to bend backward and forward.

Poor or static working positions will strain the musculoskeletal system. Sitting for long periods without proper support for the lower back will cause muscular fatigue and backache. A person lacking back support must exert muscular energy to sit up straight. This places what is termed a static load on the body, and it will lead to fatigue. Alternatively, sitting in a manner that forces the spine into a curved position will also strain the back. (See discussion of chairs in chapter 4.) Similarly, standing upright requires muscular energy. The body is not balanced while standing, so that the calves must constantly work against gravity in order to hold it up. This is why standing for a long period of time makes us fatigued. Even the most ideal posture can lead to musculoskeletal "loading" if it is maintained too long, because the human body is designed to move. Static positions are contrary to biology. We all experience the urge to move after sitting in one position for a while. This is a natural response to a biological need. Even while we sleep, we naturally shift position many times during the night. A properly designed job will incorporate the human need to move.

There are many tasks in the office that can be done either standing or sitting. For example, if you sort and open mail for about twenty minutes a day, a comfortable counter and footstool for one leg, as shown in figure 4, would be a good addition to your desk and would allow you to take a rest from sitting.

Back injuries, among the most common of all industrial injuries reported, are usually attributed to jobs that require lifting. Although office workers do not routinely do lifting, they often carry boxes or equipment around. They may be more vulnerable to back injury because they are far less exercised and less experienced in lifting than a worker who expects to do it on the job. They will certainly have had less practice in learning what position is safest for lifting. (We should note, however, that the concept of safe lifting is a misleading one in that some tasks should not be done manually at all, no matter how experienced the worker or how rugged the job requirements.)

Lifting and carrying puts great stress on the back. Carrying a bulky

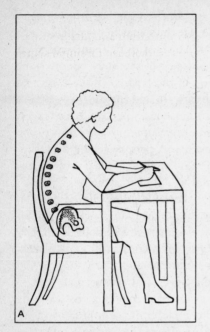
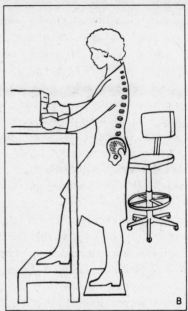

FIGURE 4. *The Spine at Work*
A. In order to maintain the spine in the least strained position, curved chairs like this should be avoided. People who write at their desks all day should use a straight-backed chair. Machine operators need a chair with a backrest that supports the lower back. Chair height should be adjustable so that the elbow can rest comfortably bent at a right angle. B. Job redesign to allow comfortable standing for certain tasks, such as mail opening and sorting, as an alternative to sitting (and vice versa), can reduce muscle strain. A footrest, proper counter height, and well-designed shoes will help prevent strain on the lower back.

or heavy load can cause injury to the joints and ligaments of the back. Sometimes ligaments can even tear or a disc rupture, both extremely painful conditions. A torn ligament or ruptured disc forms scar tissue as it heals, and this makes it particularly vulnerable to a new injury, particularly from the same motion that caused the first one. If this is a motion commonly used on the job, job and task redesign is needed to prevent permanent serious disability. Another back injury can occur when the ligaments that encase the discs tear, allowing the disc to slip out. This is called a ruptured disc and can result from a sudden rotation or bending of the spine. Most often, however, there isn't a single acute incident that can be pinpointed as the cause.

Protecting the back from injury is essential. Never lifting weights that are too heavy is a basic rule of thumb. Flexing the knees, keeping the weight close to you, and lifting in a manner that allows forward movement to avoid twisting the spine also helps prevent injury. Some recommended maximum weights for lifting are given in table 2.

TABLE 2. TYPICAL WEIGHTS IN THE OFFICE AND RECOMMENDED MAXIMUM WEIGHTS FOR LIFTING BY UNTRAINED WORKERS

Recommended Maximum Weights

AGE	MEN	WOMEN
16–18	44 lb.	26 lb.
18–20	51 lb.	30 lb.
20–35	55 lb.	33 lb.
35–50	46 lb.	28 lb.
Over 50	35 lb.	22 lb.

Typical Weights

Paper cutter	11 lb.
Copying paper, 3 reams	15 lb.
Paper-filled wastebasket	16 lb.
Large coffee machine (no water)	27 lb.
Postage meter	27 lb.
Large potted plant	29 lb.
Case of 8½ by 11 file folders	35 lb.
Electric typewriter with metal plate	43 lb.
Filled transfer file	50 lb.
Photocopying paper, 10-ream case	52 lb.
Filled 2-drawer filing cabinet	135 lb.

Strengthening both the back and the stomach muscles will help keep your back healthy and may ease a backache you already have. There are simple, nonstrenuous exercises to accomplish this. The YM–YWCA has an excellent back exercise program. You can write or telephone your local "Y" for information.

THE EYES

In a 1980 study of 2,330 people from fifteen different workplaces, 77 percent of the VDT users and 56 percent of the others in the survey said they had at least one of the eye problems listed, such as eyestrain and painful, tearing, bloodshot eyes. Potential hazards to the eyes that may cause irritation, eyestrain, and even cataracts are listed in table 3.

One major source of concern and dissatisfaction to office workers is the lighting in offices. We know from research that uncomfortable lighting can cause eyestrain, or visual fatigue, which is an equivalent term. Reading without adequate light, reading small print over long periods of time, and even reading with distractions such as noise can also strain the eyes. While it is generally believed that visual fatigue does not contribute to long-term deterioration of the ability to see, eyestrain can cause symptoms such as eye irritation, watering, and reddening of the lids. Visual fatigue can cause temporary deterioration in the eyes' ability to focus on different visual distances. Eyestrain can also cause headaches as the nervous system is overloaded and the stress spreads to the head and neck, particularly if the head and neck muscles are held in a static position. The eyelids often feel heavy during an eyestrain headache.

To understand the relationship between how the eye works and the possible effects of the office environment on the eyes, we need to focus on both the act of seeing itself and the structure of the eye and of the muscles that allow it to move (see figure 5). The images that are perceived by the eye are produced after the light enters through the cornea. The eye is like a camera, with the light focused by the lens, which covers the center of the eye, and projected onto the retina, the eye's "film." The retina contains many nerve fibers, which interpret the light signals, convert them into nervous impulses, and transmit them along the optic nerve to the brain. The brain, in turn, translates the electrical impulses from the optic nerve into a "perceived" image. Scientists have unraveled bits and pieces of the action of light on the receptors in the eye, but the exact mechanisms are still not known.

A delicate muscle structure allows the eyes to function. Six muscles permit the eyeball to rotate, to follow moving objects, and to focus on particular objects. Another muscle is the iris, which is the colored part of the eyeball. It controls the size of the black pupil in the center of the eye. The pupil is not an actual structure but rather an opening that allows the light to enter. The size of the pupil changes in response to

TABLE 3. EYE HAZARDS IN THE OFFICE

EYE IRRITATION	EYESTRAIN, OR VISUAL FATIGUE*	CATARACTS
Adhesives	Direct glare from light fixtures	Infrared light
Ammonia (from blueprint machines)	Frequent changes in viewing distance	Microwaves
Cigarette smoke	Inadequate lighting	
Excessive heat	Poor-quality photocopies, computer print-outs, carbon copies	
Formaldehyde (insulation, carbonless copy paper, plywood)	Reading small script or numbers	
Garage and traffic fumes	Reflected glare from paper, equipment, and other surfaces	
Irritating dusts		
Low humidity		
Methanol (from spirit duplicators; causes blindness if ingested)		
Ozone (from photocopiers and other electric machines)		
Ultraviolet light		

*As we age, our visual acuity, adaptation, and accommodation decrease, making us more sensitive to these hazards.

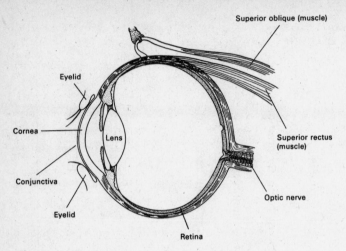

FIGURE 5. *The Eye and the Muscles That Move It*

the amount of light available: it will be wide open in darkness and minimum size in bright light. The term "adaptation" is used to describe the eye's ability to adjust to different lighting conditions.

The problem becomes worse as we get older because the vitreous humor, the fluid that fills the eyeball between the lens and the retina, becomes more opaque, which tends both to decrease the contrast and to increase the scattering of light inside the eye itself, which impairs acuity.

The ciliary muscle controls the shape of the lens and thereby the eye's focusing action. The changing lens shape allows the eyes to adjust to different viewing distances; this adjustment is called accommodation. When a person's lens does not change shape appropriately, his or her ability to perceive objects either close up or at a distance (near-sightedness or far-sightedness) will be impaired. Defects in lens shapes are, of course, a common human condition; many of us wear eyeglasses to correct such defects. Since the lens thickens gradually as we age, we generally have to change the corrections in our glasses over time. A thickening lens reduces visual acuity, or the ability to discriminate fine details. The average person sustains a seeing loss of 25 percent between the ages of twenty and sixty. Put another way, there is on the average a 50 percent reduction in light reaching the retina at age fifty and a 66 percent reduction at age sixty. Therefore, older workers need more light to see than younger workers.

The lens of the eye can be permanently damaged by exposure to ultraviolet, infrared, and microwave rays, as well as other sources of radiation. The lens is vulnerable to the heating effects of radiation because it has no blood supply of its own to carry out the function of dissipating heat. A lens exposed to radiation becomes opaque, blocking the light from entering. This condition is called a cataract and will require surgery if it progresses sufficiently.

Eye exposure to radiation and to some irritating chemicals can also cause the membranes that cover the eye, the conjunctiva and the cornea, and the eyelids to become bloodshot, irritated, and swollen. Because the eyes are so sensitive, even minor irritation can be painful. Injury to the cornea can lead to loss of sight because the scar tissue that forms in the healing process will destroy the transparency that is absolutely necessary for the cornea to function.

It is possible for workers to be exposed to microwaves if they work in or near the very tall buildings on which transmitters have been erected, but this is not a widespread problem for most office workers. If you work in such a building, however, you should check with the health authorities in your area to see what the levels are and whether your building has been shielded.

THE LUNGS AND RESPIRATORY SYSTEM

The lungs are the most important route by which toxic substances enter the body. Environmental toxins can get into the bloodstream through the lungs and affect other parts of the body, or they may exert their adverse effect directly on the lungs themselves. The office environment can contain a variety of substances and conditions that are injurious to the respiratory system. These are shown in table 4.

The lungs are part of the respiratory system and perform the vital function of transferring oxygen from the air to the blood. Oxygen is, of course, essential to life, and no organ can survive for long without it. The respiratory system consists of a major breathing tube, the *trachea*, or *windpipe*, which connects to the nose and throat. This tube branches into two other airways, the main *bronchi*, one in each lung, which branch out further into medium-sized, then smaller airways, the *bronchioles*. These tiniest airways end in delicate air sacs, *alveoli*, which resem-

TABLE 4. KINDS OF LUNG DISEASE AND SOURCES IN THE OFFICE

ALLERGIC RESPONSES

Caused by natural materials and some chemicals. The victim will experience wheezing, cough, pain, and shortness of breath. In some cases, may lead to chronic bronchitis.

Sources: Cigarette smoke
Formaldehyde and other chemicals given off by synthetics
Molds and spores in mildewed paper
Molds and spores in ventilation system

IRRITATION

Caused by caustic or corrosive substances leading to cough, excess phlegm production, discomfort, and possible increased susceptibility to infection. Extreme exposure can lead to serious acute response.

Sources: Adhesives
Ammonia from blueprint and other machines
Chemicals given off from synthetic materials
Cigarette smoke
Methanol from spirit duplicating machines
Ozone from photocopiers
Paint fumes
Pesticides

CHRONIC REACTIONS

Dust diseases that cause scarring and hardening of the lung, lung cancer, chronic bronchitis, and emphysema. These reactions are less likely in an office environment because of the comparatively low doses of toxic substances.

Sources: Asbestos
Long-term exposure to allergens and irritants
Radon released from building materials

---

ble clusters of grapes. There are millions of such air sacs throughout the lungs.

The air sacs are surrounded by tiny blood vessels. Oxygen from the air diffuses across the air-sac walls, which are one-millionth of an inch thick, to be picked up by the red blood cells and transported around the body. If these walls become damaged, torn, or scarred, their ability to transfer oxygen is impaired, and ill health, such as heart disease or chronic bronchitis and emphysema, will result.

Some substances found in the office are irritating to the respiratory

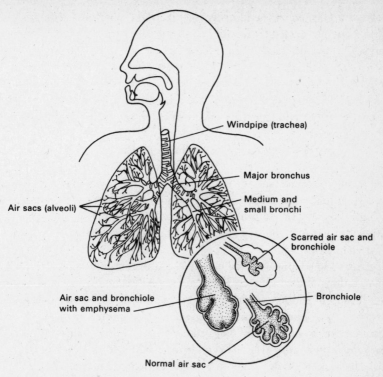

Windpipe (trachea)

Major bronchus

Medium and small bronchi

Air sacs (alveoli)

Scarred air sac and bronchiole

Air sac and bronchiole with emphysema

Bronchiole

Normal air sac

FIGURE 6. The Lungs and Lung Disease

system. Ozone from some photocopiers and cigarette smoke are two examples. The airways are lined with mucus-producing glands, like those in the nose. The airways are also lined with minute fibers called cilia, which move the mucus up to the throat where it is swallowed and digested. Mucus production is part of the body's natural defense mechanism. When the airways are irritated, the glands produce more mucus in order to dissolve the substances and remove them. If the irritation is frequent the glands secrete a great deal of mucus and become swollen. The excess mucus tends to become infected, leading to chronic bronchitis, which is characterized by a hacking, phlegm-producing cough. Since the airways are also blocked by the swollen walls, it is more difficult to expel air, leading to pressure on the tiny sacs and possibly causing them to tear. This condition is known as emphysema. The stagnant, moist air in the lungs is ideal for the growth of micro-organisms. A vicious cycle of infection, reinfection, irritation, and reirritation can set in. Usually fairly high levels of irritating substances are needed to set the cycle off—higher than in most offices—but the reports of respiratory disease among office workers are increasing. The possible danger is one that workers should be aware of. Lung irritants can also injure the cilia, reducing their effectiveness in removing contaminant-laden mucus.

Breathing fine dusts in the air can also lead to lung disease, where the dusts enter the small airways and sacs and either rip them or cause scar tissue to form. Asbestos is a notorious source of occupational lung disease. Again, most office workers are not exposed to asbestos, at least at high levels, but it is a problem that may be present. We tell you how to recognize the presence of asbestos in your office and what to do about it in chapter 8.

Dusts and chemicals in the air can cause an allergic response leading to an asthma-like condition. There are several technical names for this condition, including *extrinsic allergic alveolitis* and *hypersensitivity pneumonitis*. Colorful names are given to allergic occupational lung diseases: *mushroom workers' lung*, *cheese washers' disease*, *maple-bark disease*, and *farmers' lung*. If you examine this list of diseases you will notice that all the jobs involve handling organic, living materials like mushrooms, cheese, and hay. Molds, spores, and other micro-organisms grow on these products. When they inhale these micro-organisms, many people react to the proteins they contain by an immunological defense.

We are all familiar with hay fever, which is a reaction of the immune system in people who are sensitive to pollen in the air. This type of sensitivity is inherited, and whether a person, technically called an atopic individual, develops an allergic reaction will depend on whether there is exposure to the allergen. It is estimated that about 10 percent of the population is atopic. In a hay-fever-like allergic reaction the body forms a specific antibody to the foreign sensitizing substance, the antigen. When the antibody interacts with the antigen, histamines and other chemical substances are released into the bloodstream. These chemicals cause the muscles in the airways to contract and mucus to flow, leading to the familiar wheezing, sneezing, coughing, and runny nose of the hay-fever sufferer. Once a person has been sensitized, even small amounts of the offending allergen can set off the reaction again.

Of particular importance to office workers is the allergic reaction dubbed humidifier lung. The onset of humidifier lung is much more insidious than that of other allergies. It is also not limited to allergy-prone atopic people, and conversely, not all allergic people will get the reaction. The immune response takes several hours and involves the formation of complexes in the blood. These complexes stimulate other chemical reactions, which can lead to cell injury, sometimes progressive and permanent. Nodular areas, or granulomas, can form in the lung, largely consisting of swollen tissue that sometimes becomes scarred and hardened, not unlike the scarred and hardened fibrosis caused by asbestos and other dusts. These changes are often visible on X-rays. There will be a decrease in the lung's ability to function. Sometimes the condition may progress even if there is no longer any exposure to the original allergen that set off the response.

Unfortunately the victim of this illness may not be aware of it for some years. Unlike the hay-fever sufferer, who is acutely aware of the problem but recovers completely once the attack is over, a worker exposed to the molds and spores that contaminate air-conditioner and humidifier systems may feel nothing until long after the onset of the disease.

Allergic responses can also occur from ordinary dust. Many of us experience this dust allergy in our homes, particularly during spring-cleaning binges. A microscopic creature, the dust mite, is believed to be responsible for the dust allergy, although other causative agents may be present. These tiny creatures live on human dander (skin or hair scales), food particles, pollen, and so on. Personal experience with hundreds of office workers has established for us that many offices have a dust problem, particularly in storerooms. One can expect dust allergies to afflict susceptible people who handle musty, dusty files and papers.

Finally, there are many chemicals that are potent sensitizing agents. Some, like formaldehyde (described more fully in chapter 4), can cause a response similar to humidifier fever. Others produce a skin reaction known as contact dermatitis.

THE SKIN

The skin protects the internal organs from foreign substances. It has remarkable defense structures, yet skin disease is the most widely reported occupational illness. The skin, as shown in figure 7, consists of two layers covered by a tough material, keratin, that is resistant to many dusts, germs, and chemicals. The inner layer contains hair follicles, blood vessels, sweat glands, and other glands that produce a protective wax. The outer layer, the wax, a layer of nonliving cells, and the keratin cover act as a carrier, guarding the inner skin layer and the rest of the body from harmful physical and chemical agents.

Some toxic substances irritate the skin, others produce allergic skin reactions, and some do both. Skin allergy, or contact dermatitis, will produce the same symptoms—reddened, rough, cracked skin, sometimes with open sores (eczema)—that characterize irritant dermatitis; but as with other allergies, only some people, those who are sensitive, will develop it. For example, not everyone who is exposed develops a reaction to poison ivy, a well-known cause of contact dermatitis. About 20 percent of the work force can be expected to develop allergic contact dermatitis if they come into contact with sensitizing chemicals.

Table 5 shows some of the chemicals found in office work that can cause an allergic skin response. This reaction, like the allergies in the lung, involves an immune response. Most of the chemicals listed can attach themselves to the protein in the skin, converting the body's own protein into a new structure, which now becomes "foreign" to the immune system. An antibody-antigen reaction takes place. Once the

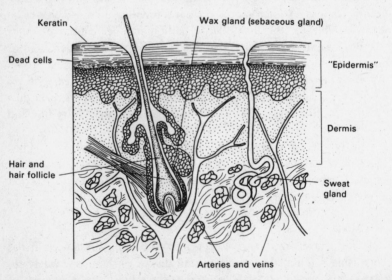

FIGURE 7. *Microscopic Cross-Section of the Skin*

TABLE 5. OFFICE CHEMICALS THAT AFFECT THE SKIN

ADHESIVES, BOOKBINDING
animal glues
benzoyl peroxide (plasticizer)
polyvinyl resins
shellac

ADHESIVES, CARDBOARD BOX
phenolic resins (phenol-formaldehyde, melamine-formaldehyde)
rubber adhesives

ADHESIVES, GLUE (ALL-PURPOSE)
animal glues
camphor
dibutyl phthalate
fillers (inert)
formaldehyde
glycerine
gum arabic
nitrocellulose (camphor as a plasticizer)
oil of wintergreen
phenol
phenolic resins
polyvinyl resins
sulfur

ADHESIVES, LIBRARY PASTE
defoamer
dextrins

Dowicide antifungus agents
formaldehyde
glucose
glycerine
oil of wintergreen
starch
water

CLEANERS, COFFEEPOT
alcohols
alkyl aryl sodium sulfonate
sodium bisulfate
sodium metasilicate
tripolyphosphate

CLEANERS, OFFICE MACHINE
pine oil
rosin soap
solvent naphtha

CLEANERS, TYPE (BLANKET AND ROLLER)
antioxidants
carbon tetrachloride
perchloroethylene
petroleum distillates
plasticizers

CLEANERS, TYPEWRITER
carbon tetrachloride
methylene chloride
perchloroethylene
trichloroethylene

DUPLICATING PAPER
diazo compounds with spectral absorption in the range of 3,500 to 4,500 A (dialkylanilines, phenylmorpho-lines, and others)

COATINGS, PAPER
butadiene-acrylonitrile copolymer
carnauba wax
castor oil
dibutyl phthalate
latex rubber
melamine-formaldehyde resins
methylmethacrylate resins
nitrocellulose (camphor as a plasticizer)
vinyl copolymers

ETCHING COMPOUNDS
ammonium salts
chromic acid
EDTA and other organic chelating agents
ferric chloride
gum arabic

TABLE 5 (*cont.*)

halogenated aromatic
   sulfonamide
nitric acid
sodium hydroxide

INKS, BALL-POINT
   PEN
aluminum stearate
castor oil
dyes
hydroabietyl alcohol
mineral oil
oleic acid
rosin
sulfonamide
   plasticizer

INKS, COLORED
driers (cobalt
   abietates and
   naphthenates)
linseed oil
odor-masks
   (coumarin,
   essential oils)
pigments (titanium
   dioxide, copper
   and gold salts,
   chrome yellow,
   molybdenum
   orange,
   phthalocyanine
   blue, nigrosine)
solvents (turpentine)
surfactants

INKS, DRAWING
   OR INDIA
acetone
alcohols

ammonia
camphor
carbon black
resins
shellac

INKS,
   DUPLICATING
alcohols
dyes
glycols
methyl salicylate
resins

INKS,
   FLEXOGRAPHIC
acrylic resins
casein
chlorinated rubber
hydrocarbon solvents
nitrocellulose
   (camphor as a
   plasticizer)
polyamid resins
rosin
shellac
triphenylmethane
   dyes (methyl
   violet, etc.)
zein

INKS,
   FLUORESCENT
dibutyl phthalate
fluorescent dyes
   (rhodamine,
   thioflavin)
ketones
polyester resins
urea

INKS, FOUNTAIN
   PEN
alcohol
dyes
gallic acid
glycols
iron salts
oxalic, tartaric,
   and citric
   acids
phenol
sodium hydroxide
surfactants
tannic acid
thymol

INKS,
   INDELIBLE
aniline
carbon black
cashew-nut oil
   resins
cresol
dyes (nigrosine)
solvents

INKS, MARKING
castor oil
coal tar dyes
cresol
phenolic resin
   (cashew-nut oil,
   phenol-
   formaldehyde)
petroleum
   solvents

INKS,
   MIMEOGRAPH
carbon black
castor oil

TABLE 5 (*cont.*)

glycols
lanolin
nitrocellulose
(camphor as a
plasticizer)
rosin

*INKS,
MIMEOGRAPH
CORRECTION
FLUID*
dibutyl and diethyl
phthalate
dyes
ethyl alcohol
nitrocellulose
(camphor as a
plasticizer)

INKS, NEWSPRINT
aliphatic
hydrocarbon
solvents
carbon black
mineral oil
rosin

INKS, PRINTING
alkyd resins
benzidine yellow
carbon black
chlorinated rubber
(gravure inks)
chrome yellow
cobalt,
manganese, and
lead soaps

linseed oil
(tung, oiticica,
and soybean
oils)
lithol red
methyl salicylate
mineral oil
petroleum solvents
phenol-
formaldehyde
resins
rosin

*INKS, STAMP
PAD*
acetone
aniline dyes
cresol
glycerine
glycols
phenol
resins

INKS, STENCIL
dyes (organic and
inorganic)
petroleum solvents
resins (rosin,
phenolics)

INKS, WRITING
alcohol
eosin
gallic acid
glycols
iron salts
sodium hydroxide
tannic acid

thymol

*PAPER, FILLERS
AND COATING
MATERIALS*
acrylic resins
alum and milk of
lime (satin white)
aluminum sulfate
barium sulfate
calcium carbonate
calcium sulfate
casein
cellulose nitrate
chlorinated rubber
(neoprene)
clay
formaldehyde
glycerol
lithopone
petroleum waxes
polyesters
polyvinyl acetate
polyvinyl chloride
rosin
rubber latex
sodium silicate
starch
talc
titanium dioxide
varnishes

*SOLVENTS, INK
THINNERS*
butyl benzyl
phthalate
di-2-ethylhexyl
phthalate

SOURCE: Exerpted from R. M. Adams, *Occupational Contact Dermatitis* (Philadelphia: J. B. Lippincott Co., 1969).

immune system has "learned" to react against this foreign combination of skin protein and chemical, it becomes so sensitive that it will react against even tiny quantities of the combination. In some cases, even if the chemical is no longer present, the reaction continues against the already inflamed skin.

The prevention of skin disease is obviously best accomplished by eliminating direct contact with injurious chemicals. But there are other practices that can help:

1. You should wash your hands regularly after handling irritating or allergenic substances, such as after carrying out a maintenance chore on an office machine. A mild soap should be available, and if you end up washing your hands frequently, a good-quality lanolin hand cream should be supplied to replace the oils in the skin that have been washed away. If washing during the day is really impractical, there are "waterless" cleansers that should be supplied and that can be kept in your desk drawer.

2. Wherever possible, the least irritating supplies and chemicals should be used.

3. In some cases, as for short jobs like adding chemicals to a photocopying machine, protective gloves can be worn. A box of surgical or disposable plastic gloves can be hung on the wall near the equipment. Most people find it difficult to wear gloves for a long period of time because they are clumsy and uncomfortable and make the hands perspire, which makes them more vulnerable to chemical hazards.

4. As with all other hazards discussed here, a clean and well-maintained workplace will limit the extent of exposure to irritating or allergenic substances.

Stress

Stress can cause unhappiness and ill health. Studies have documented a host of patterns that are common to people in stressful situations. The stressed person will not feel good, will be anxious, nervous, and possibly depressed, may possibly have unnecessary feelings of guilt and shame, irritability, and moodiness. People under stress may not like themselves very much; their self-esteem may be low. They may be bored and apathetic. Stressed people often feel very lonely. They may have an increased tendency either to eat excessively or not to eat enough. Exposure to stressors can cause a person to take inadequate care of his or her personal health. Stress prompts other unhealthy, self-destructive behavior. People may turn to drinking, cigarettes, or other drug abuse as a means of coping with stress. There is increased accident proneness, or perhaps inappropriate impulsive behavior such as nervous laughter or outbursts of anger. People may feel restless or even begin to tremble.

Some of these behavioral effects will spill over into relationships with friends and family and affect performance on the job. Stressed workers may be absent excessively or may be unable to complete the work required of them. They may have difficulty getting along with their co-workers. They may leave their jobs because they are so dissatisfied. One sign of a stressful workplace is that large segments of the work force are afflicted with these symptoms. Such a workplace may be characterized by excessive absenteeism, low productivity, poor interoffice relationships, high labor turnover, and an excessive accident rate.

Some physical health effects associated with stress include chest and back pains, sleep disorders such as insomnia and nightmares, and digestive-system disorders such as diarrhea, indigestion, and loss of appetite. There may be a loss of normal sexual interest or an inability to perform normally. Migraine headaches, menstrual-cycle irregularities, or even the cessation of menstruation, skin rashes, and faintness are all associated with the stress response. Finally, serious life-threatening diseases like coronary heart disease, the major cause of death in the Western world today, ulcers, diseases of the circulatory system, and many other chronic diseases are in part attributable to stress.

UNDERSTANDING WHAT STRESS DOES

All living things, even plants, respond biochemically to the demands of their environment. Sometimes the responses are physically noticeable: a person may blush in an embarrassing situation, or feel cold and clammy and have a sensation of "butterflies" in the stomach when frightened. There will also be unperceived physical responses. Virtually every major organ system is involved in stress. For example, the blood pressure will usually rise when a person is exposed to high levels of noise. The stomach will secrete greater quantities of acid. The heart will begin to pump faster. Whether the source of the demands is happy, like excitement at a football game, or sad, like the death of a loved one, or a physical stressor like noise or extreme heat or cold, the human body will respond with a similar set of biochemical reactions called a general stress response.

The stress response is sometimes called a "fight-or-flight" reaction in an attempt to relate the response to its primitive function. Confronted by a physical threat, such as a wild animal in the jungle, the body understandably activates its alarm system so that maximum energy is available for meeting and combatting the emergency, or for fleeing from it, if that is the logical alternative. And although the energy involved in coping with stressors is not measurable in the same way that we calculate mileage on our cars, its effects can be observed by the ever-increasing incidence of disease and disabilities that are related to stress.

Although the pathways of the stress response are normal biochemical processes, the end physiological result of continual adaptation to stressors will be at best "wear and tear" and at worst stress-related disease. In addition, the stress response affects the body's general resistance to all diseases and its ability to recover. There is probably not a single ailment, from the smallest cut on the finger to major diseases like cancer, whose progress is not affected by stressors. A person under stress will not recover as rapidly as the person with peace of mind and a serene, less demanding environment.

The mechanisms of the stress response are controlled by the same nerves and glands that orchestrate the day-to-day functioning of the body. Glands produce and release hormones into the bloodstream. These are extremely potent chemicals that act as messengers to every organ and system, beginning, stopping, and otherwise modifying their actions. Most biological functions depend on specific hormones for direction.

The nervous system begins in the brain, which acts as central control with pathways extending down the spinal cord. The nerves branch out from the spinal cord and eventually link up with every muscle, vein, artery, and organ in the body. Major nerves lead to the major organs, and tiny nerves to the smallest parts of the body. When the brain transmits an electrical impulse, it stimulates the production of chemicals directly at the microscopic nerve endings and junctions. These chemicals are equivalent to the hormones produced by the glands, except that they remain localized at the nerve junctions instead of circulating throughout the bloodstream. The nervous system and the glands are not independent of the external environment. While we do not think about making the heart beat, the lungs breathe, or the hormones circulate, the

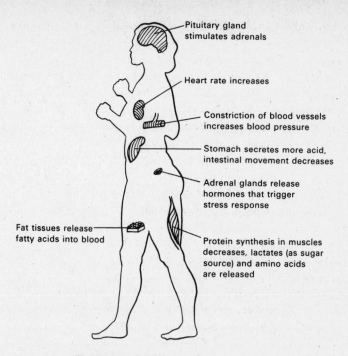

Pituitary gland stimulates adrenals

Heart rate increases

Constriction of blood vessels increases blood pressure

Stomach secretes more acid, intestinal movement decreases

Adrenal glands release hormones that trigger stress response

Fat tissues release fatty acids into blood

Protein synthesis in muscles decreases, lactates (as sugar source) and amino acids are released

FIGURE 8. The Body's Response to Stress
Stress mobilizes body reserves for energy production. The response is an increased utilization of normal biological pathways, as shown. The hormones secreted in response to stress influence blood pressure.

stressors in our surroundings can profoundly affect the functioning of the autonomic nervous system and the glands, and thereby alter respiration, heartbeat, and hormonal activity.

As an example, when the brain responds to stress, it automatically sends a signal to the vagus nerve, which stimulates the secretion of gastric acid in the stomach. Usually the lining of the stomach wall can withstand the extreme acidity of the stomach. But at the same time that stressors are stimulating the secretion of more acid, the steroids produced by the stress response are decreasing the ability of the intestinal lining to protect itself from stomach acidity. This may be one way that stress exacerbates ulcers. Less serious but very disturbing and fatiguing are the indigestion, diarrhea, and loss of appetite (or sometimes the urge to overeat) that are frequently caused or aggravated by stress.

Many aspects of the stress response, however, are not yet understood. For example, one component of the stress response is a rise in blood pressure resulting from a comprehensive series of biochemical changes. Hypertension, or chronic high blood pressure, is also associated with stress, although the relationship between the instantaneous rise in blood pressure caused by the stress response and chronic disease is not clear. It is interesting that studies correlate as much of a relationship between heart disease and stress as between heart disease and physical factors such as cholesterol levels. It is ironic that we as a society seem much more eager to reduce the fat in our diet than we are to develop social methods to decrease the levels of stress in our lives.

Other diseases of the circulatory system, such as coronary heart disease (damage to the major arteries of the heart) and stroke, have also been related to stress. But as with so many other chronic diseases, stress is but one of a complex array of causative factors. Family history, occupational environment, and aspects of personal life-style such as smoking all contribute to the development of these diseases.

Nor can science explain the death of a spouse from "natural causes" just a few short weeks after the death of a lifelong marriage partner. It may be that science will never explain such phenomena, and perhaps that is good. Some stressors are natural and some are even fun, while others are simply unavoidable. A meaningful way to look at stress is to recognize that extraordinary or continuous unwanted stress costs us energy, deprives us of tranquillity, facilitates the occurrence of some diseases and causes others outright, and prolongs the time of recovery from any disease. It is logical to try to minimize exposure to stressful conditions and to eliminate them from our working environment as much as possible.

CHAPTER 3

VIDEO DISPLAY TERMINALS
The Computer Connection

In 1980, approximately 10 million people worked on video display terminals. The video display terminal, or VDT, provides the link between the human being and the computer. It is also called a word processor, a VDU (video display unit), or a CRT (cathode ray tube). A benign-looking machine with a modified typewriter keyboard and a television-like display screen, the VDT is connected to the computer by a cable or a telephone line, which serves as the umbilical cord for the transfer of information between the terminal and the computer. The VDT is rapidly replacing the typewriter for correspondence and reports, the bookkeeping ledger and calculator for accounts, and other systems for sorting and retrieving files, inventory and customer records, reservations, and so on. It is predicted by experts such as the Arthur D. Little Corporation that by 1990, 40 to 50 percent of all American workers will be making daily use of terminals and that there will be more than 38 million workstations with terminals in the factories, schools, and offices of the United States. When you add to this the 7 million portable terminals that are projected to be toted around by sales representatives and others, and the 34 million terminals at home, it appears that most Americans will be firmly anchored to a computer for their livelihood very soon.

Newspaper offices were among the first workplaces to be dramatically affected. Where once typesetting was done by hand or by use of a manual typesetting machine, now there is computerized phototypesetting. Reporters' typewriters have been replaced by VDTs. Stories can be written on the VDT, automatically transmitted to editors, edited, retransmitted to the reporter, and then turned into type. Advertising, internal communications, accounting, and storage of archival materials are all computer-based operations in newspapers now.

Changes comparable to those in the newspaper industry have taken place in banks, insurance companies, and various other industries. Businesses using reservations have been revolutionized by computers. Airlines and railroad ticket agents use telephone headsets plugged directly into computers. The computer automatically assigns incoming calls to available reservation agents. A VDT displays information on fares and schedules, and keeps track of seat availability, fare changes, even information on weather conditions. Reservations are entered by the agent on the VDT.

Long-distance telephone operators are similarly at the beck and call of the computer. When a call requires the intervention of an operator, the computer automatically assigns the call and generates a *beep-beep* signal in the operator's headset while data such as the numbers dialed are simultaneously displayed on the VDT. The operator obtains additional information from the customer and types it into the terminal. Ticket agents usually can control the rate at which they receive incoming calls by pressing a control key signaling acceptance of their assigned call. Operators have no control over the rate at which calls are assigned to them, and the time it takes them to complete a call is closely monitored.

Unfortunately, the explosion of computer technology and its office applications have not been accompanied by the planning and design needed to make VDT use safe and healthful. Consequently, as more workers spend longer periods of time using video display terminals, complaints about discomfort and other health effects are mounting. The majority of complaints have centered around eye problems, such as visual fatigue, soreness and itching, tingling, and tearing of the eyes. Back and neck aches and other strains, largely due to uncomfortable work positions, are also prevalent. In fact, the Stellman–Columbia Uni-

versity Office Health Study found that word-processing machine operators who used video display terminals for more than half the working
day reported two to three times as many muscular aches and pains,
particularly in the hand, wrist, upper back, and neck, as did clerical
workers with similar duties who did not use VDTs. Other stress-related
symptoms and job dissatisfactions were also more prevalent among the
VDT-machine users.

There has also been a great deal of publicity about the clusters of
birth defects reported among video display terminal operators and about
the possibility of radiation exposure from using the VDTs. We have
already discussed in chapter 1 the problem of the lack of adequate studies
in occupational health and the difficulties in carrying out a good study.
Many questions remain about the relationship between pregnancy outcome and VDT work. First, there is the question whether the clusters
of defects are related to the VDT work or whether they merely occurred by chance and had nothing to do with VDTs. This question
deserves serious and immediate attention and can be answered by a
well-designed study comparing several thousand VDT operators with
an equal-sized, matched group of office workers who do not operate
machines. Second, if the clusters are related to VDT work, it must be
determined what is causing the effect. The levels of radiation emitted
from most VDTs are extremely low, especially in comparison to the
relatively lax (or nonexistent) standards for occupational exposures. The
likelihood that radiation exposure led to the clusters (if they are real)
does appear to be fairly remote, but the question of the kinds and levels
of radiation exposure arising from VDTs is complex, and we discuss it
in detail in this chapter as we systematically review the safety and health
hazards of VDT work.

Visual Aspects of VDT Work

The circuitry of the VDT and its physical
design are controlling machine factors in the degree of visual comfort
you have during VDT work.

THE MACHINE

How much strain and stress you experience reading a VDT screen is
determined by the brightness of the characters on the screen, the degree
of contrast between characters and background, how long the characters

last, and how much they wave or flicker, as well as by the shape of the letters.

A good VDT will have both adjustable brightness and contrast controls, which means that you will be able to adjust the brightness of the screen and of the characters to the level of light in the office. Some workers may have offices with natural light, which will of course vary during the day, and it is important to be able to adjust the brightness of the screen accordingly. Some users find it soothing to be able to shift contrast and brightness from time to time. And most important, not everyone finds the same brightness and contrast levels best suited to him or her. The ability to make adjustments to meet individual needs is therefore critical.

The steadiness of the letters on the screen is determined by the way in which the characters are generated and maintained. The images are produced by the cathode ray tube, or CRT, an evacuated glass tube that, when powered by electricity, shoots electrons from a "gun" at the rear of the tube toward the screen at the front. The screen is coated with phosphors that emit light when they are energized by the striking electrons from the electron gun. The operator sitting in front of the screen will see a bright spot where the electrons have struck and energized phosphors. Each character on the screen will be made up of many energized spots. For example, it requires 15 phosphors to produce the letter A on many machines. In order to keep the characters legible, electrons continually "refresh" the images at a specific "refresh rate." If not refreshed frequently enough, the characters on the screen will flicker as they start to fade. VDTs come with different refresh rates; the minimum needed for comfortable viewing is listed in table 6.

The shape of the letters on the screen affects how easily they are read. In general, "squared" letters are easiest to read. Some VDTs come only with upper-case (capital) letters, which are harder on the eyes than upper- and lower-case letters combined, particularly for long documents. It is also best if the text display does not extend all the way to the edges of the screen, because the sharpness of the characters usually declines at the edges. The characters should be at least the minimum heights listed in table 6, and there should be a space equivalent to at least 1/2 character between words and 1 character between lines.

Some of the specifications for VDTs are very technical, and understanding all the physical principles behind these requirements is far beyond the scope of this book or your needs for setting up a healthful

VDT station. We will provide only a brief description of how a VDT works and how some of its working characteristics are related to the circuitry. Additional data that will be helpful for the intelligent purchase of a VDT are given in table 6. This table includes both the characteristics you can see when you sit down in front of the unit, such as screen color, and the electronic specifications that must be obtained from the manufacturer. A good rule of thumb is not to purchase any equipment from a manufacturer or supplier who either cannot or will not supply these specifications.

OFFICE LIGHTING AND GLARE

Video display terminal work requires different lighting arrangements from the average office. There is no agreement among experts on the

TABLE 6. RECOMMENDED VISUAL CHARACTERISTICS FOR VDT SCREEN DISPLAYS

Screen Contrast and Brightness	
Screen color and character	Dark green with lighter green or yellow characters, or black with white characters.
Screen luminance (brightness)	Screen luminance should be adjustable across a wide range to a minimum of approximately half the level in the office. The machine should also have contrast adjustability, since both of these characteristics depend on user preference.
Letter Size and Legibility	
Character generation	A 5 by 7 or 7 by 9 dot matrix.
Character refresh rate	40–60 hertz minimum for low to medium persistence phosphor, with higher levels preferable.
Character size (for normal viewing distance of 70 cm or 28 inches)	Minimum height: 3.1–4.2 mm. Maximum height: 4.5 mm. Width/height ratio: 3:4–4:5.
Spacing	Between words: ½ character height. Between lines: 1 character height.

ideal lighting level for VDT work. There are, however, some good basic principles that can be applied. One generalization is that lighting levels at the lower end of the lighting spectrum are preferred for VDT work over the very bright lights that are characteristic of many offices.

When planning the lighting for VDT work, or placing a VDT into an existing office, you must take into account where the light sources from windows and light fixtures are with respect to both the screen and the VDT user's eyes. The object is to keep light from shining directly either onto the screen or into the eyes. Thus, a VDT should never face a window but should always be placed at right angles to it. Windows in offices that house VDTs should be fitted with blinds or curtains for better control of background lighting levels.

Direct artificial light should similarly be avoided. Artificial light should be shielded, usually coming from concealed lighting reflected from the upper walls. This is illustrated in figure 18 and is more fully discussed on pages 91–94. Many office workers will at once recognize that this is not the kind of lighting they have in their offices. Usually a large overhead fixture shines unremittingly down onto the work surface, often resulting in a glare problem.

The elimination of glare is paramount in easing the eye burden of VDT work. All equipment and furniture that surrounds the VDT workstation should be made with a matte finish to minimize reflection of light off the surface and hence glare. The need for matte finishes includes the walls and floors, as well as the furniture and office equipment. The VDT screen itself can be a major source of reflected glare. Screens produced with fine-grained anti-reflection coatings, called antiglare displays, can reduce glare. Some companies sell antiglare polarizer filters that fit on most VDT screens. However, some people have found that the antiglare screens reduce the resolution of the screen image and hence may solve one visual problem while introducing another. It is not possible to provide a list of "good" screens since the products available change so rapidly. Your best bet is to purchase equipment from a vendor that will permit you to exchange the products until you are satisfied. This may cost a little more, but it will be worth it in the long run.

YOUR EYES

Approximately 20 to 30 percent of the population has minimal visual defects such as astigmatism and near- or far-sightedness that go unnoticed. The increased VDT work load may make the user aware of these

TABLE 7. LIGHTING, GLARE, AND VDT WORK

Lighting Levels	Overall lighting should generally be at the lower end of the scale of 30–150 footcandles recommended for the office.
Artificial Lighting	Room fixtures should be shielded, and indirect light is best. Concealed lighting that is reflected from the upper walls is preferred (see figure 18).
	Individual local desk lighting should be shielded and fitted with a dimmer so that individuals can adjust levels to their own preference.
Windows	Windows should be fitted with adjustable blinds or curtains. VDTs should be placed at right angles to windows, not facing them.
VDT Casing and Other Surfaces	Matte, not shiny, finishes should be used to minimize reflection.
VDT Screens	Screens should be coated with fine-grained anti-reflection materials.

defects. For example, someone entering data will alternately look at the screen, the keyboard, and the document source once every 0.8 to 4 seconds. This is a change of direction approximately 15 to 75 times a minute. Blurred vision, itching and dryness of the eyes, headaches, dizziness, and ocular pain may all indicate that a visual defect needs correcting. Normally, eyeglasses will solve the problem. However, VDT users may need to have special corrective lenses prescribed that are appropriate to VDT work.

In particular, anyone who needs reading glasses with strong corrections or who wears bifocals may need lenses specifically prescribed for the viewing distance that she or he sits from the screen. In many cases, especially if you work on a VDT that has no movable parts, this distance will be different from the distance for which your optometrist or ophthalmologist has prescribed your lenses.

The particular problem that bifocal wearers may encounter is that whether they see the keyboard and the screen characters best through their upper or their lower lens, they will have to bend their necks. If they are best able to view the keyboard through the upper lens (for longer-distance vision), they will have to bend their head and neck toward the screen. If they need to view the screen through the lower lens (for closer vision), they must bend head and neck backward. Either position may lead to neck and back aches. Further, if the screen is to be viewed through the upper lens, it may be necessary to push it back in order to bring it into the focusing range of the upper lens. This will reduce the apparent size of character images, which will strain the eyes.

"VDT glasses" should be prescribed by a competent practitioner who is fully aware of the range of focus that the VDT operator requires. You should measure the distance between your eyes and the screen, keyboard, and source documents and give these measurements to your practitioner. We have provided a diagram of the distances to measure in figure 9. If the person who prescribes your lenses does not know how to take these measurements into account, go to a different one. Some unionized VDT users are covered by contracts that provide for free eye examinations and new prescriptions. In these cases and in that of people who work for large companies where many will need examinations, it also makes a good deal of sense to develop a list of practitioners who are knowledgeable about the visual requirements of VDT use.

Even people who do not wear corrective lenses should have an eye examination before embarking on extensive work using a VDT. There should also be regularly scheduled eye examinations, at least biannually, thereafter. Because the effects of VDT work are so little understood, it would be a good idea to keep a record of these examinations. If you belong to a union, the union should obtain permission from its members to keep a file of the results of these examinations for the group, and concerned employers may similarly want to keep track of what is happening to their employees. It may be that in fact no long-range changes in visual acuity will result from the use of video display terminals. However, unless we begin to collect the appropriate data (at the same time, of course, that we seek to improve working conditions), we will never know what the actual effects are. The history of occupational health is unfortunately replete with examples of workers serving as experimental animals in the discovery of occupational diseases.

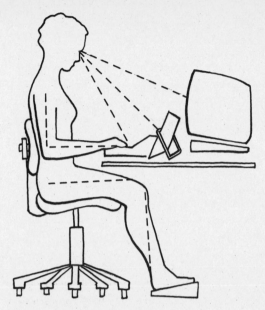

FIGURE 9. *VDT Work Positions*
For greatest comfort, the elbow and knee should bend at
90-degree (right) angles. Both a footrest and an adjustable
chair can help you achieve the right position. Table height
should be adjustable, for an ordinary desk will not provide
the correct position. A document holder and an adjustable
screen will allow you to experiment and find the least
fatiguing reading distance. Various authorities recommend
different distances, from 18 inches for reading to 28 inches
for the screen. The dotted lines show the distances you
should measure to report to your optometrist or
ophthalmologist during an eye examination.

The Workstation: Avoiding
Muscular Aches and Pains

In addition to the visual problems that we
have discussed, working at a video display terminal can cause a variety
of back and neck aches, sore arms, and other muscle strain. The major
reason for these aches and pains is that the average VDT workstation

has usually not been designed for bodily comfort and does not conform to the mechanical needs of the human body. In fact, most VDT workstations have not been "designed" at all. It is all too common to see a VDT simply plunked down into an office that is already crowded and uncomfortable. As a consequence, people are obliged to sit for long periods of time in awkward or unnatural positions. But even with careful design, a job that requires long periods of sitting and repetitive motions will be tiring to the muscular system, not to mention the mind. An appropriately designed workstation will minimize the strain of these movements.

Repetitive movements of the head and neck, either up and down or from side to side, may lead to neck and upper-back pain, particularly when the movements involve more than one joint at the base of the skull. Technically, bending the head forward more than 20 degrees, backward more than 10 degrees, or to the side more than 45 degrees will cause you to move more than one joint. If you rotate your head slowly, you can feel the movements of these joints. Muscular strain in the neck often causes headaches as well, probably because the nerves to the back of the scalp travel in a path with the neck muscles. If you continually contract these muscles, the nerves will be irritated and pain in the head will result.

If we translate the biochemical requirements of the body into practical VDT workstation terms, we can see that adjustability of the components, which include the machine itself, the desk on which it is placed, the surrounding work surfaces, and accessory equipment such as document holders, will permit you to avoid repetitive eye, head, and neck motions.

A VDT screen that can be both tilted and rotated will allow the user to optimize the viewing angle and background illumination while minimizing glare on the screen, and to set up the VDT and the source document in the most comfortable working arrangement. Some otherwise well-designed VDTs cannot be rotated. This deficiency can be compensated for with a stand that rotates the machine. This is an economical solution if the capital investment in an otherwise good VDT has already been made.

The VDT keyboard should definitely be detachable from the screen. When the keyboard is detachable and the screen can both be rotated and tilted, a VDT user can make frequent postural changes during the day and avoid the muscular strain of static work positions. The thinner the

FIGURE 10. *A Model VDT Workstation*
A VDT workstation should be equipped with: a document
holder; enough space to work comfortably; adjustable task
lighting; a screen that faces away from the window; a window
with adjustable blinds; proper working height. The VDT will
have a thin detachable keyboard, a screen that tilts and rotates,
and optimum contrast and visual characteristics as described in
the text.

keyboard is in depth, the better. A thin keyboard will reduce strain on the hand and arm muscles and will allow a higher desk top to be used. A higher desk top will allow the source document to be held closer to the eyes, which makes for ease of reading. Keyboards that are as thin as 33 mm (1 1/3 inches) have been designed.

The VDT keyboard should be constructed of a material that has a matte surface to reduce light reflection and glare. It should be engineered to have a slight slope; most people find a 10-to-15-degree angle ideal. There should be a palm rest that does not interfere with using the keys.

THE WORKSTATION
The design characteristics of desks, chairs, and workstations in general are discussed in chapter 4. Because of the great demands that the repeti-

tive movements of VDT work make on the human body, it is of paramount importance that the components of the VDT workstation work together, complement each other, and fit the human body in all its various sizes and shapes.

TABLE 8. BIOMECHANICAL RECOMMENDATIONS FOR VDT WORKSTATIONS

Keyboard	Must be detachable from VDT. Should be as thin in depth as possible. Should be slightly sloped (10–15 degrees). Should have palm rest and optimum layout.
Screen	Should be able to rotate and tilt to user preference.
Document Holder	Height should be adjustable: for full-size screens, should be on same level as screen; for small screens, should be above. (N.B.: small screens are inadequate for heavy VDT use!)
Desk	Should be of appropriate height to permit elbows to be at right angles. Should have sufficient surface and storage space for work and personal belongings.
Chair (Footrest)	Same as in general office (see fig. 16).

Static electricity may also be a problem in a VDT work environment. Many offices, particularly in the winter, have a good deal of static electricity in the air, which can be discharged against the chassis of the VDT. This can be uncomfortable for the operator, and may also interfere with the operation of the VDT. To reduce the problem, antistatic carpeting is available, and there are also grounding devices that can be attached to VDTs and other equipment. Several manufacturers provide conductive floor mats to place under equipment or in the work area, as shown in figure 11.

Static buildup has recently been blamed for an outbreak of skin problems in Great Britain and Norway, where VDT operators complained of skin irritation and facial rashes. Although the evidence was circumstantial and the cause of the outbreaks not fully identified, when antistatic carpets were installed, the skin problems disappeared.

FIGURE 11. Static Control in Workstations
Equipment malfunctions, such as occur at the supermarket counter or bank teller's window, can be avoided by using conductive mats, which ground both the users and the static-sensitive equipment. The mats help prevent annoying static-electricity shocks. They can be used successfully at VDT workstations as well.

Radiation: Will Your VDT Zap You?

One of the most frequently asked questions about VDTs is whether they emit harmful levels of radiation. Some of the questions initially arose because of an incident where two young men at the *New York Times* who worked on VDTs developed cataracts at a very early age, an extremely rare event. This was particularly noteworthy because cataracts are known to be caused by occupational exposure to radiation. However, measurements carried out on those machines, as well as on other VDTs, have found radiation levels well below those accepted by many authorities as leading to cataracts.

Recent reports of miscarriages and birth defects associated with VDT use have again brought the question of radiation emissions to the forefront. Between May 1979 and May 1980, fourteen women employees who worked in one section of the *Toronto Star* newspaper gave birth to babies. Seven of these mothers had operated VDTs during their pregnancy. Four of their babies had birth defects: blindness in one eye, a clubfoot, a cleft palate, and a heart defect. Publicity surrounding this cluster of birth defects led to reports of other such clusters among women who used VDTs during their pregnancy, and also, not surprisingly, led to strong and contradictory statements by experts.

The *Ottawa Citizen* reported the following in 1982: Dr. Walter Zuk, head of the X-ray section of the Canadian Radiation Protection Bureau, stated, "Basically VDTs have got to be the nonhazard of the century as far as radiation is concerned." But Dr. Ian Marriot, the Canadian Health and Welfare's senior consultant for public service health, said that birth defects associated with VDT use "are a cause for concern. It could be a statistical effect, but it may not be just chance. I think the numbers are large enough so that we'll have to think twice about it."*

To add to the confusion, the *New York Times* recently reported on a new major area of concern among electronics-age experts: the leakage of radiofrequency radiation leading to espionage of state, military, and business secrets. The article reported that "every computer ever made constantly and inadvertently emits radio waves. The signals . . . come off screens, chassis, wiring, and power lines." Companies such as Wang Laboratories are advertising new methods to ward off the intelligence evils of radiofrequency radiation leakage with statements like: "You've always felt confident with Wang. Now you can feel safe." How is the formerly reassured VDT operater, continually proffered guarantees of radiation safety, to feel now about nationwide coverage of the radio-

*Laura Robin, "VDT: Paradox of the Workplace," *Ottawa Citizen*, April 6, 1982.

frequency leakage from VDTs that is causing a security uproar in the military and business world?

Clearly the radiation question is an issue whose time has come and which deserves some in-depth analysis. And we should say at the outset that this is a very difficult section to write because so many of the facts are not yet known. We can only present the available data and then make what we believe to be prudent but not alarmist recommendations.

WHAT IS RADIATION?

Let us begin with some basic definitions. The term "radiation" is generally used in this context to refer to electromagnetic energy that travels through the air in the form of waves. At one end of the energy spectrum are X-rays, also known as ionizing radiation. These are powerful beams that can rip apart the electronic structure of cells and cause serious biological harm, including cancer, birth defects, and premature aging. The higher the levels of exposure to ionizing radiation, the more likely is such an effect. Exposure to ionizing radiation is measured in units called rems, and in this discussion we will use two dosage rates: rems per year and millirems per hour (abbreviated as mrem/hour). (A millirem is one-thousandth of a rem.)

Radiation that is lower in energy than X-rays is called non-ionizing and includes visible light, infrared radiation, microwaves, and radio waves. At the lowest energy end of the spectrum are the electromagnetic waves that carry house current and other low-intensity electrical energies. This is called extremely low frequency radiation, or ELF. The energy spectrum for electromagnetic radiation is shown in figure 12. The lower the frequency, the less intense the energy of the waves and, it has been thought, the less likely there will be a biological effect. Recently, however, evidence has been mounting that microwaves, even at quite low levels, can have a variety of biological effects, including problems in normal fertility among both men and women exposed to it. There are virtually no data on the biological effects of ELF radiation, and it is believed by many people that the energy is so low it simply cannot interact with the human body. All of these conclusions are based on "models" and theory. No well-designed studies exist to answer the question of biological effects on living, breathing beings. Non-ionizing radiation is generally measured in units of watts per square centimeter of surface area and abbreviated as W/cm^2, or mw/cm^2 where the unit is milliwatts or one-thousandth of a watt.

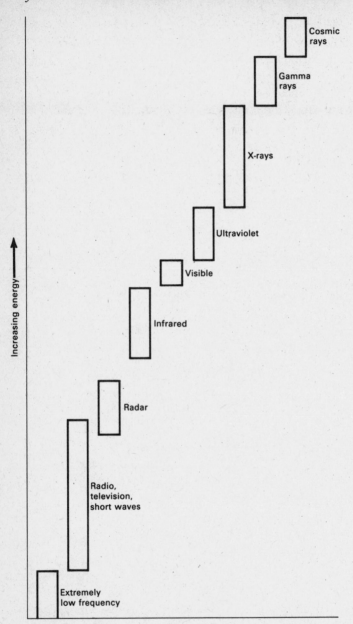

FIGURE 12. *The Energy of Different Types of Radiation (the Electromagnetic Spectrum)*

To summarize, we are basically discussing three types of radiation, each associated with different energies and biological effects:

1. Ionizing radiation, or X-rays, the most energetic and most biologically powerful, known to cause cancer, birth defects, and other severe outcomes
2. Microwaves and radiofrequency non-ionizing radiation, much less powerful but now associated with adverse effects such as fertility problems and blood abnormalities, although the evidence is still not as powerful as for X-rays and the effects are not as great
3. Extremely low frequency non-ionizing radiation (ELF), even less energetic than radiofrequency and thought not to be capable of interacting with the human body, although virtually no data exist to verify the lack of biological effects

SOURCES AND LEVELS OF IONIZING RADIATION IN VDT WORK
The primary source of X-rays is the cathode ray tube, which generates the electrons that create the image on the screen. This is also a major source of X-rays in television sets. This source can be completely enclosed and most operator exposure eliminated.

In 1981 the Bureau of Radiological Health of the Food and Drug Administration released the results of its radiation surveys of video display terminals.* The report stated that VDTs "emit little or no harmful radiation under normal operating conditions" and that detectable emissions were "well below any existing national and international standards." Since no standards have been specifically set for VDTs, the FDA based its analysis on the standards in effect for emissions from television screens. Under the conditions used for testing television sets, 8 of 91 VDTs tested in an earlier series of measurements, or almost 10 percent, exceeded the 0.5 mrem/hour television cathode ray tube standard. For the 34 additional units tested the FDA reports that "none of the 34 VDT's emitted radiation above 0.5 mR/hr." This is true; however, in looking at the data it can be seen that one VDT in this series emitted 0.42 mR/hour,† below the standard but still a significant amount of radiation. We have presented the findings of the FDA survey, including manufacturers, models, and emissions measured, in table 9.

*An Evaluation of Radiation Emission from Video Display Terminals. DHHS–FDA Publication no. 81–8153 (Rockville, Md.: U.S. Department of Health and Human Services, February 1981).
†Milliroentgens (mR) are approximately equivalent to millirems.

TABLE 9. RADIATION EMISSIONS FROM VIDEO DISPLAY TERMINALS

Manufacturers Participating in the VDT Evaluation and Identifying Codes

	Code		Code
Advanced Systems Route 73 Berlin, NJ 08009	ADSY	Chuo Musen Company, Ltd. 11-9-12 Ohmori-Nishi Ohta-Ku Tokyo, Japan	CHUO
Astronautics Corp. of America 907 S. First St. Milwaukee, WI 53204	ASTR	Cinematronics, Inc. 1044 Pioneer Way Suite B El Cajon, CA 92020	CINE
Audiotronics Video Display Div. 8299 Central Ave. NE Spring Lake Park, MN 55432	AUVI	Computer Optics Berkshire Industrial Park Bethel, CT 06801	COMO
Electronic Display Div. Ball Brothers Research Corp. P. O. Box 4376 St. Paul, MN 55164	BABR	Conrac Corporation 600 N. Rimsdale Ave. Covina, CA 91722	COCO
Fernseh Division Robert Bosch Strasse 7 6100 Darnstadt Postfach 429 West Germany	BOSC	Control Data Corporation Miniperipheral/Terminals Div. 2401 N. Fairview Ave. St. Paul, MN 55113	CODA
Bunker Ramo Corporation Trumbull Industrial Park Trumbull, CT 06609	BUNK	Electrohome Limited 809 Wellington St. N. Kitchener, Ont. Canada N2G 4J6	ELEC

ELST
Elston Electronics
P.O. Box 25
Phelps, NY 14532

FOUR
Four-Phase Systems, Inc.
1933 Vallco Parkway
Cupertino, CA 95014

HITA
Hitachi, Limited
Yokohama Works
292 Yoshida-Cho
Totsuka-Ku
Yokohama, Japan

IBMC
IBM Corporation
Old Orchard Rd.
Armonk, NY 10504

IKEG
Ikegami Electronics (USA), Inc.
37 Brook Ave.
Maywood, NJ 07607

LEXI
Lexitron Corporation
9600 Desoto Ave.
Chatsworth, CA 91311

MOHD
Mohawk Data Sciences Corp.
1599 Littleton Rd.
Parsippany, NJ 07054

MOTO
Motorola Data Products
Display Products
1155 Harvester Rd.
West Chicago, IL 60185

NENI
NEC America, Inc.
130 Martin La.
Elk Grove Village, IL 60007

ONTE
Ontel Corporation
250 Crossway Park Dr.
Woodbury, NY 11797

REDA
Redactron
100 Parkway Dr.
Hauppauge, NY 11787

SCEL
SC Electronics
530 Fifth Ave.
St. Paul, MN 55101

TECP
Teleram Communications Corp.
100 Ford Rd.
Denville, NJ 07834

TETE
Telex Terminal Communications
3301 Terminal Dr.
Raleigh, NC 27611

TOEI
Toei Musen Co., Ltd.
12, Wakamatsu-Cho
Shinjuku-Ku
Tokyo 162, Japan

VYDE
Vydec, Inc.
130 Algonquin Pkwy.
Whippany, NJ 07981

WANG
Wang Laboratories, Inc.
836 North St.
Tewksbury, MA 01876

TABLE 9. (cont.)

	Code
Wells-Gardner Electronics Corp. 2701 N. Kildare Ave. Chicago, IL 60639	WGEC

	Code
Zenith Radio Corporation 6001 Dickens Ave. Chicago, IL 60639	ZERC

IONIZING RADIATION DATA

MANUFACTURER	MODEL	RADIATION (IN MILLIROENTGENS/HOUR)*	MANUFACTURER	MODEL	RADIATION (IN MILLIROENTGENS/HOUR)*
ADSY	TV-5	0.0	BABR	TU-8C(1)	0.0
ASTR	160600-4	0.0	BABR	TU-8C(2)	0.72
ASTR	160400	0.0	BABR	TG-H12(1)	0.0
ASTR	160600-5	0.0	BABR	TG-H12(2)	0.0
ASTR	160200-4	0.0	BABR	BHL5C	0.0
AUVI	940-04(1)	0.0	BABR	THC17C	0.4
AUVI	C921-01	0.0	BABR	TV-12(1)	0.0
AUVI	900938-02	0.0	BABR	TD-12M	0.0
AUVI	900949	0.0	BABR	TTL15	0.0
AUVI	951-01	0.0	BABR	TV-12(2)	0.0
AUVI	940-04(2)	0.0	BABR	TCR-19	0.0
BABR	TD15C	0.0	BABR	TU-8C(3)	0.96
BABR	HR15	0.0	BABR	TU-8C(4)	0.66
BABR	TTL-150	0.0	BOSC	MC37BB	0.0
BABR	TV120	0.0			

Code	Item	Value	Code	Item	Value
BUNK	549272	0.0	ELEC	D01-402	0.0
CHUO	MV-98	0.0	ELEC	K30-501	0.0
CHUO	QDM-9M	0.0	ELEC	K31501	0.0
CHUO	QDM-12K	0.0	ELST	DM10-09AO	0.0
CINE	VBS-3	0.0	ELST	DM20-12AO	0.42
COCO	2000-23/C	0.0	FOUR	7101	0.0
COCO	DZB 15/N	0.0	FOUR	7111	0.0
COCO	ENA 9/C	0.0	FOUR	5115/7111	0.0
COCO	5722C13	0.0	HITA	CD-12	0.0
COCO	5222/N19	0.0	HITA	VM-172U	0.0
COCO	6122/N19	0.0	HITA	VM-172AC	0.0
COCO	SNA23/C	0.0	HITA	VM126-AV	0.0
COCO	5512/C12	1.6	HITA	VM-905U	0.0
COCO	RHB19	0.0	HITA	VM-173U	0.0
COCO	5522/C12(1)	.65	IBMC	3278-2	0.0
COCO	RQB14/C	0.0	IKEG	TM25-8	0.0
COCO	SNA23/C	0.0	IKEG	DM-511H	0.0
COCO	ANB12	0.0	IKEG	MV900REVD	0.0
COCO	QQA14/N	0.0	IKEG	TM20-8	0.0
COCO	5522/C12(2)	1.15	IKEG	DM121V39	0.0
COCO	5211/C19	0.0	IKEG	PM-950	0.0
COCO	CC-115A	0.0	IKEG	DM202-2	0.0
CODA	8277	0.0	IKEG	DM121-V39E	0.0
COMO	V15702	0.0	IKEG	PM-121T	0.0
ELEC	EVM-1710	0.0	IKEG	MV-17EX	2.0
ELEC	K20-401	0.0	IKEG	TM10-2(1)	0.0
ELEC	V05-301	0.0	IKEG	TM10-2(2)	1.2
ELEC	C21-402	0.0	IKEG	TM14-1	0.0
			LEXI	VT112	0.0

IONIZING RADIATION DATA (cont.)

MANUFACTURER	MODEL	RADIATION (IN MILLIROENTGENS/HOUR)*	MANUFACTURER	MODEL	RADIATION (IN MILLIROENTGENS/HOUR)*
MICO	BB132	0.0	NENI	FVM-95A	0.0
MICO	C3910(1)	0.0	ONTE	OP-1/R	0.0
MICO	C3412	0.0	ONTE	OP-1	0.0
MICO	M-6940	0.0	REDA	V591-6022	0.0
MICO	C3910(2)	0.0	SCEL	5M916C	0.0
MOHD	2491	0.0	SCEL	5EC920	0.0
MOTO	XM-286HB	0.0	SCEL	3M912	0.0
MOTO	M1000-155	0.0	TECP	2277 MARK II	0.0
MOTO	M2000-155	0.0	TECP	2277	0.0
MOTO	XM-353-27	0.0	TETE	277D	0.0
MOTO	M3000-140(T)	0.0	TOEI	TMC-17M	0.0
MOTO	M3000-140(AN)	0.0	TOEI	TMC-12M	0.0
MOTO	M4000-140(T)	0.0	TOEI	TMC9M	0.0
MOTO	M4000-140(AN)	0.0	VYDE	1400	0.0
MOTO	KV106LM	0.0	WANG	12WP	0.0
MOTO	MD3000-240	0.0	WGEC	19V1001(2)	0.0
MOTO	XM705-25	0.0	WGEC	19V1001(1)	0.0
MOTO	MD-4000-240	0.0	ZERC	D12PF-1	0.0
MOTO	XM360-10	0.0	ZERC	D12-NF-1	0.0
MOTO	XM351-207	0.0			

SOURCE: Adapted from table in Bureau of Radiological Health, Food and Drug Administration, *An Evaluation of Radiation Emission from Video Display Terminals*, HHS-FDA Publication no. 81-8153 (Rockville, Md.: U.S. Department of Health and Human Services, February 1981).
*This measurement reflects the maximum stable reading obtained for any surface.

It is difficult to evaluate these findings. Since the highest emission levels measured by the FDA were 2 mR/hour, or almost one-half the maximum allowed, at a typical usage rate of 6 hours per day for 50 weeks per year, the total average exposure would be 3 rem/year, which substantially exceeds the 0.5 rem/year limit for the general population. A pregnant woman operating such a machine for 36 weeks of her pregnancy could be exposed to levels in excess of those recommended by the government for pregnant women.

It is also important to mention here that sperm are very vulnerable to ionizing radiation and that, in fact, more adverse reproductive outcomes have been associated with radiation exposure in males than in females. All attention to date on the issue of reproductive health and VDTs has been focused on the female employee. All discussions here include *all* workers!

It is clear that for most of the models tested there is no detectable ionizing radiation. However, *most* models were not tested, and if only

March 22, 1982

FACTS ABOUT XEROX VISUAL DISPLAY TERMINALS (VDU's)

Summary
Xerox standards require rigid design testing, quality checks during manufacture, and research to back up a strategy that allows us to produce VDT's that are safe for use by anyone. For additional information, please call J. C. MacKenzie, Corporate Director of Environmental Health and Safety, at 716–422–9266 or 8*222–9266.

COMPARISON OF XEROX 850 VDT RADIATION
LEVELS WITH CURRENTLY ACCEPTED STANDARDS

Radiation Region	Exposure Standard	Xerox 850	Reference
X-ray	0.5 mr/hr.	Same as normal background	[b]CFR 1020.10
[a]Ultra violet			
Actinic (200–300 nm)	1×10^{-7} W/cm²	None detected	NIOSH, [c]ACGIH
Near (320–400 nm)	1×10^{-3} W/cm²	1.9×10^{-7} W/cm² (5000 times less than the exposure standard)	NIOSH, ACGIH
[a]Photochemical (400–1400 nm)	1×10^{-2} W/cm² sr	2.7×10^{-6} W/cm²sr (3000 times less than the exposure standard)	ACGIH
[a]Visible infrared (700–1400 nm)	1×10^{-2} W/cm²	5.1×10^{-6} W/cm² (2000 times less than the exposure standard)	ACGIH

[a]Measured at screen face (worst case)
[b]Code of Federal Regulations
[c]American Conference of Governmental Industrial Hygienists
  (Threshold Limit Values for Chemical Substances and Physical Agents in the Workroom Environment–1980)

FIGURE 13. *Excerpt from a Xerox VDT Factsheet*

1 in 34, or 3 percent, do emit, there can be a substantial public health problem. Your protection against unknowingly being exposed to ionizing radiation is to operate only those models for which the manufacturer will provide emission-level data such as supplied by Xerox in figure 13. As with the Xerox machines the levels should be either zero emissions or emissions that are indistinguishable from background levels in the environment.

There are some other safeguards, such as never using a machine that is not operating properly. Also, it helps to remember that the machines were tested by the FDA while operating under the most extreme electronic stress with the protective device removed, not typical operating conditions by any means.

We do not believe there is widespread cause for alarm about the emission of ionizing radiation from VDTs. But we do emphasize that full knowledge about *your* machine and model is both your right and your need. It is also important for VDT users to place their potential problems in perspective in comparison with other workers *known* to be exposed to ionizing radiation, such as hospital workers or those employed in the nuclear-energy industry. For such occupationally exposed people the government has seen fit to declare a yearly exposure standard ten times higher than that of the general population, or 5 rem/year in comparison to the 0.5 rem/year limit for the general population. We believe that the 5 rem/year standard is inexcusably lax and that no workers should be put at greater risk than other people. We take small comfort that at least a more stringent standard is being applied to office workers.

SOURCES AND LEVELS OF NON-IONIZING RADIATION IN VDT WORK

We now turn to the question of non-ionizing radiation, which is generated by the high-voltage systems and the horizontal beam deflectors in the equipment. Most measurements have found little radiofrequency and microwave radiation emitted from the sets. Ninety-five percent of the non-ionizing radiation emitted is extremely low frequency radiation (ELF), such as the radiation that carries the current in your home. Power densities of up to 200 mw/cm^2 have been measured, generally from the front of the VDTs.

It is very difficult to give either reassurances or warnings about ELF radiation because virtually nothing is known about it, despite the fact that we are literally enveloped in it as a result of the mass electrification of our lives. The energy of the beams is, however, very low, so that they should not produce effects similar to those of those of ionizing radiation. There are some fairly good experimental models, which show that the beams interact only in a very limited way with the body.

This discussion, unfortunately, is not very helpful for the VDT user who sits in front of the screen all day—or for that matter, for the parent who may allow children to spend hours in front of a VDT at home, or for the home hobbyist. Therefore we have decided to take the prudent course. It is possible to shield VDTs and to block the non-ionizing radiation from entering your work environment. At the beginning of this discussion we mentioned recent controversies about information stealing that can result from radiofrequency leakage from VDTs. The military and other security-minded agencies are embarking on a program to limit leakage. For example, one can cover all external parts of the VDT (including the screen) with a fine mesh that effectively blocks the radiofrequency signal. Such meshes are quite inexpensive, and in its story on the leakage problem, the *New York Times* showed a drawing of an Apple computer encased in its fine-mesh apparel.

We believe such modifications are needed now, and that they should not be limited to a case-by-case modification program. As the *Times* reports, custom modification can greatly increase the cost of an individual word processor, but assembly-line modifications would add only marginally to overall production price. In the meantime, you can and should contact your VDT manufacturer to learn how to adapt your model in this way.

Again, to give some perspective on the problem, and not to cause alarm among VDT users, the likelihood that the ELF from the VDTs is wreaking environmental damage upon us is not great. The exposure, however, is unnecessary and avoidable and its elimination should be incorporated into the basic design of the VDT.

OTHER RADIATION

The phosphors on the screen can generate infrared, ultraviolet, and of course visible radiation. The levels emitted are so very low that they do not appear to be meaningful by even the most stringent standard.

OTHER POTENTIAL EMISSION PROBLEMS

One area that was investigated by the Food and Drug Administration and that has not received substantial attention is that of ultrasound emissions from VDTs. Unlike radiation, ultrasound is a mechanical form of energy. It is actually sound with a frequency beyond the range that the human ear can perceive.

The FDA found average ultrasound levels of 68 decibels. They refer to a recommendation of 75 decibels made by a British researcher, since no country has legislated a maximum exposure standard for ultrasound. We believe that 75 decibels is not a stringent enough standard. Since some of the effects associated with ultrasound, although at a higher level, include ringing in the ears, headaches, fatigue, and other symptoms similar to the complaints of VDT operators, the question of controlling the ultrasound level is worthy of follow-up by manufacturers, regulators, unions, and others concerned with the problems of VDTs.

RECOMMENDATIONS ON RADIATION AND VDTS

To conclude what is clearly a controversial and difficult subject, we provide the following recommendations, made not so much from a position of certainty as from a knowledge that some policies must be set now.

1. Only equipment for which the manufacturer can and will supply data on emission levels for all forms of radiation and other emissions should be used.

2. Only machines that more than meet minimum standards should be used.

3. All machines should be shielded with a metal casing or painted with highly electrically conductive paint to minimize non-ionizing radiation.

4. There is an urgent need for a study on the clusters of birth abnormalities that have been observed in order to determine whether they occurred by statistical chance or are due to some agent in the workplace. Because of the anxiety that the issue has induced, we recommend that if other jobs are readily available, a pregnant employee be permitted to switch. However, if another job is not available, we do not believe it necessary for pregnant workers or men planning paternity who know that their VDT models do not emit radiation to stop doing VDT work.

5. We recommend that a study of the relationship of birth defects and VDT work be designed to include the possibility of male reproductive effects, since males are known to be affected by working conditions as well. This area must be clarified.

6. We recommend that studies on the effects of ultrasound be

undertaken immediately and that methods for absorbing this unnecessary mechanical pollution be developed and made available to
the consuming public.

7. We recommend that work practices be instituted in each
workplace using VDTs that provide adequate rest breaks and time
away from the machines. The stress and the visual and biomechanical
health and safety hazards associated with VDT work, as well as any
possible radiation effects, would all be lessened by decreasing the
duration and intensity of exposure to these machines.

Stress, Computers, and VDTs

This discussion of video display terminal
work would not be complete if we did not take note that the closely
timed, repetitive, and often boring work can make many jobs that
routinely use VDTs stressful and dissatisfying. Several studies of automated work environments confirm this.

Since VDTs were introduced into the workplace at the end of the
1960s, the most numerous jobs, like all office jobs, are at the bottom rungs
of the office ladder. These workers, usually women, have a minimum
of decision latitude. In many ways their work is indiscernible from
factory work, and in some ways it is even worse. Factory workers
generally make more money than office workers. They can usually talk
to one another and make up informal work groups more easily than
switchboard operators or clerical workers in processing or data-entry
pools. Also, many factory workers belong to unions that can protect
them against arbitrary management decisions and help them to seek
better wages, working conditions, and management processes.

Many of the people who operate switchboards, enter data, or type
on word processors are paced, monitored, and evaluated by machines.
Data-entry clerks, for example, are usually required to type a minimum
number of keystrokes per second, and there is an upper limit for the
number of errors that is tolerated. The computer automatically measures the productivity of the worker and also keeps a permanent record
of performance. This is called a machine-paced job and is analogous to
the automobile assembly line where cars come down the line at a prescribed speed and each worker is required to weld his weld or twist his
bolt as the auto passes before him. The paced environment is believed
to be among the most stressful workplaces. Workers whose speed is

controlled by a machine are found to experience greater job dissatisfaction and to show more symptoms of stress.

Automation of the office, with computers handling more and more tasks, is relentlessly pushing the rationalization of office work processes up the office job ladder as previously prized secretarial and management skills give way to computers, semiconductors, and silicon chips. In the words of Philip Kraft in a recent *Computerworld* special report, "When stripped to its essentials, the effort to create the office of the future is no more than an attempt to make the office of the present look like the factory of the past." One of the ways Kraft and others have described the conversion of the office into an automated factory is by breaking the jobs of the office into small discrete tasks and then dividing these tasks among the employees, not necessarily in a way that makes sense to the individual but instead in order to increase the efficiency or productivity of the whole operation. Thus, rather than seeing a project through from start to finish, an employee may be charged with carrying out only one small segment of it. "This is white-collar factory work, but it is still factory work," says Kraft.

Kraft goes on to describe how such changes affect management, who, he says, have "mixed feelings" about it. "On the one hand, manag-

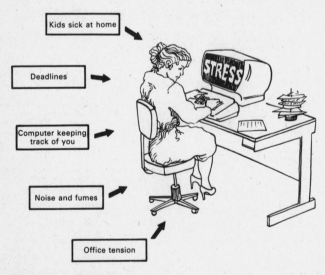

FIGURE 14. *Office Stress*

ers are trained and hired to implement precisely the sort of deskilling and standardization I have been talking about. On the other hand, many managers may feel uncomfortable turning skilled people into extensions of machines. Even if they have no particular objection to deskilling other people, they may suspect that there is less glory and less money and probably less chance for advancement in managing unskilled people than in managing skilled people."

So the implications of automation are not limited to clerical worker, the blue-collar factory worker, or the fast-food-counter cook. Even the manager will feel a substantial impact of office automation, "and for the same reasons," according to Kraft. Kraft also points out that, when the work carried out by clerical workers is "routinized, standardized, and then given to machines," the management of such work is in turn "supervised by low-level, low-paid workers." We would like to add that it may not be supervised by a human at all, since the computer itself can pace a worker, send her warnings, and keep precise track of her comings and goings.

Clearly, the changes thus far introduced into the workplace are deserving of immediate radical reform, though for many VDT operators *any* attempt to improve working schedules will be a welcome relief to the continuous, physically uncomfortable, visually tiring, and monotonous work they do. Two different but modest suggestions of job design come from the British Association of Scientific, Technical and Managerial Staffs (ASTMS), a union for professional workers, and the U.S. National Institute of Occupational Safety and Health (NIOSH).

ASTMS recommends that for work requiring day-long VDT operation, "operators should work a maximum of two hours followed by a 30 minute break. No more than four hours should be worked in any one day." This is clearly a recommendation that involves larger questions of job redesign and sharing so that a VDT operator can use other skills and perform tasks that facilitate rotation during the day.

NIOSH, on the other hand, is less demanding in its approach and recommends that "a 15 minute work-rest break should be taken after one hour of continuous VDT work for operators under high visual demands, high workload or those engaged in repetitive work tasks." The NIOSH report concludes that "while there is no research evidence that this work-rest schedule will be sufficient to deal with all the reported problems, it is felt that this schedule should be tried before more disruptive schedules are implemented."

These proposals are part of a total program that includes universal testing of machines, job rotation, and individually designed and adjustable work environments. The suggestions may appear radical and unrealistic, but they can hardly match the already radical change that has accompanied the introduction of the computer and the video display terminal into the white-collar environment of modern industry. It is no more radical than bringing 10 million VDTs into the office in less than a decade and assigning more than 20 million workers to spend collectively more than 25 billion hours per year operating this equipment, and auditing trillions of keystrokes each year to keep track of the pace and productivity of the computerized office.

CHAPTER 4

TOOLS
OF THE TRADE
Office Furniture, Supplies,
and Equipment

Furniture and office equipment are the tools of the office worker just as the wrench is the stock in trade of the plumber. Unfortunately little attention has been paid to optimizing the design of either the wrench or office furniture and equipment for worker well-being.

Finding a Chair That Fits

Any survey would show that sitting, whether at a desk, switchboard, or typewriter, is the most common characteristic of office work. Obviously, a chair that fits is essential to health.

There are four key factors in a well-designed chair: height, seat, backrest, and construction materials. Since office workers are not cus-tom-ordered off a shelf to meet certain specifications and hence come in all sizes and shapes, office chairs must be adjustable to individual dimensions and biomechanical needs.

It is not difficult to tell whether you and your chair are suited to

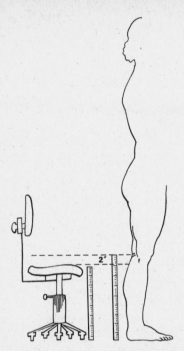

FIGURE 15. *Measuring Correct Chair-Seat Height*
The height of the chair seat should be two inches
less than the distance from the floor to the crease
behind your knees.

each other. When you sit on your chair, your hips and knees should bend at right angles and your feet should be flat on the floor. Whether you can achieve this posture will depend on the height of the chair, which in turn must be adjustable to your own height and the length of your legs. The highest point of your chair seat should be approximately 2 inches less than the distance between the crease behind your knee and the floor when you are standing up. This knee-crease-to-floor distance is known as the "popliteal height," and your chair must conform to this individual physiological requirement. You should measure your own popliteal height and that of your co-workers to see how well it matches your chairs. (Persons who feel shy about doing this can of course make their measurements at home.) Your chair should have a knob for adjusting the seat height. If your seat height is incorrect, change it, then label the chair with your name and consider it your personal piece of office equipment to use for the time you are assigned to your workstation. If your chair is the wrong height and is not adjustable, you must add this problem to the list you should be making as you read this book.

Seat height is particularly critical if your job entails moving your feet to operate a foot pedal on a dictaphone, a door buzzer, and so on. An incorrect height will strain the muscles in your back and may even lead to muscle-joint disease. Dictaphone transcribers sometimes experience backache when they have to extend their foot out to the foot pedal from a too-high chair, resulting in a swayback posture. This problem will be solved by an adjustable foot pedal that can be positioned directly under the knee, as well as by appropriate chair and keyboard height.

An important feature of chair design is support for the spine. Your chair should allow you to sit up straight without bending your spine. For you to assume this position without undue effort, the back of the chair should make firm contact with your back 4 to 6 inches above the seat. The shape of the backrest will depend on the job you do. For the desk worker who writes, reads, or sits and does not operate a machine, a firm, straight-backed chair that allows the body to assume an un-strained position is appropriate. For the typist or VDT operator, on the other hand, who works sitting with hands extended, the best backrest will be small and kidney-shaped, fitting snugly into the small of the back. To accommodate routine body movement, a backrest should tilt back and forth. If frequent body rotations are required by your job, a backrest that meets the back too high or does not move may cause bruises. At the very least, if you don't turn black and blue, you will be uncomfortable. In a job involving frequent sideways motions to reach for papers or answer the telephones, an adjustable backrest can make a real difference in the way your entire body feels at the end of the workday. You might also consider evaluating how a workstation that requires all this sideways motion might itself be changed to be both more pleasant and efficient, and less straining.

A job that requires a great deal of movement will also be eased by a chair that moves along the floor easily. If your workspace floor is covered with carpet that impedes movement of your chair, then you should have a floor mat. On the other hand, slipping and sliding can also be a problem. In general, it is better not to have casters on your chair, since these can cause strain on the calf muscles as you continually try to anchor yourself in place. They can also cause accidents. If casters are absolutely necessary to accomplish your tasks, you should be able to secure the chair by locking the wheels in place.

For the chair to be stable, it should have a five-pronged base rather than the four-pronged type that is common in the United States and is probably responsible for many chair accidents. It is interesting that in the Federal Republic of Germany, five-pronged chairs are required by law.

A good seat will slant slightly backward, just enough to allow you

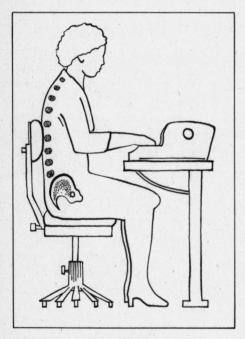

FIGURE 16. *A Chair That Fits*
A well-designed chair will allow you to assume a
position with knees and elbows bent at a 90-degree angle.
The seat height should be adjustable and the backrest
should provide firm support for your lower back. A
five-pronged safety base will give the chair stability, and
locks on the casters will keep it from sliding.

—possibly even posturally "encourage" you—to lean back and use the backrest. It should not be so slanted, however, that you find yourself falling back into the seat, which will force you to strain to reach things and make sitting up an effort. The edge of the seat should be scrolled so that it does not dig into the back of your legs, and the entire seat should swivel, particularly if your work requires frequent sideways movements. A swivel seat allows you to continue to use your backrest as you turn.

Seat size is critical. A chair seat that is too long front to back will force you to lean forward in order to work and place unnecessary pressure on the lower back and thighs. This can impede circulation and aggravate, or even cause, circulatory problems such as varicose veins or hemorrhoids. The well-designed seat should end 5 inches behind the crease in your knee when you are sitting straight and using the backrest.

The material used for the seat should be porous in order to allow normal body heat to dissipate, and textured to prevent you from sliding forward. Wool and rayon fabrics are best. Synthetic and plastic seat covers do not allow body heat to escape. The heat and perspiration problem will be exacerbated if you wear layers of clothing made from synthetic materials. For example, a woman wearing nylon or acetate underpants, nylon pantyhose, an acetate slip, and a polyester skirt and sitting on a vinyl chair seat is effectively in contact with five layers of plastic, which will trap body heat and cause excessive perspiration. In addition to discomfort, problems like rashes and irritation can occur. There are some examples in the medical literature of bladder infections and vaginitis that have been partly attributed to this cause. If this is one of your problems, an immediate part of the solution is to switch to cotton and other natural fibers in your clothing.

Aside from causing discomfort and possibly ill health, poorly designed chairs impede work efficiency. Research has shown that at least 40 minutes of productive time are lost each day because of poor workplace design, some attributable to the chair. Another study has demonstrated that workers who improvise their seating arrangements with pillows, cushions, and backrest devices brought from home, spend several hours a week adjusting these makeshift devices for comfort. A cost-benefit analysis that took such "productivity" losses into account would probably justify an immediate outlay for new chairs.

The Desk

Just as a chair must fit the person who sits in it and correspond to the needs of the job, so too a desk must accommodate both user and task. There must be room for easy handling of constantly needed papers and documents. Telephones, calculators, and other equipment should be readily accessible. Desk clutter is not only unpleasant to look at but can lead to postural strains as the worker contorts his or her body reaching for needed items.

To determine proper surface size and arrangement, make a list of all the typical tasks routinely carried out and the materials and equipment needed to do them, and then calculate the space needed. Vertical space organizers and other aids are available in a variety of shapes and sizes. You might also want to consider taking some of the machinery or papers off the desk to reduce clutter and excessive sideways motion. An example of the contrast between well-designed and poorly designed workspace is shown in figure 17.

Your desk is the proper height when it allows your hands and forearms to be at right angles to your body while you are sitting upright and using the desk surface. This right angle–horizontal position places the least strain on the muscles and hence is the least fatiguing. You should also be able to assume a comfortable reading distance and position. If you are using machines, a document holder will allow for more flexibility.

Unfortunately, most desk heights are not adjustable and are designed to fit the average person, usually male. This generally means that you will have to adjust your chair height to attain the necessary horizontal forearm position. Adjusting chair-seat height may not work, however, because if you make the seat too high, you may then not be able to rest your feet on the floor while maintaining your thighs in a horizontal position. This will be exchanging one problem for another. If you must raise your seat to reach your desk, you may then need a footrest. For comfort and safety the footrest should be adjustable for height and angle of inclination and should never be left in the aisle where someone may trip over it and be injured. The height of a typewriter table should be lower than the desk, as is standard. Plunking a typewriter or VDT on a writing desk will result in a very strained and uncomfortable working position.

Another spatial desk requirement is for freedom of movement. A

FIGURE 17. Designs in Office Space
A. This poorly designed workstation has the following problems: chair too low; four-pronged chair base; appliance cords exposed; inadequate storage and filing space; poor lighting; nonadjustable VDT; attached VDT keyboard, surface too high; crowded work surface.

B. A well-designed workstation is characterized by: document holder; adequate work surface; adjustable lighting sources; blinds on the windows; VDT screen placed at right angles to the window; detachable, thin VDT keyboard; proper working height.

desk must provide room between the thighs and knees and the desk. There must also be adequate clearance behind the chair for getting in and out easily and gracefully.

The surface finish of the desk will affect how much light is reflected. Light bouncing back into the eyes can be a problem. Matte finishes should be obtained. The manufacturers can provide an exact reflectance value, which should be kept between 0.25 and 0.45. The edges and corners of the desk, as with all furniture, should be rounded and smooth to prevent injury.

Office Equipment

PHOTOCOPIERS

No office is complete today without a machine for duplicating letters and documents. Photocopying has become a way of life in the office. A properly designed, installed, and maintained machine is not a hazard, but like all office equipment that requires chemicals for processing or has a high-voltage source, a photocopier can cause indoor air pollution, and may also expose the user to excessive noise and light or even to toxic chemicals if it malfunctions. Understanding how photocopiers work will help you to understand where hazards may arise.

Many photocopiers operate by an electrostatic process. The drum of the copier is coated with a chemical (such as selenium) that has the special property of being able to accept an electrical charge. The photocopier drum is housed in a totally dark area inside the machine where it becomes charged by an electrical impulse. After the drum is charged, a document is copied by reflecting a very bright light from the document surface. (The intense light is one potential hazard.) The amount of light that is reflected from the surface will vary with the writing on it. An area without any writing will reflect all the light that hits it, while areas with printing will absorb the light. The reflected light will thus be an "image" of the document being copied.

The reflected image next hits a series of mirrors and is focused by a camera lens onto the surface of the charged drum. The chemical on the drum loses its charge when light hits it. But since the light has only been reflected from areas of the original document with no printing, the surface of the drum will still be chemically charged in the same areas where there is printing on the original document. The drum surface now has become a chemically charged "mirror image" of the printed page.

Next comes the development process. In development, a special powder, the toner, passes across the drum. It contains an electrically charged chemical that adheres to all the oppositely charged areas on the drum—the areas with printing on the original. This chemical now has, in turn, become the mirror image of the printed page. A piece of paper passes near the drum, and by an electrostatic process the chemical image goes through an intense heating process that bakes the chemical image permanently onto the surface. In the final step, excess powder is removed from the copy and the machine delivers a finished photocopy to the user. If the photo-reproducing chemicals are "wet" instead of dry, they will have been suspended in a solvent, often an alcohol, which is also evaporated during the heating process. The fan cools the paper and machine.

In some machines, this complicated process is repeated and hundreds of copies are made in a very few minutes, really a wonder of technology.

Chemical Hazards in Photocopying. Ozone, a sweet-smelling gas, is given off by equipment that uses a high voltage, including photocopiers. Ozone is formed from the oxygen normally found in the air when it is energized by high voltage. According to most experts, ozone can impair lung function and increase the natural resistance of the airways during breathing, making breathing more difficult. It can decrease one's resistance to infection. Laboratory animals exposed to bacteria and low levels of ozone are more susceptible to disease than control animals exposed only to bacteria. Heat and other stresses worsen this effect. Ozone can also aggravate already existing lung disease and can be particularly irritating to people who already have a sensitivity to other substances or are prone to asthma. Finally, ozone can produce a host of biochemical changes in the blood, including increasing the fragility of red blood cells. However, no one understands the long-range implications of these changes for human health. Research indicates that ozone may be a mutagen, meaning that it may change DNA, the genetic material controlling cell duplication. This could make an exposed individual more likely to develop cancer, but no adequate research has yet been done to answer this question.

Because of its chemical potency, relatively strict standards have been set for human exposure to ozone, although they were not set to protect against its possible mutagenic effects. Both the current U.S. Occupational Safety and Health Administration (OSHA) and the Environmental Protection Agency standards are 0.1 parts per million (ppm) average exposure over a given day. This is equivalent to about 1 drop of liquid in 500 quarts of water. The American Conference of Governmental Industrial Hygienists, an independent standards-making organization, has recommended a ceiling (or maximum exposure) level of 0.3 ppm. A level of 10 ppm is immediately dangerous to life and health. Ozone can be smelled by most human beings at a level of 0.01 ppm, which is far below the OSHA standard. Ozone decomposes to oxygen in a relatively short time, usually between 3 and 15 minutes depending on environmental conditions.

One study of photocopier machines found ozone levels that ranged from 0.08 to 0.202 ppm. After routine maintenance ozone emission dropped to nondetectable levels. Another survey carried out in an office by the National Institute of Occupational Safety and Health (NIOSH) found levels of ozone sufficiently high for them to recommend that copiers be removed from areas where workers sit or work routinely.

The principal solution to the ozone problem (as well as to heat and other problems) is good ventilation. Most manufacturers have minimum specifications for the space and the ventilation requirements of the machines they sell. The Xerox Corporation, for example, publishes a "space/environment/electrical" manual for all its equipment. You should not buy equipment if such data are not readily available. If you already have the machine in place, you should request the specifications from the manufacturer and compare them with the actual setup in your office.

There are some commonsense rules to follow. No one should sit in the path of the exhaust from a photocopier. In fact, there is little reason for anyone to sit near a copying machine at all, since it will at the least be noisy and generate heat, even if it does not emit ozone. If you smell ozone, the levels generated may still be below those considered unsafe by all laws. A dosimetry badge or a detector tube may not be sensitive enough for the levels of ozone generated by many photocopiers. Some machines have ozone-limiting devices installed at the factory. Others can be equipped with filters that capture the ozone before it is emitted into the air. If you believe you have an ozone problem, you should ascertain whether such a filter is available for your photocopier. Larger machines can be fitted with flexible ventilation ducts such as are used for clothes dryers, placed near the exhaust stream from the machine.

Excessive ozone emission may mean that your machine needs servicing. If servicing doesn't work, there are two alternatives. One is to relocate the machine to a larger, better ventilated area, and the second is to get a different model. Since so many photocopiers are rented, substituting a different model may not be that difficult.

Toners. Toners are made up of a fine particulate powder called carbon black. The powder is suspended in a solvent or, in dry toners, mixed with polymers. Exposure to toners is usually minimal. However, since some of the chemicals are potentially hazardous, simple and inexpensive precautions should be taken. People who routinely maintain equipment have a far greater likelihood of chemical exposure than users, and they should be trained to use safe procedures and be provided with protective gloves. Face masks are probably unnecessary. If there is so much dust that you need a face mask, there is something seriously wrong with your machine and it should be returned to the manufacturer. Spent toner and other large quantities of chemical waste from machine maintenance should be carefully disposed of in sealed plastic bags to reduce exposure on the part of custodians. People who service photocopiers need special health and safety training from the manufacturer, since they are exposed to the highest levels of chemicals.

The most likely source of chemical contact for routine users is toner dust. If dark toner dust appears on the paper, or around the machine area at any time (probably indicating that the dust trap within the machine is defective or that the toner-reclaim container is full), machine usage should be stopped immediately and the machine maintenance contractor called. All skin contact with or breathing of toners and other photocopying chemicals should be avoided.

These precautions are necessary because some chemicals that are used in toners—or that have been used in the past—have been found to be mutagens. That is, when subjected to laboratory tests involving bacteria, they altered the genetic material of the bacteria. Most scientists agree that there is a high correlation between mutagenesis and carcinogenesis, meaning that most chemicals that alter genetic material may also cause cancer. Two positive mutagens have been discovered in photocopier chemicals. After tests showed that nitropyrene, a trace contaminant of the carbon black in Xerox toner, was a mutagen, the company removed it from its product. TNF (trinitrofluorenone), is also a mutagen, and was removed from the IBM photoreceptor drums, which contained very small amounts of it. Small levels of TNF were detected in spent toner from these machines. Similar chemical compounds may be present in the chemicals used by other manufacturers. The presence of such mutagens in toners does not mean that people who operate photocopiers are going to get cancer. The amount of toner that will adhere to the finished copy is very low, on the order of approximately 30 ug/per page (which is 30 millionths of a gram or about 1 millionth of an ounce). In the worst case that has been published, about 0.04 ug/per cubic meter was found in the air, also an extremely small amount.

Ironically, the mutagen discovered in the Xerox toner was an impurity in the carbon black and not a chemical needed for the photocopying process itself. Xerox Corporation arranged with the manufacturer of the carbon black to remove the culprit chemical from the carbon black supplied both directly to Xerox and to manufacturers of "licensed" products—that is, chemicals that are sold for use in Xerox machines but are not produced by Xerox. This was an effort on the part of the corporation to eliminate potential exposure of their service representatives.

However, "licensed" products that are manufactured by other companies, but whose tricky labeling makes them appear to have been made by a larger manufacturer, may be inferior products, and often do not come with appropriate warnings or product safety information. The parent corporation has been required, like Xerox, to grant the "license" by court ruling in an effort to limit monopolies. Unfortunately, the courts have not ensured that the substitutes are as safe or as well tested as the original. If the label on the products used in your office for photocopiers or other machines is unclear, or does not have an address or a phone number to call for product safety information, then you should speak to your management about spending a little more for supplies and purchasing materials for which material safety data sheets are supplied.

Solvents. Some photocopiers use liquid toners rather than toners in powder form. The solvent usually consists of simple chemicals called isoparaffinic hydrocarbons. Continued exposure to solvents can lead to defatting of the skin and consequent skin irritation. While the reaction is usually mild, such as a slight irritation of the nose and upper respiratory tract, some very sensitive people may experience an allergic response, or hypersensitivity, causing severe irritation.

Some copying equipment operates by transmission of electrical signals to electrosensitive paper that has been treated with a chemical coating. Some people may be sensitive to the coating materials and develop skin reactions. They should avoid contact with the paper, using surgical gloves or finger pads if necessary when inserting and handling the paper. As with other copying processes, this equipment and paper should be used only in well-ventilated areas, a warning extended by the manufacturers. To learn the identity of all chemicals used or emitted in photocopying processes, it is usually necessary to write to the machine manufacturers, specifying the model number of your machine and the exact trade names of products used with it. The information is often provided in the form of material safety data sheets.

Other Chemicals. The drum in most machines contains particularly toxic chemicals, such as cadmium and selenium. Usually there is no reason to handle or remove the drum, since it will be serviced by representatives who must have extensive safety training. If it is your job to service the machines, then you should be aware of the precautions you must take to avoid any contact with the drums. Old drums should be removed and returned to the manufacturer for disposal.

Bright Lights. The light intensity needed for reflection of the document image is very high. All manufacturers recommend that the document cover be kept down for all copying. However, sometimes the speed of copying, the quantity, or a bulky book or other bound document makes keeping the cover down inconvenient or difficult. The user's eyes will then be exposed to high-intensity light for short periods of time. Little is known about the long-term effects of such light exposure. As with other occupational conditions to which a person may be exposed for many years, prudence is the wisest course. If your machine will not operate without the cover closed, do not override this protective device.

Noise. Many office copier machines produce noise, a necessary aspect of the heating/cooling stage of copy development. Typically some of the larger, multiple-copy machines operate at 80 decibels (dBA). Smaller machines will operate at levels that range from 70 dBA to 78 dBA. The current OSHA standard is 90 dBA. NIOSH recommends 85 dBA, the level set by many countries around the world. Isolation of the machine, sound-absorbing materials, and other strategies that can eliminate noise exposure are discussed in chapter 7.

OTHER MACHINERY IN THE OFFICE

It is beyond the scope of this chapter to describe the many types of machinery that may be used in a specialized office. However, when ordering a piece of equipment, care should be taken to determine and prevent potential health hazards.

If a machine uses or generates toxic chemicals, it must be operated in well-ventilated areas. For example, blueprint machines can generate ammonia fumes, particularly irritating to the eyes. Spirit duplicating machines give off methanol (also called methyl alcohol or wood alcohol). In confined spaces the levels of alcohol have been found to greatly exceed the OSHA standard of 200 parts per million. Many schools use these inexpensive duplicators.

If the machine will contribute to the noise and heat load of the office area, special care should be taken to increase ventilation and to reduce noise levels. Such a machine should be isolated, and only those workers who must have direct access to it should be located in the immediate area. Examples of particularly noisy machinery are folding machines, collators, addressing and postage machines, coin-sorting machines, computer printers, and printers for word-processing equipment. Again, see chapter 7 for a discussion of methods and materials for reducing noise and vibration. If you work near these machines you should find out how noisy they are. If the noise level is close to or exceeds 80 decibels, you are working in an "industrial noise" environment. Contact the resources listed in appendix B for more help and information.

All office machines should meet the electrical safety requirements of organizations such as the Underwriters' Laboratory and bear an approved seal. If the equipment doesn't, then don't use it. Never override automatic shutoff switches, and never violate injunctions not to open certain machine areas. Call a service person. Attempting to fix what is wrong yourself is foolish, and neither workers nor employers should attempt it.

Only heavy-duty electrical connections should be used. Never use a "cheater" to convert a three-pronged plug into a two-pronged plug. The third prong grounds the machine and keeps the operator from receiving an electrical shock. All cords should be inspected regularly and frayed or worn cords replaced. Many machines use high voltages, and they should be treated with a great deal of respect.

Whatever machinery is used in your office, you should be instructed not only how to use the machine properly but also about any hazards associated with its use. If the machine appears to be malfunctioning, work should be halted and a repair person called. Routine maintenance of machines, as recommended by the manufacturers, is essential to the safe operation of equipment. The dates of maintenance should be posted on the machines.

Paper

The chemical revolution has not passed paper manufacturing by. Modern paper manufacture employs dozens of chemicals. There are increasing numbers of reports in the medical literature of allergic reactions to the various chemicals in paper. Some of these chemicals are listed in table 5, on page 33. A few of these substances have recently been shown to be carcinogens as well.

Carbonless copy paper has been responsible for a large number of health complaints and skin reactions like those experienced by

> a 21-year-old woman who had a 1-1/2 year history of intermittent eruption of the face and neck. She worked as a clerk in a college registrar's office and at specific times during the academic year, carbonless forms were used for student registration. Within 24 to 48 hours after using these forms, she had developed a pruritic [itching], erythmatous [reddened] and edematous [swollen] dermatitis.*

Exposure to light can often worsen the situation, as can cold and wetness.

Individuals who have developed an allergic sensitivity to formaldehyde have particular difficulty in eliminating contact with papers manufactured with this chemical. Most papers, including those used in books, magazines, and newspapers, contain traces of the formaldehyde employed in the manufacturing process. Some newsprint has a 0.02 percent

*James G. Marks, Jr., "Allergic Contact Dermatitis from Carbonless Carbon Paper," *Journal of the American Medical Association* 245 (June 12, 1981): 2331.

formaldehyde content, and some paper towels have been measured at 0.03 percent. Even the paper used on most dermatologists' examining tables contains formaldehyde.

Paper can also be a source of eyestrain if it is glossy or provides an inadequate contrast between the printed letters and the background. Papers that are highly glossy will reflect back light, causing "blind spots" when you try to read the printed material. Some poor-quality photocopy papers have notoriously high reflectance. In general, glossy papers should be avoided and matte ones substituted to reduce glare.

Improving the contrast between the paper and the printed words improves legibility. The combination of high-grade light-colored paper and dark matte ink provides the best contrast. Researchers testing reading performance for papers and inks of various contrasts and reflectances have found a fourfold drop in reading performance from matte paper with matte ink to glossy paper with glossy ink. Colored paper often lowers contrast; care should be taken to make sure contrast is adequate before ordering colored stationery.

If you have identified paper as a culprit in dermatitis or visual fatigue, there are some relatively easy solutions. Since different brands of paper use different chemicals, you will probably be able to substitute a nonallergenic brand. After you've identified the particular chemical causing the problem, probably with the help of a dermatologist, write to various paper manufacturers to ask if their products contain the chemical. (You might want to try out a small quantity of the paper just to make sure.)

When buying office paper, especially if you are considering a large purchase, it is always a good idea to test a small quantity first. Let typists try it out and see if readability characteristics are good.

Other Chemicals in the Office

There are chemicals in various other office products like glues, cements, cement thinners, liquid correction fluids, and so on. Some of the chemicals, such as formaldehyde, trichloroethylene, and epoxies, are potentially toxic, but the levels emitted and the percent composition in most office products are small. The likelihood of a lung reaction or cancer or other chronic disease from this source is remote, far lower than in almost any industrial process. However, if the chemical is an allergy-causing agent like formaldehyde, as we have already discussed, even very low levels can cause a serious problem. (See tables 3 and 5.)

There are two other important exceptions. The occasional user of a product like rubber cement is almost assuredly in no danger of chronic illness, but if your job involves long periods of cutting and pasting, then there must be sufficient ventilation to keep you from being overexposed to the fumes emitted by the volatile solvents in the product. A newspaper paste-up room, for example, should have specially designed ventilation. Or if you have file drawers full of carbonless copy paper, there is a good chance that the level of effluent will build up to near-toxic levels.

Another important exception to the generalization that office chemicals do not represent a grave danger occurs when your office is part of an industrial site or near laboratories, garages, or other sources of chemical fumes. Recently the offices and laboratories in a building at Rutgers University in New Jersey had to be closed because of contamination of the air by diethylstilbestrol, a synthetic female hormone known to be a cancer-causing agent and associated with other adverse effects. The chemical had made its way through the ducts from the experimental areas to the offices and other laboratories.

Other instances of chemical contamination of office areas have been reported in the scientific literature and the popular press. An even more tragic accident occurred in 1943 when two young Canadian secretaries died from exposure to diethyl mercury, a chemical painted on seeds to prevent them from developing fungus growths. The chemical is volatile and had seeped through the burlap bags containing the seeds. The women sat at desks near the piles of bags; after inhaling the contaminants for some months, they were poisoned and died.

If you work in an office that is near a factory or laboratory, you may want to reassure yourself that the air you breathe is not contaminated and that the fresh-air inlet to your building does in fact supply clean air. If you have suspicions that there may be a problem, you should contact the appropriate resource, listed in appendix B, and learn your rights and the identity of the chemicals in question.

CHAPTER 5

SHEDDING
SOME LIGHT
ON THE ISSUE
Lighting in the Office

In a recent survey of office workers run by 9 to 5, the National Association of Working Women, lighting was chosen by most of the respondents as the most important physical aspect of their work environment. This is understandable, since 85 percent of the information we receive from our surroundings is perceived through the eyes. Lighting affects our ability to see as well as our comfort, safety, efficiency, and even our mood.

Some information on the relationship between lighting and efficiency is available from research on the effect of different lighting levels on worker productivity. One study of office efficiency showed a 28 percent drop in keypunch productivity when lighting was reduced to half its original level, which was far below any level recommended for office work. When the lighting was restored, the rate and accuracy of the work returned to its original level. Another study involving the same doubling of lighting up to the currently recommended levels showed a savings of $52,900 in an office with 100 keypunch operators. The subject of this book is not, of course, workplace productivity. The productivity studies, however, show that lighting has a very considerable impact on the worker as measured by job performance. We must therefore assume that lighting has as much of an effect on worker health and safety even if no comparable studies have so far been conducted in this area.

How Much Light Do You Need?

How much light is appropriate depends on the visual preferences and capabilities of the office worker, and on the type of work being done. In general it will not be possible to devise one system that will meet everyone's needs. For example, a worker who has been operating a machine all day may need a different light level later in the day than in the morning, and a different intensity than her colleagues. To accommodate such variations a good lighting system will allow individuals to control how much light they want for particular tasks. This means that overhead lighting fixtures should constitute only part of the light source and that the balance of the light should come from individual lamps or lighting fixtures, a scheme referred to as nonuniform lighting. A lamp with a free-swinging arm is very good because a person can shift the position of the lamp to match the position of the work on his or her work surface.

The finer and more detailed the seeing tasks, the higher the level of light needed to perform accurately, comfortably, and efficiently. Reading or transcribing from poor copy demands more than twice as much light as is needed for reading from clear copy. The speed with which you have to read or "see" things will also change the amount of light you need. If you must scan a prescribed number of data entries in a given length of time, you will probably require more light than if your job requires only casual reading.

Corridors need comparatively low levels of light, usually just enough to provide security and to prevent accidents. Conference rooms, photocopying rooms, or stockrooms may also require less lighting since the work carried out there may involve little concentrated reading or other detailed work. It may also afford a good break for the eyes of workers who normally work under much higher light levels. Table 10 gives the levels of illumination recommended by the Illuminating Engineering Society, and generally recommended by standards-making organizations to provide an environment for efficient visual performance. These levels are the standard ones used by

TABLE 10. RECOMMENDED LIGHTING LEVELS

The current lighting recommendations from the Illuminating Engineering Society are given in illuminance ranges rather than single values. The higher values are generally required for workers over forty, for work requiring high speed or accuracy, and where the reflectance of task background is less than 30 percent.

TASK OR WORK AREA	RECOMMENDED LIGHTING LEVEL (IN FOOTCANDLES)
Reading	
High contrast or large size (such as typed originals, handwriting in ink, and good-quality photocopies)	20–50
Medium contrast or small size (such as medium-pencil handwriting and poor-quality photocopies)	50–100
Low contrast or very small size (e.g., handwriting in hard pencil on poor-quality paper, and very poor-quality photocopies)	100–200
Building entrances (outdoors)	5
Conference rooms	20–50
Drafting and graphic design	
High-contrast media	50–100
Low-contrast media	100–200
Elevators	10–20
Libraries	
Active stacks	20–50
Book repair and binding	20–50
Card files	50–100
Mail sorting	50–100
Offset printing and duplicating	20–50
Parking garages (indoors)	5
Stairways and corridors	10–20

SOURCE: Adapted from *Illuminating Engineering Society Lighting Handbook. 1981 Reference Volume* (New York: IES, 1981).

AUTHORS' NOTE: These levels are recommendations. Individual comfort should be the main guide. Non-uniform lighting that provides individual workstations with a light source in addition to the general source is preferred.

most lighting designers and incorporated in many building codes.

The quality of light is another factor to consider in office lighting. Even in an office where the amount of light provided is appropriate, the arrangement of the lights may be such as to give rise to a sensation of excessive brightness or harshness. An ideal lighting system will combine natural and artificial light. According to several studies, this combination improves color perception and also contributes to a sense of well-being.

Another method for improving the quality of light is to combine direct and indirect lighting. Indirect light is reflected from ceilings or walls, whereas direct light shines directly from the fixture onto the workspace. One way to have good office lighting is to have one-third of the recommended task lighting as general lighting (which could be indirect lighting) and the remaining two-thirds coming from individual direct sources such as swinging-arm lamps.

Avoiding Glare and Shadows

Glare is caused by light shining directly into your eyes or bouncing off a surface and reflecting into your eyes. Anyone who has tried to read a glossy magazine under a direct light and tilted the paper in order to read has experienced glare. If you can see what you are doing more easily with your hand shielding your eyes from the lighting system, then chances are you have a direct glare problem. To do something about glare you have to figure out where the offending light is coming from. Try placing a mirror on your desk or other work surface and looking at the images in the mirror. If you can see exposed light bulbs or any bright light reflected in the mirror while you are sitting or standing in your normal working position, the lamp or other object being reflected is probably causing the glare.

One logical solution is to change the location of either the light source or the workstation. Since most lighting fixtures are built into the ceiling and are very difficult to relocate, rearranging workstations makes more sense. In general, workstations should be between rows of lighting fixtures. If it is not possible for the light to be at the side of the desk, then it should be centered directly over your head rather than over the desk, or worst of all, directly in front of the desk. Figure 18 illustrates these principles.

The glare problem can also be tackled by shielding the light source

A   B

FIGURE 18. Lighting Designs
A. A well-designed office will provide individual task-lighting sources.
Both indirect and direct lighting sources will be present. Concealed
lighting reflected from the upper wall is preferred. The work surface will
be at right angles to a window, equipped with shades and two overhead
lighting fixtures. Surfaces of walls and furniture will be matte to
minimize reflections. B. A poorly designed lighting scheme results in light
shining or reflected directly into the eyes, as shown by the arrows.
Fixtures directly overhead or in front of the work area will cause glare,
as will the unshaded window in front of the desk in the illustration.
Minimal use of low-reflective surfaces has been made in this office.

with plastic or other devices that spread out the rays. This is called
diffusion. Some of the devices, logically called diffusers, are placed on
the sides and bottom of the fixtures. Plastic or frosted glass shields can
also be used. Another way to cut down glare is to cover the lamp with
a gridlike series of baffles that keep your eye from making direct contact
with the bare bulb and also diffuse the light. These are the methods
commonly used in offices. The efficiency range of the various shielding
devices can be ascertained, and your purchasing agent or consultant

should ensure that the most efficient device is being used. These shields are relatively inexpensive, and should be changed if they are not doing the job required.

If you are lucky enough to work near a window, it is important to realize that natural light can also cause glare. Just as with lighting fixtures, the best position is for you to sit so that the light comes into the room at your side or rear. If you face the window, you need an easily adjustable shade that can be opened or closed as the sun changes position. Climbing on your desk to move the shades or doing battle with the cords is unsafe.

Glare can be greatly reduced by eliminating shiny, reflective surfaces on furniture and equipment. The same is true of paper quality, as discussed in chapter 4 but worth repeating here, since the likelihood of your being able to change the paper or cover a shiny desk with a piece of blotter paper is much greater than that of redesigning the lighting fixtures. The extent to which a surface bounces back or reflects the light is called its reflectance, and most suppliers of equipment or materials will supply information about the reflectance of their products. The following surface reflectance levels are generally recommended:

Ceiling	0.70 to 0.90
Walls	0.40 to 0.60
Furniture tops	0.25 to 0.45
Office machines	0.25 to 0.45
Office equipment	0.25 to 0.45
Floors	0.20 to 0.40

There are literally hundreds of colors and surface finishes available that meet these criteria.

Shadows are the second problem that can arise from direct light. Shadows can be formed only by direct light. Outdoors, you have to be in the sun, a source of direct light, in order to cast a shadow. There are no shadows on a cloudy day, when the sun is shielded. One solution, therefore, is indirect lighting, which provides a shadow-free environment. Individual task lighting that can be moved is another method for combatting shadows, as in drafting rooms, where shadows are a common complaint. Besides, the fineness of drafting requires strong light. To illuminate the entire room at that level would be excessive for most other tasks and probably uncomfortable to work in for a full day. A better lighting plan might use general, indirect lighting to provide 50 footcandles, and individual swinging-arm lamps for the recommended additional 150 footcandles for drafting.

In the new open offices, task lighting is a necessity since the partitions separating the workspaces will almost always cast shadows from overhead lights. Providing additional individual light fixtures will eliminate the shadows. Again, the best are lamps with free-swinging arms. Unfortunately, many of the modular workstations have immovable lighting fixtures built in as part of their design, making it almost impossible to deal with the shadow problem or to move light to match the task.

Fluorescent Lighting

Fluorescent lights are widely used in offices because they are much more energy- and cost-efficient than incandescent bulbs. A fluorescent tube puts out about four times as much light as an incandescent bulb of the same wattage. One reason is that incandescent bulbs use up a lot of their energy generating heat rather than light, another drawback for use in offices, where the extra heat is certainly not needed in the summer months.

Fluorescent lighting is very controversial in some circles. People have attributed many ill effects to it, and popular magazines often run articles about health effects ranging from discomfort to serious illness. A recent study in the British medical journal *Lancet* reported on an association between melanoma, a very serious form of skin cancer, and fluorescent light. The study is hardly definitive, and to date little evidence exists to show that fluorescent light causes diseases like cancer. There are reports in the medical literature of skin rashes and other skin reactions thought to have been caused by fluorescent-light exposure in highly sensitive people, but again there is little reason to expect this to occur in any but exceptional cases.

Many kinds of fluorescent bulbs do give off ultraviolet radiation, most of it very low-level. We are all exposed to ultraviolet radiation when we are in the sun, and it is this component of the sun's rays that causes sunburn. Some scientists carrying out specialized research with ultraviolet-sensitive chemicals or cells have found that the ultraviolet rays given off by the fluorescent bulbs in their laboratories have interfered with their research. They generally shield the bulbs with a yellow cover that absorbs the rays. In most office situations the white plastic shields on the fluorescent bulbs will absorb virtually all the ultraviolet radiation. If you have an unshielded fluorescent tube in your office you probably should have it covered with a plastic shield. Although we do not believe that ultraviolet radiation from fluorescents represents a health threat, the shield will not only absorb it but will also prevent glare, and so is useful in any case.

We are not as certain about the psychological and comfort effects of fluorescent lighting as about the radiation. Unfortunately, no well-designed large-scale study has been carried out. Many individuals have indeed complained that sitting under fluorescent lights detracts from their sense of well-being. It may be that they are feeling the same discomfort that people report experiencing in overlit offices. According to many experts, much emphasis in the past has been on flooding the workplace with light with little attention to people's needs or comfort.

In addition to overillumination, it may be that the color of the fluorescent bulbs is not one of the more modern "warmer" varieties. "Cool white" bulbs, which lack deep red and are slightly greenish, are still the largest sellers. Bulb manufacturers have altered the wavelengths of the light generated to create a less harsh feeling. Substituting these bulbs for the "cool white" variety can readily be done in any office. The yellower bulbs that closely mimic sunlight are considered best by some people.

Another common complaint about fluorescent bulbs is their flicker, or rapid fluctuations in the light. Flicker can be caused by a number of different things. Old bulbs may be wearing out; the solution is good maintenance with a regular schedule for changing bulbs before the flicker problem develops. If changing the bulbs doesn't work, the circuit should be investigated. A faulty lamp circuit, usually with a starter switch that needs to be replaced, will increase the flicker.

Most of the electricity in offices is alternating current (AC), which means that it goes on and off many times a second. This causes both fluorescent and incandescent lights to go on and off rapidly—usually so rapidly that it is not noticeable. If a room has many lights on the same circuit, however, they may flicker exactly in unison. In this case the flicker will be noticeable to many people and will almost certainly be annoying. The circuitry should be changed.

Still another problem can be a humming noise, called ballast hum,

FIGURE 19. *How to Measure Light in the Office* *A light meter can be used to measure surface* *and room light. Be sure not to let your* *shadow fall between you and the area you are* *measuring.*

which is caused by the magnetic field generated by the electric current's expanding and collapsing. Humming ballasts should be replaced with quieter varieties if the hum is audible and annoying.

Maintenance of the lighting system is needed if it is to continue to provide good lighting to office occupants. At a minimum, maintenance includes cleaning and changing the bulbs regularly. Even in a clean, unpolluted office, where the air is filtered and the outdoor air relatively pure, there can be a drop in the light level of approximately 5 percent per year due to undusted bulbs. The lighting fixtures should be cleaned at least once a year, and more often where the air is not clean.

The light bulbs should be changed before they burn out, because they will become progressively weaker. Most large buildings maintain a regular schedule for light-bulb replacement, since the lifetime of the bulbs can be estimated quite well.

Taking Measurements

You can easily measure lighting levels using a light meter as illustrated in figure 19 and compare them with the levels shown in table 10. Remember, however, that most of these recommendations are derived from experiments in laboratory settings, usually using young volunteers, and that your own comfort and ability to work efficiently must determine how much light you need.

CHAPTER 6

PREVENTING THE TOWERING INFERNO
Fire Safety in the Office

More than a year after the city of New York passed more stringent local laws governing fire safety in office towers, only 167 of the city's 851 towers, defined as buildings taller than 10 stories, have met all the law's requirements. The law requires that elevators descend automatically to the lobby in case of fire. Many elevators are heat-activated and are literally drawn to the floor where the flames are. Alarms, two-way communications systems, and stations to ease evacuation, coordinate fire-fighting efforts, and control panic are also specified. The New York City Council passed the law in 1973 after five people had died in two separate fires in 1970. Suits by landlords kept the city from enforcing the law until 1978, when landlords were given until September 1982 to comply. The *New York Times* reported on October 30, 1982, one month after the deadline had passed:

> Five people were injured in a fire at the 51-story Marine Midland Building. . . . The building's elevators had heat-activated controls instead of the automatic system, and one of them went to the floor

that was on fire instead of the lobby and jammed open. The landlord was among those given extensions of the deadline for compliance. A subsequent survey of all office towers, most of which are in Manhattan, showed that five of six landlords had not complied.

New York City has some of the strongest codes and strictest enforcement of fire laws in the country. What does this news story portend for office workers across the land, particularly in the newer cities where fire codes are notoriously lax? We are afraid that it means the "Towering Inferno" will one day be more than a fictional film. Several hotel disasters have already proved the point. Poor planning clearly extends beyond the office to the very buildings themselves. And strict fire-safety inspections and drills should be part of every office's operating procedure. They are not.

Nationwide, 64,000 fires were reported in offices and banks between 1970 and 1974. Monetary losses exceeded an estimated $236 million, and hundreds of people were hurt or lost their lives. Much of this injury and loss could have been prevented relatively easily by appropriate fire-safety planning and personnel training, or by simple changes in interior design and the installation of warning and sprinkling devices. More difficult but still essential changes that could save lives and property are stricter building codes, inspections, and enforcement.

Fueling the Flames

For a fire to start, two elements are necessary: something to burn, and oxygen to support the combustion. Wood or paper was the original material ignited in more than half the office fires between the years 1970 and 1974 analyzed by the National Fire Protection Association (NFPA). About 8 percent arose from burning textiles like draperies and seat cushions.

The amount of combustible material inside a building that will support and spread a fire is called the fuel load. If you look around your office, you will be surprised at the potential fuel load of your surroundings. The vinyl covering on the walls, the furniture, the rugs, the papers and books, the files, the plastic wastebaskets and containers, can all ignite, the fuel load supporting and spreading a fire. It is calculated by itemizing every combustible item and then using the figures in table II,

TABLE 11. WEIGHTS FOR CALCULATING THE FUEL LOAD

ITEM	SIZE	WEIGHT TO USE*
Officer's desk (wood)	6' by 3' by 30"	195 lb.
Officer's chair	Standard	65 lb.
Secretary's desk (wood)	6' by 3' by 30"	195 lb.
Sideboard	37" by 18"	100 lb.
Secretary's chair	Standard	45 lb.
Credenza (wood)	7' 6"	215 lb.
	5' 6"	160 lb.
Sofa	3 cushion	170 lb.
	2 cushion	110 lb.
Chair	1 cushion	70 lb.
Coffee table (wood)	3' by 3'	50 lb.
End table (wood)	2' by 2'	26 lb.
Conference table	10' by 3'	200 lb.
Conference chair	Standard	36 lb.
Clerk's desk (wood)	Standard	150 lb.
Planter (wood)	3' by 2'	50 lb.
File cabinet (wood)	5' by 2' by 2'	110 lb.
Carpet		1 lb./sq. ft.
Carpet underlayment		1 lb./sq. ft.
Doors	24" by 80" by 2"	56 lb.
	30" by 28" by 2"	68 lb.
	34" by 28" by 2"	77 lb.
	36" by 80" by 2"	83 lb.
	38" by 82" by 2"	138 lb.
	30" by 44" by 2"	98 lb.
Wood panel	35" by 93" by 2"	94 lb.
Wood panel	38" by 93" by 2"	103 lb.
Wood panel	20" by 93" by 2"	84 lb.
Wood panel	4' by 8' by ¼"	50 lb.
Draperies and misc.	Room—16' by 20'	200 lb.
Contents of		
Officer's desk		178 lb.
Secretary's desk		180 lb.
Credenza		560 lb.
File cabinet		650 lb.
Carton of paper		50 lb./cu. ft.
	8½" by 11" paper—1" thick	3 lb.

TABLE 11. (cont.)

ITEM	SIZE	WEIGHT TO USE*
	8½ " by 14" paper—1" thick	4 lb.
	8½ " by 11" looseleaf binder—1" thick	4 lb.
Wastebasket contents		3 lb.
Wood picture frame	30" by 40"	5 lb.

SOURCE: Excerpted from Citicorp's *Safety and Fire Prevention Manual.*
*If the item is plastic, multiply the weight by 2.

supplied by Citicorp, a pioneer in fire safety, to add up the total. Figure 20 also illustrates how to do this. It is both informative and disconcerting to realize how quickly the fuel load adds up to a dangerous level.

The maximum safe fuel load has been defined as 15 pounds per square foot. If the fuel load in your office can be kept below this level, there is a good chance that you can get the people out of a burning area and isolate the fire—that is, provided building construction allows you to isolate burning areas. There may also be certain areas in your building, like warehouses or storage areas, where the 15-pound-per-square-foot level cannot be met. These areas require special fire protection.

Special care must be taken with plastics. Most plastic materials are far more dangerous when burning than wooden articles of equivalent size and shape. Simply using the fuel-load figures in table 11 would seriously underestimate the potential danger. Citicorp recommends doubling the weight of the article if it is plastic. This is prudent advice for a start, in the absence of more definitive scientific data upon which to base recommendations, but it may still not be good enough to provide a margin of safety.

THE PERILS OF PLASTIC
Many synthetic materials can be particularly deadly during a fire because they give off extremely toxic fumes when burning. Some, like the cyanide that is evolved from burning urethane, a common upholstery stuffing, can be deadly at very low concentrations. Or the carbon monoxide emitted by vinyls when they burn can incapacitate you and severely limit your chances of getting out of a fire in time. The searing

A   B

FIGURE 20. Office Furnishings as Fuel for Fire
Using the values given in table 11, we have carried out a sample
calculation for the office areas shown:

Office A: Weights of	Office B: Weights of
Wood clerk desk	Wood officer desk
Secretarial chair	Officer chair
Credenza	2-cushion sofa
Carpet	1-cushion chair
Carpet underlayer	Side table
Door	Carpet
Draperies	Carpet underlayer
Wood paneling	Door
Desk contents	Wood paneling
Credenza contents	Desk contents
File-cabinet contents	Paper
Paper	Wastebasket contents
Wastebasket contents	Looseleaf binder
Wood picture frame	Plastic plants and pots
Plastic plant and pot	Wooden picture frame

2,953 pounds ÷ floor area of 200 square feet = 14.7 pounds per square foot

1,842 pounds ÷ 400 square feet = 4.6 pounds per square foot

fumes of hydrochloric acid that will also be given off will cause you to cough and make it extremely difficult to keep your eyes open to find your way out.

Because of the high flammability of so many plastics, most are made with chemical flame retardants. Unfortunately, while this does indeed keep the flames down, it usually causes the plastic to smolder instead, producing even larger quantities of deadly smoke. Some new plastics are being synthesized and products manufactured from them that are more inherently flame-resistant and that will significantly reduce the problem. But most of these products are still in the developmental stage and are not commercially available, particularly at a reasonable cost.

Too little is known about the increased fire risks arising from the growing use of plastics in building materials and furnishings. Some of the scientific evidence available is disturbing. For example, researchers conducting studies under the aegis of the National Bureau of Standards concluded that smoke from plastics is, in general, six times more lethal than smoke from Douglas fir, a commonly used wood. They found that burning plastics always gave off irritating and asphyxiating fumes, and that some of the smoke contained potent chemicals toxic to the nervous system. A nervous-system toxin will severely limit your ability to escape from the fire. Other chemicals present in much of the smoke had the ability to injure the liver, kidneys, and heart even at very low levels.

Tests exposing animals to smoke showed that the toxic smoke from plastics was released more rapidly, killing more quickly than smoke from wood. In addition, unlike wood smoke, some of the plastic-generated smoke caused immediate acute effects such as severe corrosion of the eyes and severe pulmonary-tract irritation at very low levels.

HIDDEN HAZARDS

Many unexpected sources of fire and fume hazards are right before your eyes, like the plastic wastepaper basket that has replaced the old-fashioned metal basket in so many offices. A plastic wastepaper basket will easily melt and generate fumes. In addition, a carelessly tossed cigarette butt can lead to a fire, which the old metal basket would simply have contained. Here the hazard is seen but unperceived, but there are also unseen and unperceived fire hazards in your office building. The urea-formaldehyde foam that may insulate your walls is highly flammable and will both spread the flames and be a source of deadly fumes when burning. It is difficult to increase its fire resistance, since the chemicals needed for this tend to make it more brittle and difficult to use.

As an ironic aside here, it should be mentioned that the almost perfect insulating material is asbestos because of its qualities of inertness and resistance to extremely high temperatures. But as discussed in chapter 8, "Indoor Air Pollution," asbestos is unfortunately a deadly chemical that causes cancer and lung disease and has been responsible for the deaths of thousands of workers who applied asbestos to insulate buildings and ships, among other jobs.

Also hidden in the walls is a building's electrical wiring. The NFPA analysis of office fires found that at least 20 percent of the fires it studied began in the electrical distribution system. Many building codes now permit the use of plastic tubes or conduits to cover the wires. When these conduits burn, they generate high levels of carbon monoxide, hydrochloric acid, and other chemical fumes that can be deadly, or at the very least disabling.

PCBS—A NEW HAZARD IN OFFICE BUILDINGS

In the early morning hours of February 5, 1981, an explosion and fire in an electrical transformer in New York State's eighteen-story office building in Binghamton sent oily soot billowing up from the basement. The ventilation system sucked in the smoke and soon spread the soot through the ductwork behind the walls and in the suspended ceilings and over the surfaces and even inside cabinets and closets. Luckily the building was unused at the time and there were no fire-related deaths or injuries, but a massive cleanup effort was needed. It was discovered that 180 gallons of coolant fluid had leaked out of the transformer. The fluid contained polychlorinated biphenyls, PCBs, which are particularly poisonous synthetic substances, among the most toxic and long-lasting known to man. PCBs cause cancer, birth defects, liver damage, and other diseases. What is more, the heat of the flames caused some chemical reactions to occur, and the deadly substances called dioxins and dibenzofurans were formed.

Several days into the routine cleanup the potential danger of the situation was realized. Chemical tests showed levels of PCBs in file drawers that were as high as 74.5 ug/m³. The National Institute of Occupational Safety and Health recommends a standard of 1 ug/m³ for PCBs. Levels of 273 parts per million of dibenzofurans and 4 parts per million of dioxins were measured as well in the pervasive soot. Clearly a crisis was at hand.

To date the Binghamton State Office Building remains closed, and no one is quite sure how to detoxify it. Including fire fighters and cleanup crews at the early stages of the disaster, 479 persons have claimed they were exposed to the toxic soot. Lawsuits totaling more than $1 billion have already been filed claiming negligence on the part of the state. A resolution of the crisis is not yet apparent.

Although the Binghamton disaster appears to be the first on this scale, there are surely others waiting to happen. PCBs were commonly used as a coolant in capacitors and transformers for many years, and the Environmental Protection Agency has estimated that there are approximately 140,000 transformers nationwide like the one in the Binghamton building. As a result of the tragedy, New York State decided to replace transformers containing PCBs in its office buildings at a cost of about $20 million. (Disposing of the old coolant will not be easy—there doesn't appear to be a completely safe and acceptable way of doing it, but several promising new techniques are being tested.) The Canadian government banned such transformers after a similar but smaller incident in Toronto in 1979. But the problem is still largely unrecognized and unresolved.

Reducing the Risk

There are some practical steps that can be taken to reduce the potential havoc of fire. These are listed in the survey in appendix A. One obvious course of action is to reduce an excessive or unnecessary fuel load. The large stacks of papers and forms that abound in most offices are a major source of fuel. Keeping these unused records and papers in fire-resistant storage files or vaults will not only protect lives but cut down on office clutter.

Another possibility is to furnish offices only with flame-retardant items and materials. The safety department of Citicorp and the Port Authority of New York and New Jersey have recommended that the vast number of properties they control purchase only materials that generate lesser amounts of fire, smoke, and toxic gas. Furniture and furnishings should be purchased only after a manufacturer's affidavit certifying that all materials are flame-resistant, and stating their expected durability, is received. Performance under fire conditions should be an essential qualification that is listed when bids are solicited for office supplies. Of course, insisting on fire retardance is still a compromise, because with the smoldering and toxic-fume production there may be no immediate solution.

Some things should not be purchased at all. Plastic decorations are an unnecessary source of fuel and toxic gases. Some natural products also give off extremely hazardous fumes when burning.

Smoke Detectors and Sprinklers

An essential first step in reducing the danger from a fire is to realize that the fire is burning. The NFPA analysis showed that only about one-third of office fires originated in the main work areas. Fourteen percent started in storage areas, another 14 percent in structural areas such as suspended ceilings, and 13 percent in service areas. This means that it is possible, even likely, for a fire to burn for some time and spread a considerable distance before a building's occupants become aware of it unless adequate detectors and warning devices are in place. Detectors and alarms linked to sprinkler systems can put out, or at least largely control, a fire in the early stages before major damage or injury has occurred. NFPA found that in office buildings with sprinkler systems, 97.4 percent of the fires were satisfactorily controlled.

The types of fire detection and sprinkler systems required depend on the number of people in the building, the number of floors, and the type of occupancy (offices only, offices and manufacturing, restaurants, etc.). Often local building codes will specify or affect what system is to be installed.

There are two types of smoke detectors: photoelectric, which detect visible products of combustion, and ionization, which detect invisible products of combustion. Photoelectric smoke detectors may be preferred since ionization detectors contain minute sources of radioactivity, although the Consumers Union does not consider this a problem of any significance. Both types offer approximately the same level of early-warning protection. An alternative to a smoke detector is a heat detector that will be set off when a particular temperature is reached or when the rate of temperature change is greater than normally expected.

Both smoke and heat detectors are generally located at ceiling level, where they can be seen and where they are exposed to the smoke or heat generated by a fire. Others should be placed inside air-handling systems to detect fires in venting, heating, and cooling systems. The spacing and the area coverage for detectors depends on the particular manufacturer's specifications, since they vary. The detectors are, of course, hooked up to an alarm. In addition to these automatic devices, each general work area should be equipped with manual alarms as well, so that if a fire is detected by a worker, she or he can set off an alarm.

Automatic sprinkler systems are one of the most effective ways of guarding against loss of life and property from fire. Sprinkler systems are located at ceiling level and can be visible or concealed. The NFPA has a standard for sprinkler systems; generally, each sprinkler head should cover approximately 200 square feet. Sprinklers should also be installed in combustible spaces *above* ceilings, where fires may spread.

It is an astounding fact that one of the most frequent reasons for unsatisfactory sprinkler performance is that the sprinkler control valves were closed, so that the system could not automatically respond to a fire. Valves are closed for many reasons, such as inspections and servicing. They must be reopened immediately, and a good sprinkler system will have a warning light or alarm that remains on whenever a valve is closed. It is ridiculous and dangerous to work in an office with a sprinkler system that cannot operate because it is turned off. The system should also be inspected at least annually by a trained professional to ensure that other mechanical problems are not present.

Unfortunately, many buildings do not have sprinkler systems, and many building codes, particularly in the newer cities, do not require them. It is commonly assumed that retrofitting a building with a sprinkler system is inordinately expensive, but the actual cost is comparable to that of some luxury items, like plush carpeting, that are frequently installed in offices. It is also disheartening that many insurance carriers discourage the use of sprinklers by requiring stiff additional premiums for protection against water damage if a sprinkler is present.

In addition to a sprinkler system, an office should be equipped with multipurpose fire extinguishers. The size of the office will determine how many are needed, and the NFPA provides ratings and details on coverage. Your local fire department should also be able to give you this information. In general, no one should have to walk more than 75 feet to reach an extinguisher.

Inspecting the fire extinguisher should be a regular procedure. For example, at least once a year the extinguisher should be weighed to make sure it still contains carbon dioxide or other fire-fighting chemicals, and the cylinder strength should be checked by a hydrostatic pressure test. The dates of the inspections should be clearly indicated on the extinguisher tag. Hoses and valves must also be routinely inspected. These factors are all detailed in appendix A, section II.

One note of caution: Never allow the use of the extinguisher to substitute for calling the fire department and for following all the notification routines in your office. First, what may appear to be a controllable fire can rapidly get out of hand. Second, it is important that the appropriate fire-safety authorities be aware of each fire that occurs, no matter how small, so that they can analyze the cause and determine whether fundamental changes in an operation or material are needed.

A number of highly technical codes and standards have been incorporated in laws that govern design and materials allowed in office-building construction. Codes specify such features as number of persons per 22-inch unit of exit width; travel distance to an exit; number of exit signs; maximum flame-spread ratings for interior finishes; requirements for fire alarms and sprinkler systems; emergency communication systems. The codes vary from area to area of the country, and code specialists are necessary to interpret their provisions to building architects. More details can be obtained from the sources listed in table 12 or from your local fire department.

DESIGNS FOR CONTAINING FLAMES

Keeping a fire contained in the smallest area possible requires walls and doors that prevent the spread of flames. For example, there are codes that require that the doors enclosing a "fire area" be able to resist flames for three hours and that the doors enclosing stairs or elevators resist flames for one and one-half hours. Buildings that have discrete airtight areas are called compartmentalized. Compartmentalization is accepted as an alternative to sprinklers in many building codes. But unless compartmentalization is carefully planned and preserved, it may not be adequate.

Changing construction styles have aggravated the fire potential of buildings. Since World War II, building materials such as heavy stone and brick have been replaced by lightweight steel framing that is covered with fireproofing materials like asbestos. Lightweight construction

TABLE 12. BUILDING CODES GOVERNING FIRE SAFETY

GEOGRAPHIC AREA	NAME OF CODE	ADMINISTERING ORGANIZATION
Western U.S.	Uniform Building Code	International Conference of Building Officials, Inc. 5360 S. Workman Mill Rd. Whittier, CA 90601
Eastern and Midwestern U.S.	Basic Building Code	Building Officials and Code Administrators International, Inc. 17926 S. Halsted St. Homewood, IL 60430
Southern U.S.	Standard Building Code	Southern Building Code Congress International, Inc. 900 Montclair Rd. Birmingham, AL 35212

materials do not provide a "heat sink" or reservoir that helps to disperse the intensity of the flames.

For the open office that has no floor-to-ceiling walls, the concept of "equivalence" has emerged. This concept is based on the theory that if fire-safe areas cannot be defined on individual floors, then a building must be vertically compartmentalized—that is, entire floors must be isolated. This is accomplished by the use of negative air pressure in the stairwells, the automatic sealing of elevator shafts with airtight doors, and other complicated techniques.

Even if compartmentalization is effective and successfully contains the flames, smoke and toxic gases may still spread beyond the fire area into elevator shafts and even stairwells, the very path the building occupants must take to escape the blaze. This has occurred even when the shafts remained closed. It is surprising just how great the airflow can be through openings in floors and walls, and particularly the vertical openings in buildings.

The amount of poisonous gas that can infiltrate these areas will depend on the height of the building, how tight the exterior walls are, the amount of air leakage between the floors, and the differences in temperature between the air inside the building and the air outside the building. (This means that a fire and the spread of gases may behave very differently in the winter than in the summer, even in the same building.) The danger from smoke and gas rises with the height of a building because the natural movement of air is upward. This is known as the stack effect. No perfect solution exists to the problem, but one way to mitigate the stack effect is to construct a vertical smoke shaft that extends the length of the building, with vents to the outside on every floor which can be opened in the event of a fire. The shaft operates like the flue of a chimney, drawing smoke from the fire into the outside air. If it is very hot outside, the smoke shaft will not work well; nor will it function properly if windows have been broken, or doors left open, on the floors where the fire is.

It should be obvious by now that the codes and the state of the art of fire safety have not kept pace with the innovations of architects, designers, and chemists. Unfortunately it has been the history of fire regulations that they follow disasters. In fact, the nickname applied to the fire codes is graveyard laws. Factory fire and safety laws followed fast upon the tragic Triangle Shirtwaist Company fire, which claimed the lives of more than 140 people who were unable to escape a blaze because they had been locked into the factory. Many people consider that the Triangle Fire ushered in the "golden age of labor legislation" in 1911. Let us hope that a similar high-rise office disaster is not needed before the age of fire safety in the office is ushered in.

Getting Out Safely

Being prepared for a fire emergency is serious business. The orderly evacuation of a building requires planning and practice. Since elevators cannot be used, adequate stairwell exits must be available, and a priority system for evacuation must be established so that the stairwells do not become clogged with panicked people trying to escape. Excellent communications during an emergency will be necessary, particularly in a high-rise, where those in the greatest immediate danger must leave first. Good communications will prevent panic from setting in. People who know and understand what is going on will be far less likely to act irrationally, endangering themselves and others. An emergency loudspeaker and telephone communications system should be available, in the event that building power is disrupted. There should be a single central source for all instructions. There must be a written evacuation plan for each floor, and a map posted that clearly and understandably shows the exit routes for building evacuation. A warning sign prohibiting elevator use should be plainly posted at each elevator door. It is generally recommended that all workers on a floor gather at a specified area on hearing the alarm, to await the instructions of the fire warden.

Each floor of a building should have a person designated as a fire warden, and there should be a deputy warden for each 7,500 square feet of space. Two searchers per floor should also be designated. It goes without saying that the designated wardens and searchers must be fully aware of all the emergency facilities and how to use them properly.

Fire drills and regular inspections are the key to preparedness. The survey in appendix A gives the items that must be inspected. Fire drills should be held at least four times a year and include full rehearsals for every aspect of an emergency. In some cities this may be a requirement. The fire department should be invited for a practice session so that they can become familiar with the layout of your building. It is the job of the fire warden to inspect the exits and the paths and doors leading to them *daily* to make sure that they are completely unobstructed. Fire extinguishers, hallway and exit emergency lights, and signs should also be inspected routinely. Deputy wardens should assume the inspection duties if the fire warden is absent. The job of searchers is to look for people in lounge areas, coffee rooms, and bathrooms and to make sure that all occupants leave the floor during an evacuation. The searchers must also be aware of people with disabilities who may be in need of special assistance during an emergency. Supplying wardens and searchers with armbands and whistles can help to assure an orderly procedure.

Only people who will take the job seriously should be assigned specific tasks. All others must, of course, be persuaded to learn what procedures to follow. The local fire department can help here with talks and illustrations of what will happen if you do not prepare for an emergency.

CHAPTER 7

HABITABLE SPACE?
The Office Environment

Of the people surveyed in one large modern office building by our Columbia University research team, 34 percent could not decorate or personalize their work areas in any way. They couldn't even hang a picture or keep a plant. Ninety percent could not control the number of people passing by their desk area, and 69 percent had no say over whether others could come directly up to their desk at any time without permission. Eighty-four percent of the office workers reported that they were always in the view of someone else and had no way to avoid this contact; 80 percent also reported that they had no control over whether their work or conversations were overheard. The overwhelming majority of office workers could not alter the ventilation (88 percent), open the windows (96 percent), adjust the lighting (83 percent), rearrange the furniture or equipment (75 percent), or change the temperature (75 percent). These results are typical of other modern offices surveyed.

Clearly, most of the people we studied have very little control over the physical environment at work. In this chapter we will discuss how various kinds of office arrangements and amenities and physical factors like noise, ventilation, and climate control relate to health and safety and how they can be improved.

Office Design

Office design has changed over the years to accommodate the ever-growing numbers of office workers and to provide a setting for their supervision that accords with newer concepts of management and productivity. Figure 21 illustrates this evolution of the office. It is interesting to explore the ways that trends in management style and office automation are related to these changes. For example, the original core office design provided middle-management people with private areas near the staff they supervised and directed, the latter usually sitting in open, factorylike pools. As many middle-management functions are being eliminated by computers, so too the core design is rapidly being replaced by cubicles and work areas that place people around machines rather than supervisors. The open office described below is a design interpretation of a more egalitarian management approach where interpersonal relations and communications are ostensibly bolstered by the removal of walls.

Architectural and furniture fashions also have had a profound effect on office design. The sleek, Space Age look of the 1970s and 1980s has eclipsed the marbled, highly detailed architecture of the early twentieth century. Modular, portable furniture and partitions can be attributed in part to the use of prefabricated materials and rapid construction methods, in addition to the flexibility they provide.

THE MAZE OF THE OPEN OFFICE

A recent advertising supplement to the *New York Times* illustrated the "ideal" office of the 1980s: a computer terminal at virtually every desk, geometrically arranged dividers to break the space into cubicles, modular furniture, and even workers on roller skates, zipping around the open space. This design is an "open," or "landscaped," office. The concept of the landscaped office first appeared in Germany in the early 1960s and was called the *Bürolandschaft*. It was defined as an office where rigid walls gave way to free-standing screens, hung panels, or modular T-shaped units demarcating individual workspaces. Rationales for the open office included improvement of the information-processing and communications functions of the modern office and the democratization

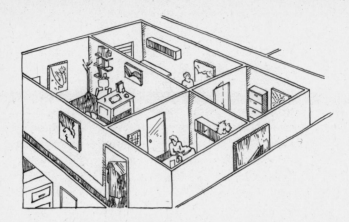

A

B

C

D

FIGURE 21. Evolution in Office Designs
Office designs have changed with both building and
management styles: A. The traditional "single office concept,"
with secretarial offices next to executive offices. B. The
"bullpen," with a pool of secretaries surrounded by individual
offices. C. The "executive core" design, with executive offices at
the hub surrounded by clerical pools, was not popular for long.
D. The latest design, the open-landscaped office, mixes executive
and clerical workstations, separated by dividers.

of office space. European researchers predicted that an increase in staff
productivity and morale and a decrease in absenteeism and renovation
times would result. There were also less idealistic justifications. The
open office makes supervision easier, or as one designer put it in a
September 1979 *Science* article, "it gets the manager out of the corner
office and into the work area where he can better control his employees."

Reduced overhead is another plus for open office design. Because
they allow for more centralized heating and cooling systems, open
offices lead to savings in energy costs. Also, more people can be fit into
any given office space, and there is greater flexibility in the rearrange-
ment of work spaces as companies expand or change work tasks. In a
1967 study commissioned by the U.S. government's General Services
Administration (GSA), the following savings for landscaped offices
were predicted: 11 people could fit into a space where only 10 people

could fit in a conventional office; 71 cents would be saved on initial occupancy installation such as partitions and floor coverings for each square foot of open office space; and annual maintenance and replacement costs would be reduced by 46 cents per square foot. Another GSA study recommends the following per-person square-foot space allocation for landscaped versus conventional offices:

	CONVENTIONAL OFFICES	LANDSCAPED OFFICES
	(in square feet)	
Executive	500	400
Middle-management	300	244
Supervisor	150	125–85
Minimum (clerical)	60	45

It is worth noting that the GSA has thus determined that clerical workers need one-eighth the space of executives in a conventional office, while in a landscaped office they need only about one-tenth the space. This constitutes, of course, an increase in the inequality of space allocation and contradicts one of the premises of open-plan theory. The widely adopted Basic Building Code of the Building Officials and Code Administrators International (BOCA) requires only 400 cubic feet of office space per office occupant. With a 10-foot ceiling height, this represents a space of 5 by 8 feet. However, most architects base their plans on a 100-square-foot per-person minimum.

Open office design is also a practical response to the costs of office construction and rental. Open floors in multistoried buildings are readily modified to suit new tenants or to set up new projects that require different space arrangements. Using easily moved partitions eliminates the expense of knocking down walls or engaging in expensive interior construction. Such "temporary" furnishings also qualify for accelerated depreciation, since they are not classified as "real property"; this results in a hefty tax advantage.

The claims made for the superiority of the open office have been largely unsubstantiated. Part of the problem may be that landscaped offices have been planned by designers with an eye for aesthetics but little knowledge of what makes a satisfactory workspace. The lush greenery of potted plants and tasteful color schemes may look good to an interior decorator but be unsatisfactory to work in. As one researcher, Dr. Malcolm Brookes of Human Factors/Industrial Design, Inc., succinctly states, "It looks better but it works worse." He studied the reactions of workers nine months after moving into a new landscaped office. The three major problems were noise, lack of privacy, and crowding. Lack of privacy is very disturbing to most individuals. Psychologists who study privacy note that it is essential to a sense of self-identity because it creates personal boundaries. Whatever the theory, lack of privacy leads to clearly reported problems. In open offices, private conversations can be overheard and workers are distracted by viewing unrelated activities. It is uncomfortable to be always exposed to observation by co-workers or managers. It is still unclear to us whether clerical workers, who formerly worked in the large open spaces of pools, prefer the small amount of added privacy that open offices provide. Some complain that it breaks up their former work groups and limits their chances to interact while doing fairly routine work.

WINDOWLESS OFFICES

A pervasive complaint from office workers is that they see no daylight from the time they enter their work area to the time they leave at the end of the day. Modern offices have large interior spaces that provide no visual access to windows. Having a view, or even a glimpse of a window, has become a measure of status. Being able to look outdoors may, however, also be important to your health. Windows not only contribute to psychological well-being but provide "visual escape." It has been suggested that having a distant view through a window provides a physiological rest center upon which the eyes can change focus and relax their focusing muscles. Under many municipal public health codes, windowless offices would fail to qualify as habitable space. This means that people could not live in them, even though they are required to work in them eight hours a day.

Noise

Noise, or unwanted sound, appears to be pandemic in the office, as well as in our homes, communities, and other workplaces. Our research group at Columbia University has repeatedly

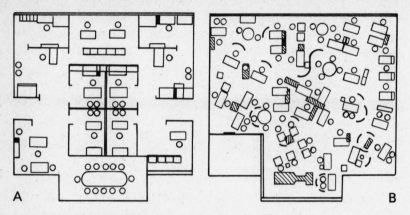

A   B

FIGURE 22. *The Myth of Office Planning*
A shows a traditional office plan; B, a plan for an open office. The plans for open offices usually change rapidly after installation. In the first open office in the United States, at Du Pont Corporation in Wilmington, Delaware, senior management personnel soon occupied corner spaces behind screens, creating for themselves closed offices. Whether because of the privacy issue or because other managers were simply not interested, no additional department at Du Pont has opted to take part in the test for shifting from conventional to open offices.

found that of all the environmental factors, noise in the office has the strongest correlation with job dissatisfaction and with the stress effects such as irritation and anxiety that were measured in the study. More than 25 percent of the dissatisfaction with the workstations studied could be attributed to noise. Other studies have obtained similar results: as noted, noise was one of the three major problems discovered by Dr. Malcolm Brookes in his study of the open office.

Office noise is rarely in the range that can cause permanent hearing loss. However, noise has other effects on the body. It can induce the stress response described in chapter 2 at levels far below those needed to affect hearing ability. Experiments have shown that a person exposed to noise will experience a rise in arterial blood pressure, changes in breathing patterns, constriction of body muscles, and an increase in sweating at levels less than one-hundredth of those associated with industrial hearing loss. Noise affects the heart, circulatory system, and digestive system, just as other stressors do.

Noise is a psychological stressor. It places a strain on the mind as well as the body, particularly when it interferes with speech and the ability to think clearly. Speech interference, or speech masking, as it is also called, was found to be a strong source of complaint among a large percentage of the people surveyed by us in one office. It is interesting that scientists investigating noise have found remarkable agreement among different people and a consistency in response when the same person was measured in repeated tests. Through such extensive surveys and tests, criteria and formulas have been developed for evaluating noisiness. These tests have been carried out in a number of environments, such as offices, homes, hospitals, libraries, and churches, as well as for various machines, appliances, and utilities. Some of these data showing the maximum amount of Perceived Noise Level (PNL), a calculated formula based on intensity, duration, and pitch of noise, are given in table 13. It is interesting to note that virtually all the environments measured exceed the maximum levels recommended in table 14.

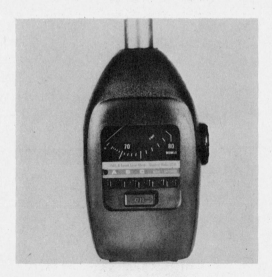

FIGURE 23. How to Measure Office Noise
To use a sound-level meter, hold the microphone on the meter at a right angle to the path of the noise, without standing in the path of the sound.

The sound-pressure or intensity levels are measured in units called decibels, abbreviated dB. Decibels are a relative measure. That is, a sound intensity of 60 dB is actually 60 dB greater than some arbitrary reference sound, given the value of 0 dB. This arbitrary zero is said to be the weakest sound that a young, sensitive human ear can hear. (Some people can actually hear better than this, and the pressure of the sound they can hear would correspond to a −dB, or negative decibel level, on this scale.)

The decibel scale is confusing because it is not linear but logarithmic. We are used to counting things on a linear scale: 20 eggs are twice as much as 10; 30 eggs are just 10 more than 20 and three times as much as 10. But if eggs were counted on a logarithmic scale, it would not work this way. A logarithmic scale is based on powers of 10. This means that each increase in 10 dB is equivalent to multiplying the intensity by 10;

TABLE 13. NOISE LEVELS MEASURED IN OFFICES

When comparing observed and recommended levels (tables 13 and 14), it is important to remember that decibels are logarithmic. Every increase of 10 decibels is a tenfold increase in intensity.

	NOISE LEVEL [dB(A)]	PERCEIVED NOISE LEVEL [PNdB]
Office		
Conference room		
With air conditioner	58	70
With fan only	52	62
Executive office		
5 machines on	64	73
No machines on	46	52
Ventilating equipment on	47	53
Ventilating equipment off	40	41
Home		
Garbage disposal	81	93
Typical vacuum cleaner	74	87
Dishwasher	70	82
Stove-hood exhaust	75	88
Typical central-heating system	58	71

SOURCE: Jeanne Stellman, *Women's Work, Women's Health* (New York: Pantheon Books, 1977), p.113.

in other words, 20 dB is ten *times* as intense as 10 dB and 30 dB is ten *times* as intense as 20 dB. Since 30 dB is ten times as intense as 20 dB and 20 dB is ten times as intense as 10 dB, 30 dB is one hundred times, or 10 × 10, as intense as 10 dB. An increase from 0 to 90 dB is an increase of 10 × 10 × 10 × 10 × 10 × 10 × 10 × 10 × 10, or 1 billion times.

Noise is often measured in units called dB(A). The noise meter is equipped with a set of filters designed to mimic the human ear's reception of sound frequencies. Noise levels measured with these filters are designated dB(A) levels. Standards refer to the A-scale readings.

Loss of speech intelligibility can be particularly exasperating if your work involves talking on the telephone. You may end up making more mistakes or having to ask the person on the other end of the line to continually repeat himself or herself, a source of stress both to you and to the caller.

The levels in table 14 are ostensibly based on the needs, as judged by the researchers, of these various workers for quiet. It should be obvious that there is no scientific basis for deciding that secretaries and general office workers can and should be exposed to more noise and annoyance than executives in private and semiprivate offices. This is a social judgment, not a scientific one. And in offices where these recommendations are put into effect, it will probably be the secretaries and other clerical workers who suffer the adverse consequences of noise. If you and your co-workers perceive your environment as noisy, then you should consider that you have made your own survey, which is also valid.

HEARING LOSS

There are some serious exceptions to the generalization that office noise is not loud enough to cause hearing loss. A bank of four addressing machines was measured at 90 dBA, currently the upper OSHA limit for noise exposure during an 8-hour day. Workers in stockrooms, coin rooms, and other noisy areas are really facing "industrial" conditions and should consult the resources in appendix B for help.

QUIETING THE OFFICE

The goal of office planners is to reduce background noise sufficiently to allow intelligible speech communication in the office, yet not to make it so quiet that all privacy is sacrificed. Lowering background noise by 5 dB, which is easily achieved with acoustical screens and other sound-

TABLE 14. SOME CRITERIA FOR NOISE LEVELS ON THE JOB

Presented are noise levels and perceived noise levels for several office situations, as well as for homes and hospitals. Note that the noisy office with difficult telephone and speech communication is a typical application for secretarial spaces. These values should be compared with typical measured noise values tabulated in table 13.

OFFICE NOISE	NOISE LEVEL [dB(A)]	PERCEIVED NOISE LEVEL [PNdB]	TYPICAL APPLICATION
1. Very quiet office—suitable for large conferences; telephone use possible	35	48	Executive office (50-person conference)
2. Quiet office—smaller conferences; telephone use possible	43	56	Private or semiprivate office (20-person conference)
3. Office satisfactory for 6–8-foot table; normal voice here 6–12 feet	48	61	Medium office and industrial business office
4. Office satisfactory for 1–5-foot table; occasional slight difficulty in telephone use; normal voice 3–6 feet	55	68	Large engineering and drafting rooms
5. Unsatisfactory for conferences of more than 3; slightly difficult telephone use; normal voice 1–2 feet	63	76	Secretarial areas (italics supplied by author): typing, accounting areas, business machines
6. Very noisy and unsatisfactory	65	78	Not recommended

TABLE 14. (cont.)

OFFICE NOISE	NOISE LEVEL [dB(A)]	PERCEIVED NOISE LEVEL [PNdB]	TYPICAL APPLICATION
Home noise	40	53	
Hospital noise	40	53	

SOURCE: Adapted from Karl D. Kryter, *The Effects of Noise on Man* (New York: Academic Press, 1970), tables 40 and 41.

absorbing materials, can increase sentence intelligibility from 10 to 50 percent. It is easier to accomplish these goals and provide a pleasant acoustical environment in a traditional office with walls and doors than in an open office, where overheard conversations, the jangle of telephones, and the noise of office machinery can be devastating to the nerves. There are a number of design factors, however, that can reduce noise levels in either the traditional or the open office.

One of the simplest ways to reduce noise is to rearrange traffic routes within and between work areas. You can make a map of where workers move throughout the day and recommend changes to cut down on traffic near individual workstations. Not only will noise levels be reduced, but personal privacy will also be increased.

Since sounds are made by pressure changes in air caused by sound waves that move away from vibrating sound sources (your voice, a ringing telephone, a machine), barriers or materials that block or absorb sound waves will reduce sound intensity. Fortunately, there are many relatively inexpensive and simple methods for lowering office noise levels. The noise source can be separated from the worker by using sound-absorbing (acoustic) walls or screens. Sound-absorbing material on walls, floor, and ceilings can also help. Acoustic tiles on the ceilings, drapes, and carpets all absorb sound.

Typewriter noise levels can be significantly reduced by the use of "sound reduction option" plastic covers—available, for example, to fit IBM Selectric typewriters. Noise levels at a typical bank of three typewriters can be cut by as much as 6 dBA, a noticeable difference. The plastic covers are inexpensive and should be a part of every typist's basic equipment. A drawback is that they slightly distort copy. Computer-

A

B

FIGURE 24. *Sound-Reducing Ideas for the Office*
A. Plastic covers on typewriters and printers. B. Acoustical dividers

printer plastic covers are also extremely effective in reducing noise.

Noisy office machinery like photocopiers, postage machines, addressing machines, and computer print-out machines should always be placed in an enclosed space so that workers who are not operating them are not unnecessarily affected by their noise. To reduce noise levels for machine operators several provisions should be made. Acoustical tiles and carpeting muffle noise in the machine area. Cabinets that machines rest on should be lined with sound-absorbent material, and felt or other acoustic material should be placed under the machines. Structural support can be added to cabinets to eliminate vibration, or cabinets with absorbent spring construction can be purchased.

Any worker who is particularly annoyed by sound coming from one direction can be given acoustical screens or barriers to position so that they absorb the sound. Such movable screens are relatively inexpensive, and their design and sound-absorbing qualities are constantly being improved.

Engineers who design machines need to be educated to spend time designing quieter ones. You can help this process along by inquiring of the manufacturer (or getting your purchasing agent to inquire) what the sound levels produced by the machines are. Quietness should be a consideration in choosing machinery for purchase. All of these tactics can help reduce office sound pollution.

The sound of telephones ringing can be particularly annoying (especially if you are away from your desk and can't answer your phone or even tell if it's yours). All telephones should be equipped with a mechanism that permits you to adjust the volume of the ring to the lowest possible level. Blinking lights can also be substituted for the ring, although this may cause visual stress or divert your attention away from your daily tasks. Call-forwarding systems, which allow the transfer of calls to a designated co-worker or a recording machine, can reduce telephone noise (during a lunch break, for example) and reduce office anxiety about unanswered telephones.

SOUND-MASKING SYSTEMS

A solution to the noise problem commonly used in the open office is white noise to cover up unwanted sound. White noise is random sound of all frequencies which is used to block out other sounds. An example is static on the radio. Most white-noise generators produce a *whoosh* sound. Pink noise, which is random sound that emphasizes the higher frequencies, is also sometimes used for noise masking. High frequencies are usually more annoying than others.

It is not clear whether any adverse effects are associated with white noise at the levels it is used in offices. Some experts say there are no ill effects from low-level white noise; others say that there are. Research studies are contradictory. One study, for example, found that white noise enhanced reaction-time performance on visual reaction-time tasks, while other studies have found no such enhancement. Other researchers found that both white noise and traffic noise caused brief, repeated periods of EEG (brain-wave) desynchronization, and commented that "as matters now stand, no satisfactory neurophysiological interpretation can be offered for these findings."

At this point workers in open offices are stuck in a peculiar dilemma. Without white noise, the open office is a jingle-jangle of sounds; with white noise, it is like living on a plateau. Think of the feeling you have had when the background noise of a fan, air conditioner, or ventilator suddenly went off. Did you breathe out and find yourself suddenly relaxing? You descended from the plateau.

No one knows what the long-range effects, if any, are of constant exposure to a stressor like white noise. Only time will tell, and then only if studies are carried out. Perhaps one solution is a return to offices with walls. Another is to design quieter office machines.

Still another method is to use taped or broadcast music programs designed to cover background noise and to increase the activity levels of office workers. These programs are advertised as enhancing work-place productivity while decreasing monotony, tension, and fatigue, and are used by more than 100,000 organizations in twenty-five countries on five continents, reaching more than 100 million people. One brand features music programmed in 15-minute segments with a constantly ascending "stimulus value" over the 15 minutes. This means the music gets livelier as it progresses along the tape. The theory is that you work faster in response to the increasing tempo, rhythm, and instrumentation of the music. The data, however, show very small changes in productivity. On the other hand, there is little evidence that the music is harmful. Some individuals, however, complain that it is distracting and annoying, another intrusion into their environment over which they have no control. With the advent of small cassette tape players, you can now have your own earphones for private listening, which is probably the best solution when appropriate.

Climate Control

According to many surveys, only 55 to 65 percent of office-building occupants are comfortable with summer office temperatures and even fewer are comfortable in the winter. Temperatures that are too high or too low or humidity levels that are too dry or too damp are frequent complaints. Some office workers spend the

winter shivering through the day, trying to work in coats and sometimes even in gloves. In the summer high humidity and hot temperatures lead to discomfort and fatigue. In many ways human health, or at
least human comfort, is playing second fiddle to energy costs. Some
building managers turn off or greatly cut back on heating or air conditioning over the weekend or after work hours in order to save money.
If the systems are not started up early enough, temperatures may be
uncomfortable for the first hours of the working day. Offices where the
systems are shut off at 4 P.M. often become unbearable before 5 P.M.
quitting time. These problems have been made worse by energy-conservation measures.

Large sealed office buildings present other problems of climate control. Days of swinging back and forth between extremes may be necessary before the temperature is finally regulated, and even then only some
office areas are comfortable while others, closer to the coolers or heaters,
may be frigid or hot. Those much farther away or next to windows may
be boiling or freezing. With windows that do not open, sealed office
buildings can become ovens or refrigerators when heating or cooling
systems break down. There is often no alternative but to leave the
building until repairs have been made.

On the other hand, old is not necessarily good either. Old office
buildings, with deteriorating heating plants, may be subject to frequent
breakdowns and rarely have centralized air conditioning, or have no air
conditioning at all. In many older cities, budget crises lead to deferred
maintenance and frequent breakdowns in municipal buildings. It is yet
another irony that agencies charged with public health regulation often
house workers in buildings that are some of the worst offenders in
climate control.

The overall goal of climate control is to provide an environment that
is free from drafts and odors, and in which the air is neither noticeably
hot nor cold, humid nor dry. The American Society of Heating, Refrigeration, and Air Conditioning Engineers (ASHRAE), the body that sets
standards and criteria for heating and ventilation systems, defines thermal comfort as "that condition of mind which expresses satisfaction
with the thermal environment." The reader will notice that both goal
and definition depend very much on individual perceptions of comfort.
Unfortunately, this is not a very precise measure. Furthermore, when
people are doing different tasks, wearing different clothes, or even
working at different levels of concentration, the amount of heat they

require in order to function most efficiently will be different. Definitions of comfort thus vary from person to person and from job to job.

Human beings have two mechanisms for maintaining internal temperature in the cold. First, the blood vessels supplying the skin, hands, and feet constrict so that less heat is lost. If the constriction lasts too long the hands and feet become numb, cold, stiff, and painful, which makes tasks needing dexterity and skill, such as typing, difficult. The second protective mechanism against cold is shivering, which is rapid contractions of the muscles to generate heat. Shivering will obviously also make it difficult to do work requiring skill. Possible effects of working in a cold environment may be arthritis and an increase in virus infections, but as yet there is no scientific proof of these effects because adequate research has not yet been done.

Heat and humidity, on the other hand, lead to heat fatigue, which is characterized by lassitude, irritability, and exhaustion. This will be worse if an office worker has to endure a hot and miserable trip to and from work. The heat-stressed worker will have trouble relating to other workers and will probably bring his or her stress home.

Moisture in the air—humidity—determines how comfortable you will be. The humidity affects how rapidly your body evaporates sweat, one of the biological mechanisms by which we adapt to our environment. When the humidity is too high, people feel "clammy." They will be uncomfortable at temperatures that they could otherwise comfortably tolerate. Even paper may become soggy if humidity is high.

On the other hand, too low humidity is not good either. In addition to drying out the nose and throat membranes, it probably makes us more susceptible to upper-respiratory infections. Low humidity will also create static-electricity problems in your office. Your hair and clothing, particularly if made of synthetic fibers, will be full of static. Pushing elevator buttons may be a "shocking" experience, and machines such as VDT terminals, which generate static electricity, may be difficult to work with unless the proper antistatic precautions are followed, particularly since most buildings do not include humidification in their systems. Some measures are described on page 52.

Air movement will also affect comfort. We all would rather have a fan moving the air on a hot day, even if the temperature is unchanged, than sit in a hot, still room. This is because air movement helps the evaporation process. However, too much air movement will create drafts and will be very uncomfortable, possibly leading to muscular aches and pains.

There are various methods for measuring the temperature and humidity in your office, and guides as to how much energy different office tasks require and how much body heat they generate. We illustrate basic measurement techniques in figure 25, and summarize both the standards and recommended levels that exist for climate control in the office in table 15. A word of caution is important here. None of these standards, though widely accepted and applied, is based on anything more than surveys of what makes people comfortable. If the climate in your working environment is making you and your co-workers uncomfortable, then it needs to be readjusted until you are comfortable.

Some cities specify required office temperatures in their building or health codes. In New York City, the building code specifies that offices must be heated to 70° F., and their heating plants must be capable of this when the outside temperature is 5° F. and the wind is blowing 15 miles per hour. In some states, industrial codes govern office temperature. If your building is leased, you may also find building heating requirements in the fine print.

If the lighting, the number of people, or the equipment in your office drastically changes, then your system must be re-evaluated, because lights and people generate heat. Also, any new equipment will generate heat. For example, a video display terminal puts out as much heat as one person, so providing one VDT per person is like doubling the density of people in terms of heat load.

VENTILATION SYSTEMS

The three basics of the ventilation system are the blower, which moves the air; the ducts, which deliver it to the room; and the vents, which distribute it. The vents either supply or exhaust air (see figure 26).

The percentage of fresh air in the mix and its cleanliness are crucial to indoor air quality. Ventilation engineers rate the system by the number of air exchanges—that is, substitution of total fresh air for used air —per minute. The BOCA Basic Building Code requires a minimum of 2 air changes per hour for "offices and jails," and allows up to 75 percent of the exhaust air to be recirculated! Your municipal building department will be able to tell you the ventilation requirements for office buildings in your city. In buildings where codes do not exist or are not

A

FIGURE 25. Airflow, Temperature, and Humidity Measurements
A. A tissue, or a source of smoke such as a candle, cigarette, or smoke
tube, can be held up to a vent as a quick way to test if there is any air
movement. However, don't use smoke if you have a smoke-activated
fire-alarm system. B. An air-flow meter, or velometer, is used to measure
the amount of air entering and leaving the room through the vent
system. The instrument consists of a long probe, which is inserted in the
ceiling vents. The probe is connected to a meter, which measures the
velocity of air flow in feet per minute. Velometers are not very expensive
and, if used correctly, are quite accurate. C. How to attach a velometer
to a supply vent (left) and to an exhaust vent. D. A portable hygrometer
(to measure percentage of relative humidity) and thermometer (to
measure temperature) should be available. Check next to exhaust vents,
supply vents, spaces with little air movement, and windows to see if you
are within the "comfort zone."

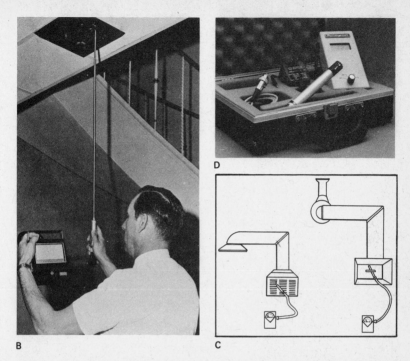

B   C

enforced, the same air may be recirculated and breathed over and over again. Energy conservation measures have tended to drastically decrease air exchange since it is expensive to heat or cool air. This has consequently increased indoor air pollution.

Ventilation systems are not designed to remove pollutants, but simply to supply and circulate fresh air. With a limited number of contaminants the ventilation system may reduce the pollution level sufficiently —but only if the system is correctly designed and in good working order. For greater levels of pollution an ordinary ventilation system will not be sufficient.

Following are guidelines for evaluating the ventilation system in your office. Some aspects are technical and need the help and advice of an expert, but many of the guides are readily followed by anyone.

The first thing to check is whether your workplace has a ventilation system, which is not as odd a question as it may seem. Some buildings actually do not have ventilation systems. You can check to see if yours does by walking around and looking for vents and ducts (see figure 27). In addition to the more familiar grilles and registers, modern office

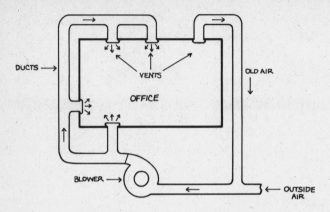

FIGURE 26. *Components of Heating, Ventilating, and Air-Conditioning Systems*
This is the typical layout of an office ventilation system. The blower moves the air; the ducts deliver it to the room; and the vents supply or remove it.

buildings often distribute air through less easily seen (but no less effective) linear diffusers and through fluorescent lighting troffers. Linear diffusers are long, narrow registers frequently found between the ceiling tiles or at the margins where walls and ceiling join. Troffers are the lighting fixtures themselves. They are effective in a heating system because they pick up the heat of the lights and distribute it during the

TABLE 15. VENTILATION RECOMMENDATIONS

Minimum flows of outside air into occupied areas	
Conference rooms	1.50 cubic feet per minute per square foot (cfm/ft²)
General office spaces	0.15 cfm/ft²
Computer rooms	0.10 cfm/ft²
Minimum air velocity	70 feet per minute
Humidity and temperature comfort zones	35–50% relative humidity
	68–80 temperature in degrees Fahrenheit

winter months. A listing of the number of vents per room should be made. Make sure you search along the ceilings, walls, and floors.

Check whether the system is on all the time. Often the air circulation in a building will stop at the close of normal business hours or on weekends even though people may regularly work late or on night shifts. In many offices, large duplicating and printing jobs are done at night, and machines can produce a high volume of pollutants, which will remain in the air if the system is shut off. You can test whether the system is on by holding a tissue near the vent. If it moves, air is being circulated.

The system may not be continuous. It may go on and off during the day. Depending on the number of people and on the work being done, an intermittent system may not supply enough fresh air. The continuity of the system during daytime operations and the length of time it is turned off before and after normal operating hours are matters of policy that can readily be changed to provide better working conditions. Unlike many of the other problems that can be present in a ventilation system, changing the timing cycle requires no structural or mechanical modifications.

Each separate room or work area should be supplied with its own vents. There should always be both a supply and an exhaust vent. You can determine which vents are bringing air in and which are removing it

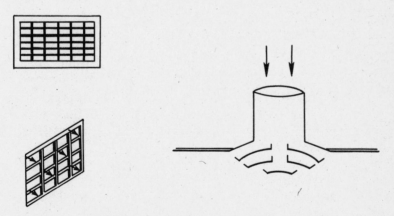

FIGURE 27. Vents and How They Work
The drawings at left show the kinds of vents you will see in your office, supplying and removing air. The drawing at right shows how air is blown through a diffusing vent.

again by holding a tissue at the face of the vent. The vents for supply and exhaust should never be right next to each other because that will cause the clean, fresh air that is blown in to be sucked out of the room before it has adequately circulated. This is called short circuiting. It is the result of poor engineering and is difficult to repair. Short circuiting may result in "dead spaces" where insufficient air or no air is replaced. You can check for dead spaces in your office by lighting a match and watching whether the smoke moves toward an exhaust vent or simply stays in one place. If it doesn't move, pollutants are not being exhausted and not enough fresh air is being supplied. Inexpensive smoke tubes are also available for this test. (Don't use a smoke test if your fire alarm or sprinkler system is smoke-activated.)

Check to see whether the vents are blocked in any way. Exhaust and supply vents will work only if the air can move freely around them. Blockage by walls, partitions, or piled-up boxes or files will obstruct the airflow and reduce ventilation efficiency.

Office areas with printing and copying machines must especially have adequate air supply and exhaust. For some machines, general ventilation is sufficient. Others require extra vents near the source of the fumes that are being emitted. Some machines such as blueprinters and photocopiers may have filter attachments that purify the air exhausted from the machines. You can request information about the availability of these attachments from manufacturers.

In some offices it is possible for the occupants to control the ventilation. You may be able to enter the fan room and to turn the blower or fan supplying the air up or down. Check with your building maintenance officer to see if you can do this.

"Zoning" problems are frequent in large offices. They occur when the sun heats offices on the west side of the building while the north and east sides are cool. Modern air systems have dampers that can be "balanced" so that the temperature in all parts of the building is comfortable. Sometimes systems require retrofitting with more valves to effectively balance the building's temperature.

Amenities in the Office

Amenities such as clean and accessible toilets, washrooms, rest areas, first-aid facilities, lounges, cafeterias, lunchrooms, and coatrooms are important. There is physical relief in being able to put your feet up for a short period in the lounge area, getting out and moving around in the fresh air, having a hot or cold drink, or resting your eyes and ears in a quiet, well-lit and decorated eating or lounging area. Meeting other people informally and talking casually affords mental relaxation.

SANITARY AND REST FACILITIES

One survey among employees in a building that housed both classrooms and administrative offices of a large Massachusetts university found that dirty restrooms were first on the list of complaints. One reason for the problem was that these restrooms were heavily used by both students and employees. Clearly a solution would have been to set aside restrooms on every other floor for use of the employees only, since they were in the building daily while the students were transient. Large retail stores have used this approach of employee-only restrooms. Unfortunately, this solution can be a double-edged sword in offices where, behind the sleek public reception areas, dingy work areas and amenities hidden from the public view have been set aside for the employees.

It is important to distinguish between sanitary facilities and lounge areas, since they have different functions. Privacy is an important consideration in the sanitary facilities. Lounges, on the other hand, are for relaxing and socializing during breaks from work, and should not be segregated by sex. Putting a chair in the toilet area does not constitute a lounge. Lunchrooms, however, can double as lounges when appropriate attention has been paid to furnishings.

EATING FACILITIES

Office workers often have to fight long lines at the lunch hour to obtain overpriced, poor-quality food. Sometimes outside restaurants and food stands are not available at all. The problem is even worse for shift workers, who may be unable to find food if their meal and break times come at midnight or other nontraditional eating times, or if it is unsafe to go out of the building at night. Unfortunately, providing eating facilities is not standard company practice. In fact, many of the office architecture books we surveyed recommended vending machines for the lunch and lounge areas as adequate, citing their low cost and space requirements. Although vending machines may do for bottled cold drinks, gum, and a few other products, they are not adequate for more substantial foods. Alternatives are available. Food-service companies can provide meals and coffee-break foods on a contractual basis, and they will even maintain lunchroom areas. The food-service industry is competitive and some comparison shopping should allow an employer to contract for pleasant meals and foods at reasonable prices. Employers can derive tax deductions for some of these expenses.

In addition to price and quality, other criteria for food service include the range of foods provided. For example, are fresh fruits and salads and beverage alternatives to coffee and tea provided? As more people are becoming diet-conscious, they are realizing that the typical "coffee break" with doughnut and high-calorie, heavy lunches add little to physical comfort, alertness, or good health. Companies that share large office buildings may want to pool their resources for a pleasant cafeteria, while still providing lunchroom and lounge areas for people who prefer to bring their lunches from home.

It is often not realized how many employees like to eat their breakfast on the premises, before they begin work. One survey of West German workers employed in 20 different "open office" firms discovered that 86 percent of the employees ate breakfast in the office building. Opening the cafeteria or lunchroom before work for breakfast is a helpful solution. The addition of a refrigerator for food storage is highly recommended. Small offices that can't afford a lunchroom can still plan a separate lounge and eating area with hot and cold water, at minimum expense.

We feel it important to add that some employers expect the women clerical workers to prepare coffee and tea in eating areas and to clean up lunchroom areas. Such unpaid tasks should not be automatic features of office work. If employees are expected to perform custodial functions, such work should be clearly written into the job description and agreed upon before commencement of employment. Tasks should either be divided among all employees without regard to sex or job level or else be compensated.

COAT AND LOCKER ROOMS
More and more workers are putting on their tennis shoes and getting outside to enjoy fresh air and exercise on their lunch hours and breaks, or walking to and from work. These "tennis-shoe armies" are taking over the sidewalks of New York. Men and women dressed in impeccable business clothes are shod in incongruous-looking tennis shoes or running shoes. They are enjoying their exercise. But what do you do

with the tennis shoes when you arrive at the office? This question is not a new one. Coatrooms should have adequate space for changing footwear, and space for drying wet garments and umbrellas. Coatrooms or restrooms can also have space for storage and changing of employer-provided protective garments and gloves for those involved in dusty or soiling work or the servicing of office machinery. It is preferable not to make coatrooms also serve as smoking areas, to prevent tobacco odors from permeating clothing. Coat areas need adequate ventilation to prevent odor and humidity buildup. Attention must be paid to security. Although locked storage should be provided at individual work areas as well, coatrooms should be secure, particularly when there is public access.

MEDICAL AND EXERCISE FACILITIES

While exercise programs and health-club facilities are rapidly becoming a part of the corporate benefits package, too few workers as yet enjoy these amenities. Much corporate interest has focused on the health of the executive corps, but other workers, such as clerical employees, need these facilities as much if not more. Although exercise is not a Band-Aid for treating workplace stress, it is an enjoyable and healthful activity. If facilities are not available at work, work-release time for exercise classes is a strong inducement for participation, and will show that a company takes its exercise recommendations seriously. Organized voluntary activities such as volleyball, softball, and bowling leagues can also encourage exercise. Employers, unions, and other worker and community organizations may want to consider sponsoring such teams, providing equipment, uniforms, and transportation. It's a good advertising as well as positive health promotion.

Some companies have also encouraged their medical staffs to become involved in such health-promoting activities as smoking reduction, diet and exercise recommendations, high-blood-pressure control, recognition and treatment of alcohol and drug addiction, and counseling for emotional problems. Frequently the medical departments screen employees for these problems and then refer them to outside agencies for treatment. In many cases there are joint labor-management-sponsored employee assistance programs, but these tend to be in the more highly unionized blue-collar sectors of our society.

It is important to sound a note of warning here. Although many companies treat employee medical records with confidentiality, there are notable exceptions and problems. An employee may be referred to the medical department by a dissatisfied supervisor who feels that poor work performance or lateness is caused by an emotional or alcohol- or drug-related problem. Some companies then inform the worker that unless he undertakes treatment he will be fired. One can understand the reluctance of employees to cooperate with such medical programs.

Also, too often the medical staff and private physicians will deal with the worker's difficulty without considering factors in the workplace that may be contributing to or even causing the emotional or substance-abuse problem. In companies where workplace health and safety programs are separate from the dispensary, such lack of communication and information may be more prevalent. A responsive and independent medical facility should be a part of every large office facility.

CHAPTER 8

INDOOR
AIR POLLUTION

The quality of the air we breathe indoors is beginning to capture the attention of researchers, government officials, and other policy makers. In 1980 the comptroller general of the United States labeled indoor air pollution "an emerging health problem." Special congressional hearings were held on the subject, and the National Academy of Science was asked to prepare and present a special report.

Indoor air pollution and the need for coping with it date back to the time humans first began to build fires inside their living spaces for cooking or keeping themselves warm. Native Americans designed and built their homes with openings to exhaust heating and cooking fumes. Other cultures far less technological than ours did the same. Unfortunately, when it comes to late-twentieth-century office buildings, some of the wisdom of our ancestors appears to have been forgotten or discarded. We have built structures that are impermeable to the outside air. Occupants of these sealed buildings cannot open windows. They must rely on mechanical devices for the circulation of the air they breathe and for the control of its temperature and humidity. To put it simply, modern office workers are almost as dependent on their office air ducts as they are on their lungs.

The ventilation system determines the quality of the indoor air by controlling the amount of outside air that is added to the building's atmosphere, its cleanliness, and the rate at which the inside air and its pollutants are either exhausted to the outside or recirculated through the building. When only limited fresh air is circulated through a building or when the outdoor air is very polluted, an indoor air-pollution problem is very likely to occur. It will be exacerbated by the substances used or produced during the normal operations of the office.

Indoor-air-quality problems do not occur only in buildings with windows that do not open. Buildings not originally designed to be sealed are undergoing a major program of "buttoning up" to reduce the high cost of energy for heating and cooling indoor air.

Indoor air pollution is produced in a number of ways. Some sources of air pollutants are natural. For example, when we exhale we emit carbon dioxide and water, which are two of the end products of our metabolic processes. Carbon dioxide is not toxic in small amounts, but it can become a health hazard if concentrations are allowed to build up. Other natural agents, such as micro-organisms, can thrive in the moist environment of a building's humidification system or water tower. If they enter the ventilation system, the outcome can be an airborne spread of disease.

Synthetic chemicals, such as the formaldehyde in pressed board or insulation materials, constitute some of the air pollution found indoors. Office machinery and supplies can release gases and chemicals into the atmosphere. Cooking and other combustion processes such as cigarette smoking, which produce carbon monoxide, oxides of nitrogen, fine particulate matter, and a variety of organic compounds, are major sources of indoor air pollution. Offices located near loading docks or over garages may have elevated carbon monoxide and diesel-fuel-emission levels, while office workers in factory locations may be exposed to the chemicals and dusts used or produced in the plants.

The levels of different air pollutants will vary from site to site and source to source, depending on how they are generated and how efficient is their removal by ventilation and maintenance procedures. Theoretically, standards have been set and systems designed to provide good air quality in office buildings. But as we all know, things very often do not work as well as planned. Sometimes, indeed, they work so poorly that indoor air quality is poorer than that of outdoor air.

Asbestos and Other Pollutants from Insulation

Some indoor air pollution is due to an ironic and potentially unhealthy aspect of energy conservation measures: contamination from the insulation materials themselves, which either may be inherently toxic or may decompose and thereby introduce toxic substances into the air. A good example of this is asbestos. Asbestos has been widely used as an insulating material because of its remarkable properties. It is nonreactive: that is, fire does not burn it and most chemicals do not interact with it. These are useful properties for the insulating and fireproofing of buildings or for the lining of ventilation and heating ducts. Unfortunately, in addition to its wonderful chemical and physical properties, asbestos also has extraordinary biological properties: it can cause cancer and the often disabling and fatal lung disease asbestosis.

Asbestos is actually the generic or family name applied to a variety of mineral silicates which are fibers of various colors, sizes, and shapes. As early as 1918 it was known that asbestos miners died at a highly elevated rate. They were, in fact, routinely denied life insurance. By 1935 many experts recognized that asbestos exposure can cause lung cancer. By 1960 it was already known that pleural mesothelioma, an extremely rare and always fatal cancer of the pleural lining of the lungs, was caused by asbestos. Yet official recognition of the hazards of asbestos was slow in coming to the United States. Indeed, it was not until 1971, after passage of the Occupational Safety and Health Act, that the first comprehensive standard for limiting occupational exposure to asbestos was promulgated. The U.S. Environmental Protection Agency has now set national standards for the application of asbestos insulation spray and the demolition of asbestos-insulated buildings. The late start by these and other regulatory agencies in limiting use of and exposure to asbestos had allowed the unimpeded use of asbestos in construction and other industries.

Most of the research on the health effects of asbestos has been devoted to studying people who experience relatively high exposures, like the workers who spray the insulation. These studies have found that approximately 20 percent of these workers die of lung cancer, 10 percent of mesothelioma, and 20 percent of asbestosis. In all, cancer accounts for approximately 50 percent of all deaths, an extraordinary rate in comparison to the United States population as a whole, where cancer accounts for approximately 20 percent of all deaths. It was found that asbestos workers who smoke multiply their chances of developing lung cancer to almost 100 times the rate of the nonsmoking nonasbestos worker.

Now that both scientific and public awareness of the toxic properties of asbestos has grown, there have been a large number of investigations to determine whether there is asbestos contamination of the air in office buildings, schools, hospitals, and other nonindustrial environments. Asbestos has generally been used in buildings in several ways. A fibrous product made from asbestos mixed with minerals like fiberglass may have been sprayed for fireproofing on beams and then covered by suspended ceilings. Or the mixture may have been sprayed onto the surface of the air plenums. A second use has been in an asbestos-based cement that is mixed with lightweight materials like vermiculite. This slurry is then sprayed onto concrete, plaster, or other surfaces and allowed to harden, where it functions as a sound absorbent. Heavily trafficked corridors, cafeterias, and auditoriums may have been treated in like manner. Asbestos materials have also been used to wrap pipes (lagging) to provide thermal insulation.

The air levels of asbestos observed in most office buildings are, of course, far lower than those found to have caused the tragic and widespread lung disease and cancer in industrial settings like shipyards and construction sites. Finding asbestos in office buildings or schools does not mean that the people who work there or the children attending the school are going to develop cancer from asbestos exposure. The development of an environmental cancer is related to the dose of exposure: the higher the exposure, the more likely the disease will occur. However, as with all substances that cause cancer, no safe lower limit for exposure exists and all unnecessary exposure should be avoided. This is particularly true for people who smoke cigarettes.

If your desk or office counter top is ever covered with a white fibrous dust, you should set about determining whether the dust contains asbestos. Many local health departments can carry out the analysis, as can federal, private, and university laboratories.

Air sampling is only one method for evaluating whether there is exposure to asbestos. Often an air sample is not necessary, especially if you know that the material in question contains asbestos. Answers to the following questions will usually provide sufficient information on how the situation should be handled: (1) How accessible is the asbestos to air movements and to areas of high activity? (2) What is its physical condition? (3) How easily does it crumble or can it be broken? (4) Is it present in the air ducts?

If your inspection or analysis shows there is an asbestos problem in your building, a strong note of caution must be introduced here before office workers or employers become overanxious and immediately set about a removal operation. Asbestos removal requires special techniques that limit the amount of the substance released into the air. Removing asbestos has often been found to be more hazardous than simply leaving it in place and enclosing or completely sealing it in. You or your building custodian should not attempt to remove the asbestos. A knowledgeable engineer or industrial hygienist should be consulted for help. The Environmental Protection Agency has published some useful information on asbestos and schools, and the National Cancer Institute maintains an extremely well-run and useful asbestos information program that is free to citizens, their physicians, and other interested parties. Addresses are listed in appendix B.

Recently a new source of airborne asbestos in offices was discovered: floor tiles containing asbestos. As traffic wore the tiles down, they were found to release asbestos fibers into the air, particularly in high-activity areas. Such tiles may need sealing with a nonporous sealant. If they are sanded prior to resurfacing, all industrial precautions, including gloves, masks, and local ventilation, should be employed.

Because the dangers of exposure to asbestos are now so well recognized, substitutes are being used for insulation, fireproofing, and other industrial applications. One commonly used asbestos substitute is fiberglass, which like asbestos is resistant to many chemicals and can endure high temperatures. Fiberglass also poses health and safety hazards, although they are not as serious as those associated with asbestos. Fiberglass is extremely irritating to the skin and to the upper respiratory tract. In some animal experiments, it has been found to cause pleural mesothelioma, the very rare cancer of the lining of the lungs also caused by asbestos. Although there is no evidence today that fiberglass will cause cancer in humans, it is wise to limit exposure to all fibrous insulation materials as far as possible. There are still other mineral insulation materials that are made of a silicate-based resin product. In most of these, the silicates are not of the toxic variety associated with lung diseases like silicosis.

Formaldehyde. In addition to the mineral insulation materials, synthetic insulation materials are also widely used. Urea-formaldehyde resin is one commonly encountered material that is usually sprayed between the inside and outside walls. Upon spraying, the resin turns into a foam, spreading out inside this interstitial space. Urea-formaldehyde resin, like many other plastic products, changes its structure with age and after contact with the air. Specifically, when the resin is made excess formaldehyde is present, and as the resin ages the excess is released. The formaldehyde in foam insulation will leach through the walls and into the air.

As a result both of adverse publicity and of the complaints that many local governments and consumer agencies have received, the use of urea-formaldehyde resin for insulation has dropped drastically. It has even been banned in the state of Massachusetts, and the Canadian government has also prohibited its future installation. However, that leaves unremedied the problems that can arise from foam insulation already in place. There are some solutions, such as the costly coating of walls and exposed surfaces with impermeable plastic to prevent the further leaching of formaldehyde into the air.

Urea-formaldehyde resin has also been used for years as the glue of choice in the production of pressed board and veneered plywoods. Unfortunately, just as formaldehyde will leach from foam insulation, so it will also leach from the glue in the pressed board. A survey in Denmark of formaldehyde levels in rooms with pressed board led the Danish government to forbid the continued use of the resin as a glue. Substitute chemicals are now used. The U.S. plywood industry is currently seeking methods to limit the emission.

Formaldehyde is chemically a very reactive substance. This property makes it useful in industry but also gives it its biological potency. At levels as low as 0.1 to 5.0 parts per million (ppm), a person may notice burning and tearing of the eyes and a general irritation of the nose and throat. Levels of 10 to 20 ppm can cause coughing, a feeling of tightness in the chest, and possibly heart palpitations. Levels above 50 ppm can cause fluid to form in the lungs (pulmonary edema) and lead to a chemical pneumonia and even death. The current occupational exposure standard is an eight-hour average of 3 ppm and a ceiling limit of 5 ppm.

Formaldehyde is also a sensitizing agent. Allergic skin disease caused by formaldehyde has long been recognized as an occupational hazard. For example, some women who sew and stitch permanent-press clothing develop severe allergic dermatitis from the formaldehyde used in the permanent-press finish on fabrics. The itching, swelling, redness, and other symptoms can occur on the hands and arms and also on the face, eyelids, and genital areas. After the widespread introduction of urea-formaldehyde foam insulation, it was confirmed that formaldehyde can cause an allergic response in the respiratory tract as well, with wheezing, coughing, and the production of mucus.

In 1979 additional information about the potentially serious health effects of formaldehyde was released in a study by the Chemical Industry Institute of Toxicology, an industry-supported basic research institute. Laboratory experiments using rats and mice exposed to comparatively low levels of formaldehyde produced an excess of cancer in the animals. The study was a preliminary one, and further work is now being carried out. However, most experts believe that formaldehyde must be considered a potential human carcinogen.

Synthetic building materials can introduce many other chemicals into the air. These are often referred to as "off-gassed" products, a term that represents an assault both on our bodies and on our language. One research report documented 48 "off-gassed" chemicals in homes that had been surveyed.

Smoking and Indoor Air Pollution

Cigarette smoke is a major contributor to the poor quality of indoor air. The gases and particulates given off by burning cigarettes contain some of the most toxic air pollutants known. For example, a major component of the tar in tobacco is benzo(a)pyrene, a potent carcinogenic substance. Burning tobacco also produces gases like the oxides of nitrogen, ozone, formaldehyde, acetaldehyde, and other toxic or highly irritating chemicals. A list of the components of cigarette smoke and their potential effects is given in table 16.

The level of air pollutants that can build up from cigarette smoke is surprisingly high. One interesting survey compared the total amount of foreign particles that could be inhaled in the nave of a church during services, when the church was filled and thirty votive candles were burning, with the amount that could be inhaled in the same church during a bingo game, when only half as many people were present as at the service but approximately 15 percent of them were smoking. The density of such particles during the bingo game was more than nine times greater than during the more densely packed but tobacco-smoke-free religious service. In a restaurant or bar where people were smoking, levels of carbon monoxide have actually been found to exceed the levels set by the Occupational Safety and Health Administration for industrial environments.

While the public by and large is aware that cigarette smoking is dangerous to the smoker, there is not an accurate public perception of the wide range of effects that cigarettes may cause. The disease most widely associated in the public mind with cigarette smoking is cancer, and indeed, cigarettes either alone or in combination with other factors, such as exposure to chemicals on the job, are a major cause of cancer. But cigarettes are also a major factor in heart disease, the leading cause of death in the United States today. Cigarettes contribute to the development of chronic lung diseases such as emphysema and bronchitis.

It is not likely that nonsmokers will develop cancer from breathing other people's smoke, called passive smoking. Some lung diseases, allergies, and general discomfort among nonsmokers are the more likely effects of tobacco smoke as an indoor air pollutant. There are several reports of a higher incidence of respiratory disease, such as pneumonia or bronchitis, in the children of heavy-smoking parents, diseases that improved or even disappeared when the parents stopped smoking. Other studies have documented allergies, upper-respiratory-tract infections, and eye irritations, among other effects, in the adult passive smoker.

Most nonsmokers are usually very unhappy about inhaling other people's tobacco fumes. In fact, in many offices cigarettes are a major source of conflict among office workers as they battle the issue of smoking at their desks. In some states court cases have been won by militant nonsmokers who sought to prevent their co-workers from smoking on the job. In New Jersey, for example, workplaces that accommodate fifty or more employees are required to establish in-house rules to protect the health, welfare, and comfort of employees from the detrimental effects of tobacco smoke. In the state of Washington, work areas in all workplaces are required to be set aside as nonsmoking areas. On the whole,

TABLE 16. SELECTED CONSTITUENTS OF CIGARETTE SMOKE AND THEIR HEALTH EFFECTS*

PHYSIOLOGICAL RESPONSE	TOBACCO CONSTITUENTS
Allergic reactions, including asthma, runny nose, upper-respiratory symptoms, hives, swelling, dermatitis, anaphylactic shock	Protein-carbohydrate complexes (glycoproteins)
Cancer and tumor promotion	Polyaromatic hydrocarbons (PAH), including benzo(a)pyrene
	Dibenz(aj)acridine and other aza arenes
	Urethane
	1-methylindoles
	9-methylcarbazoles
	4,4-dichlorostilbene
	Catechol
	Alkylcatechols
	N'-nitrosonornicotine
	4-(N-methyl-N-nitrosamino)-1-(3 pyridyl)-1-butanone
	N'-nitrosoanatabine
	Polonium-210
	Nickel compounds
	Cadmium compounds
	β-naphthylamine
	4-aminobiphenyl
	o-toluidine
Cardiovascular disease	Nicotine, carbon monoxide
Chronic obstructive lung disease, chronic bronchitis, emphysema	Particulates, gaseous components, glycoproteins

TABLE 16. (cont.)

PHYSIOLOGICAL RESPONSE	TOBACCO CONSTITUENTS
Fetal and infant morbidity and mortality	Nicotine, carbon monoxide, polycyclic aromatic hydrocarbons
Irritation, including eye itching, burning, swelling, and tearing; headache; throat irritation; nasal symptoms and cough	Particulates, carbon monoxide, other gaseous components such as oxides of nitrogen, ozone, formaldehyde, and acetaldehyde

SOURCE: Based on information from *Smoking and Health: A Report of the Surgeon General.* U.S. Department of Health, Education, and Welfare (DHEW Publication no. (PHS) 79-50066), 1979.
*It is estimated that cigarette smoke is made up of more than 2,000 particulate, gaseous, and semivolatile components.

however, while twenty-two states have enacted limitations on cigarette smoking to protect indoor air quality, these rules have been applied to public areas rather than to individual workplaces.

The prohibition of smoking in general work areas would go a long way toward clearing the air for all workers and should be encouraged. At the same time, it is extremely difficult for the addicted worker to refrain from smoking for long periods of time, particularly if his or her job is very stressful. Adequate break time and convenient smoking areas should be provided, and assistance for helping the smoker to quit should be encouraged. Smoking should not be a cause for confrontation among employees. It is to everyone's advantage to work out a solution.

Germs in the Air

One little-recognized problem is the contamination of heating and ventilating systems by micro-organisms.

For a nation that often appears to be obsessed with the sterility of its toilet bowls, we take remarkably little notice of the micro-organisms that can and do pollute indoor air. While at least some standards limiting exposure to chemical air pollutants have been set, there are no existing regulations or even systematic recommendations for controlling exposure to toxic germs.

Some of the problems related to germs in the air were recently highlighted at a scientific conference on the subject at the New York Academy of Sciences. Its organizer, Dr. Ruth Knudsin, put it this way: "Industry and laboratories can liberally spew out bacterial, viral or fungal particles into the air and into the sewer system. . . . No threshold levels of viable particles that may be emitted or to which humans can be exposed are in existence. The area of human exposure to viable particles in the environment has been totally disregarded."

It is perplexing that there are no laws governing the amount of contamination that can be added to the air by industrial and other sources, since it is in such direct contrast to the wariness with which we as a society approach the control of other infectious diseases. For example, the great majority of local governments require immunization of schoolchildren against the common childhood diseases prior to school registration. Similarly, immigration and foreign-travel laws have been stringent for many years with respect to inoculation and quarantine requirements where the chance of contraction or spread of diseases like cholera exists.

We can explain some of the neglect by examining the scientific state of the art. The theory that disease could be transmitted by microscopic organisms that were passed from person to person or from animals to people constituted revolutionary thinking a century ago. In the modern scientific age of the twentieth century, the "germ theory" basis of infectious diseases is, of course, incontrovertibly established, but it is still not clear how diseases are transmitted through the air.

A recent example of airborne contagion is Legionnaire's disease, which captured public attention during a convention of the American Legion in Philadelphia in 1976. A sudden outbreak of a fatal pneumonialike disease at that national meeting set off a massive investigation by scientists seeking to determine the cause of that tragic event. The cause apparently lay with a micro-organism, now called *Legionella pneumophila*, that was first described in 1947, although its significance remained to be discovered. This bug has subsequently been recognized as the culprit in hundreds of additional cases. Legionellosis, as the disease is called, is known to manifest itself in at least two ways. It can induce a fever accompanied by pneumonia, which if left untreated will be fatal in 15 to 20 percent of the cases, or it can induce illness and fever without accompanying pneumonia and no ensuing fatalities.

Although most people have heard about Legionnaire's disease, few people realize that previous outbreaks of legionellosis had taken place. In 1968, an explosive outbreak of fever of unknown origin occurred in the Pontiac, Michigan office of the Oakland County Health Department. On the first day of the episode one employee became ill. On the second day 66 fell prey to the illness, and the third day saw an additional 22 victims. In all, by the end of the episode 95 out of 100 employees were taken ill and 49 of 170 visitors to the building succumbed to the disease, which was given the name Pontiac fever, although its microscopic cause remained unknown.

A scientific investigation undertaken to determine the factors behind the outbreak discovered that the air-conditioning system had two defects. Spent air was collected on the evaporative condenser and exhausted from the building through an outlet duct less than 2 meters from the intake duct that supplied the fresh air for the building. A second defect was found in the air duct that supplied the cooled air to the building. This supply duct passed very close to the exhaust duct, and the common walls allowed droplets of exhausted air to collect in a puddle in the supply duct. Although the investigators could not identify any micro-organisms as having caused the epidemic, they suspected airborne spread of the disease in the Pontiac, Michigan office early in the investigation from the pattern of occurrence of symptoms. First of all, the visitors to the building had few other common opportunities for exposure to an agent that caused the disease. It was also noted that people who worked in the building and were exposed in the morning were more likely to contract Pontiac fever, or legionellosis, than people exposed in the afternoon or evening. This led to the suspicion that starting up the air-conditioning unit was somehow involved.

As is their usual procedure when epidemics of unknown origin take place, the investigating scientists from the U.S. Center for Disease Control (CDC) preserved tissue samples, assuming that a future analysis of these tissues might help to explain what had caused the outbreak, when more knowledge or better scientific techniques became available. In this case, CDC collected water samples from the evaporative condenser and exposed guinea pigs to an aerosol of it. The guinea pigs were sacrificed and sections of lung tissues frozen and stored.

Since it is the usual practice to re-examine tissue from previous similar occurrences when new discoveries are made, after the isolation and identification of the micro-organism causing Legionnaire's disease, CDC scientists re-examined samples of the frozen Pontiac fever guinea-pig lung tissue. They found *Legionella pneumophila*. There have been several other instances which support the theory that legionellosis is spread by the airborne route and that cooling towers and evaporative condensers can be the breeding ground for the germ.

Contamination of Heating and Air-Conditioning Systems

Although legionellosis is not very common, it has been comparatively well studied and serves as a good example of diseases that can be spread through the air by germs harbored in water towers, evaporative condensers, humidifiers, and other locations where water is stored for periods of time. An air-conditioning system can become contaminated when micro-organisms are sucked into the air-movement system. The humid, usually warm machine operations are an ideal growing medium for many germs and even for microscopic species of parasitic worms. Some measurements of microbial content of water-spray units have found levels as high as one million microorganisms per milliliter (about 20 drops) of water. Dense growths of microbial organisms have been found lining the walls of humidification units. When water condenses on the outside of the units or on the neighboring ductwork, microbes will often also grow on the walls. Thus air passing through the normal air-delivery duct system can pick up these germs and be contaminated.

Contamination of the air ducts can lead to the spread of infectious diseases like legionellosis, or it can lead to the spread of micro-organisms that cause allergic responses like humidifier fever. Although no one knows how widespread allergic lung responses are among office workers, there is no lack of examples. In one office where workers began to complain about intermittent chills, fever, and shortness of breath, the *Actinomycetes* bacteria, which is thought to be responsible for humidifier lung, was found; 4 out of 27 workers developed the condition. In a large office complex in the southwestern United States, several workers developed similar symptoms. Investigators found that the air-conditioning system cooled the air by sending it over an open-spray water unit. Analysis of the water revealed fourteen different types of harmful organisms, including two species of aquatic nematodes, parasitic worms that live in water. When the workers were tested for allergies, several of these micro-organisms were found to be responsible for their distress, which involved symptoms similar to those of humidifier lung.

As we have already noted, there is probably no way to desensitize a person to foreign materials. This means there will always be a reaction to the offending substance when encountered. Two steps are needed to prevent these allergies from causing suffering. One is that the air-conditioning and handling system must be kept germ-free. Another is that a sensitive worker might have to leave the job, a complex legal and philosophical dilemma involving discrimination and the Occupational Safety and Health Act.

CONTROLLING THE GERM AND ALLERGY PROBLEM

Although cleanliness of the systems is of utmost importance, it is also important to be cognizant of the correct ways to keep the system clean. It will be simply trading one occupational health hazard for another if the sterilization process is as dangerous as or possibly more dangerous than the germs. This point is well illustrated by the following advice published in a building management magazine:

> Good Breathing: A building's air conditioning, heating or humidifying unit may harbor certain airborne spores that can cause a serious lung disease known as hypersensitivity alveolitis, as well as a number of other respiratory ailments. As a preventive measure your maintenance should conduct a periodic cleaning of all these units approximately every six months by sterilizing procedures or treatment with ethylene oxide. Electrostatic precipitators or ultraviolet germicidal lamps can also be used in removing or reducing airborne contamination.

Some of this advice is good. Electrostatic precipitators appear to be useful for several air-cleaning functions. But sterilizing agents should be used only with extreme caution. Ethylene oxide is a very potent chemical that attacks the genetic material as well as protein in the body. It can cause an array of blood diseases and evidence is mounting that it also causes human cancer. It is already known to be a potent animal carcinogen. Instructing a maintenance person to spray ethylene oxide gas without additional warnings about self-protection is extremely bad advice. And the possibility that this gas may enter the general air-supply system and expose building occupants to its hazards is very real and very dangerous. It can be used only under the most controlled handling conditions. Other sterilizing agents should be accorded the same respect in handling that ethylene oxide requires, because, after all, the reason that a chemical is a sterilizing agent is that it can kill living organisms. Too often, in our use of sterilizing agents, pesticides, and the like, we humans appear to have forgotten that we too are biological creatures and susceptible to the chemical weapons we use to attack other creatures.

Radon Pollution

For many years basements and building foundations have been known to emit radioactivity, making radiation a somewhat surprising but serious element of indoor air pollution. The original source of the radioactivity in indoor air is uranium, the parent element of a family of radioactive chemical elements. Uranium is widely distributed in the earth's crust, generally at levels that range from 2 to 4 parts per million. Construction materials like concrete and bricks can be contaminated with uranium if the earth with which they are made contains this valuable but toxic element.

All ionizing radiation is potentially harmful, and the type that derives from uranium has particularly serious effects. Current energy-conservation measures are worsening the level of ionizing radiation that is present indoors, which, as with the other air pollutants discussed here, increases its relevance for office workers. Uranium miners have had their health devastated by such radiation, and the annals of occupational health as well as the history of nuclear energy are stained with the lung-cancer deaths of uranium miners. Indeed, the first human lung cancers diagnosed, just more than one hundred years ago, were among Czechoslovakian miners who worked in radon-contaminated mines.

Radioactivity is a process that originates in the nucleus of the atoms that make up a chemical element such as uranium. The nucleus is composed of positively charged particles, or protons, and neutral particles, or neutrons. The total number of protons and neutrons determines the identity of the element. For example, oxygen has 8 protons and 8 neutrons, or 16 nuclear particles. The nuclei of nonradioactive elements are stable. We can expect oxygen to always have 8 plus 8 nuclear particles. Even if the oxygen joins with hydrogen to form water or participates in some other chemical reaction, its nucleus will remain unchanged. In a radioactive element, however, the nucleus is unstable and the nuclear particles interact, decreasing in number over time.

Because the nucleus of an atom contains an enormous amount of energy, when a nuclear particle is released during radioactive decay, it emits high levels of energy—radiation in the form of X-rays and other high-energy particles. As the number of particles in the nucleus decreases, the chemical identity of the element changes. In the decay cycle of uranium, which starts out with 238 neutrons and protons, the nucleus slowly turns into radium, with 226 neutrons and protons. It takes an incredibly long time for uranium to decay. More than 4.5 billion years are needed for half the uranium present to turn into radium. This is uranium's half-life. The decay of radium is also a very slow process. The half-life of radium is 1,590 years. Slow radioactive decay rates of uranium and radium make potential exposure a perpetual problem.

When radium decays it produces radon, which is a gas and not a solid like uranium or radium. Radon gas is a major indoor air pollutant because it diffuses out of the solid walls and building foundations into the air. Radon decays rapidly, with a half-life of 3.8 days, and produces elements called radon daughters, which are particles that adhere easily to the ordinary dust in the air and are readily inhaled. When they are deposited in the lungs they wreak biological havoc because of the potent ionizing radiation they emit in the form of alpha rays. Since the half-life of these elements is short, they concentrate all their powerful energy on the lung tissue before they dissipate and turn into particles of nonradioactive lead. (It is an interesting though perhaps not essential aside that all radioactive elements eventually end up as lead, which will be the ultimate fate of the universe scores of billions of years from now.)

Lung cancer and other health effects attributable to radon contamination of indoor air will, of course, not reach the epidemic proportions that have ravaged workers in radioactive mines, but it is to be expected that radon indoors will take some biological toll of the people who inhale it routinely. Unfortunately, there are no long-term studies yet of the effects of radon contamination of indoor air in offices. Virtually all attention has been focused on the home, although most homeowners are probably totally unaware of it. For the purposes of the discussion here, we will simply extrapolate analogous residential data to the office building.

There are of course disputes about the exact health risks of radon gas, just as there are disputes about exact risks of all toxic substances. Striving for exactness often diverts the argument from the basic toxicity of a substance to technical questions of calculational methods and testing.

We will avoid those arguments here by providing some reasonable estimates. One scientist, for example, recently published a report in the journal *Health Physics* stating that "if current estimates of health effects of radon are accepted, it is concluded that energy conservation by insulation of buildings would cause at least 10,000 extra fatal cancers per year in the United States due to reduced ventilation." He based his calculations on models developed by the National Academy of Sciences, and they are probably on the high side.

A "normal" range of radon gas is unavoidable in houses, particularly in the basements, since uranium is a universal earth mineral. Some of the background rate of lung cancer in our society, that is, lung cancer that is not explained by smoking or occupational exposure, is probably due in part to radon. Clay bricks, granite bricks, and cement, particularly if made with tailings, or residue, from quarry and mining operations, will all be prime sources of radon. Houses with unfinished basements will have radon seeping in from the subsoil. Sometimes this can reach epidemic proportions, as in Grand Junction, Colorado, where tailings from mineral mines were used for the concrete foundations in many buildings, homes, and schools. In some structures the levels of radon were so high that they were unfit for human habitation and had to be abandoned. This is obviously an extreme instance.

Radon exposure is of concern to large numbers of workers whose offices are in basement floors. Many offices in hospitals and government buildings are below the ground, and radon exposure may be considerable.

Office workers may also be exposed to the gas if their buildings are constructed of granite bricks. Several years ago it was found that the Grand Central Terminal in New York had considerable radon levels. The granite brick used in the construction of the terminal is the major source of this pollution. No estimates of risk to people who work in the building have yet been made. The problem will be worse on the lowest floors of buildings, and it is unquestionably true that reduction of the ventilation in buildings significantly raises the levels of radon gas and radon daughters that are present in the atmosphere. It is not a problem to be ignored by employers and workers. Radon monitors are available, and the agencies listed in the Resource Organizations section of this book can be contacted for assistance. If excessive radon levels are discovered in your office, the walls could be sealed with sealant paints. To ensure effectiveness, this should be done by experts.

Microwaves in Office Buildings

Workers in tall office buildings such as the Empire State Building or the World Trade Center in New York City and the Sears Building in Chicago have been exposed to much higher levels of microwave radiation from radio and television broadcast antennas than most other people. Less famous buildings that house transmitters will have similar problems. Similarly, offices at or near airports will be subject to higher levels of microwaves from the radar transmissions and receptions.

Microwaves are a form of electromagnetic radiation called nonionizing radiation. They fall at the low end of the energy spectrum, having less energy than ultraviolet rays, infrared rays (heat rays), and even visible light. Microwaves are part of the natural radiant energy given off by the sun, but they are also produced by electronic devices. Microwaves are difficult to measure, and the dosage of energy they deliver depends on many factors including the frequency and wavelength, the direction waves are moving, and the size, shape, and position of the person receiving the radiation.

Microwaves cause heating of body tissue, which is the way that microwave ovens work. Animals exposed to high levels of microwaves have shown excess mortality, chromosomal anomolies, blood-system changes, and cataracts, among other health effects. However, it is not known whether humans may exhibit these health effects at the low levels of microwave exposure generally reported from industrial, broadcasting, and other radar sources.

The health effects of microwaves are controversial. Several years ago the American embassy in Moscow was bombarded by the Russians with microwaves, and newspaper reports linked high levels of microwave exposure to adverse health effects. Research in the United States discounted the connections between microwave exposure and the health of embassy personnel, but this study is disputed. There is wide disparity in microwave health effects reported in the scientific literature from all over the world, but the consensus is growing that exposure to this radiation has a wide range of potential effects.

If an office is located near broadcasting towers or radar installations, there is a relatively easy way to prevent exposure. Microwave sources can be effectively shielded by thin metal screens, and it is possible to install such screens in building walls. Adequate monitoring for leakage should also be performed by trained personnel. In this way the health of exposed workers can be protected until the many questions about the health effects of microwaves are answered.

Assessing and Measuring Indoor Air Pollution

If the chemicals listed in table 17 are present in your office, they will generally be found at levels far lower than the maximum allowed by law. This is because the OSHA levels are geared to the heavy pollution of industry. This does not mean that lower levels are safe. Many experts consider that the current OSHA levels are inadequate and too lax to protect the health of American workers. Because office indoor air pollutants are low-level, their measurement and monitoring will be complicated. Quick techniques, such as "detector tubes," which operate like a bicycle pump, pulling air through a tube containing a chemical that changes color upon contact with the toxic substance, are usually not sensitive enough for the levels encountered in the office. Ozone from photocopiers may show up, however. If you find a level of ozone that is detectable, there will be a margin of error inherent in using these tubes.

Air samples requiring more sophisticated air-sampling pumps and laboratory analysis are generally needed indoors. Even these may at times be inconclusive, as in the example discussed in chapter 1. Dosimetry badges that you can wear on your lapel over the course of the working day or longer, and that absorb pollutants onto a chemical surface, are inexpensive and can work well for pollutants like carbon monoxide or formaldehyde. The badges are sent off for rapid evaluation to a laboratory in the company that markets them. This eliminates the trouble of finding a laboratory to analyze an air sample.

We should extend two notes of caution. First, you will need some expert advice if you want to do air sampling; an industrial hygienist will probably be required. A second important point is that it is *not* your right simply to go into your workplace and take an air sample or measure noise or light levels. An employer has the right to fire you for taking air samples unless you belong to a union and have a specific clause in your contract permitting air sampling. It may seem astounding, but legal decisions stating that the air belongs to the employer have been made.

TABLE 17. MAJOR INDOOR AIR POLLUTANTS IN OFFICE BUILDINGS

POLLUTANT	SOURCES	HEALTH EFFECTS
Ammonia	Blueprint machines, cleaning solutions	Respiratory-system, eye, and skin irritation
Asbestos	Duct and pipe insulation, spackling compounds, insulation products, fire retardants, ceiling and floor tiles	Pulmonary (lung) fibrosis, cancer
Carbon dioxide	Humans' exhaled air, combustion	Headache, nausea, dizziness
Carbon monoxide	Automobile exhaust, tobacco smoke, combustion	Headache, weakness, dizziness, nausea; long-term exposure related to heart disease
Formaldehyde	Urea-formaldehyde foam insulation and urea-formaldehyde resin used to bind laminated-wood products such as particle board, and plywood; tobacco smoke	Respiratory-system, eye, and skin irritation, nausea, headache, fatigue, cancer (in exposed laboratory animals)
Methyl alcohol	Spirit duplicating machines	Respiratory-system and skin irritation
Micro-organisms (such as viruses, bacteria, and fungi)	Humidifying and air-conditioning systems, evaporative condensers, cooling towers, mildewed papers, old books, damp newsprint	Respiratory infections, allergic responses
Motor vehicle exhaust (carbon monoxide, nitrogen oxides, lead particulates, sulfur oxides)	Parking garages, outside traffic	Respiratory-system and eye irritation, headache (see carbon monoxide), genetic damage

TABLE 17. (cont.)

POLLUTANT	SOURCES	HEALTH EFFECTS
Nitrogen oxides	Gas stoves, combustion, motor-vehicle exhaust, tobacco smoke	Respiratory-system and eye irritation
Ozone	Photocopying and other electrical machines	Respiratory-system and eye irritation, headache, genetic damage
Paint fumes (organics, lead, mercury)	Freshly painted surfaces	Respiratory-system and eye irritation; neurological, kidney, and bone-marrow damage at high levels of exposure
PCBs (polychlorinated biphenyls), dioxin, dibenzofuran	Electrical transformers	Sperm and fetal defects, skin rashes, liver and kidney damage, cancer
Pesticides	Spraying of plants and premises	Depending on chemical components: liver damage, cancer, neurological damage, skin, respiratory-system and eye irritation
Radon and decay products	Building construction materials such as concrete and stone; basements	Ionizing radiation-related diseases such as genetic damage, cancer, fetal and sperm damage
Sterilant gases (such as ethylene oxide)	Systems to sterilize humidifying and air-conditioning systems	Depending on chemical components: respiratory-system and eye irritation, genetic damage, cancer
Tobacco smoke (passive exposure to particulates, carbon monoxide, formaldehyde, coal tars, and nicotine)	Cigarettes, pipes, cigars	Respiratory-system and eye irritation; may lead to diseases associated with smokers

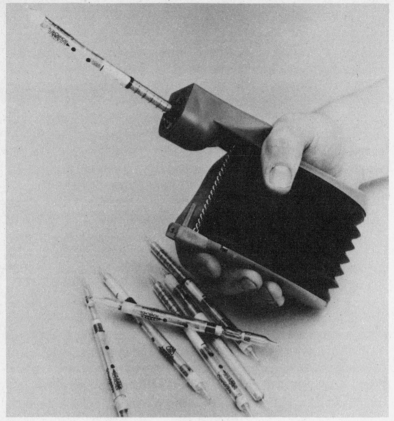

A

FIGURE 28. *Measuring Indoor Air Pollutants*
Most pollutants in the office require sophisticated testing because of their relatively low levels. Some simple methods are available for judging quickly whether higher levels are present. A. A universal tester pump comes with tubes filled with reagents that react with specific chemicals. The pump draws a measured amount of air through the tube, which then changes color, showing you how much of a chemical is in the air. The tubes can only take instantaneous samples, and cannot measure levels over time. They are also less reliable and less sensitive than more sophisticated methods, though less expensive. B. Vapor-monitoring badges are relatively inexpensive and quite accurate. You wear the badge for the length of time specified by the manufacturer, and then send it back to the company. They analyze how much chemical has adhered to the special surfaces of the badge, calculate the total amount of pollutant in your office air, and then report these results to you.

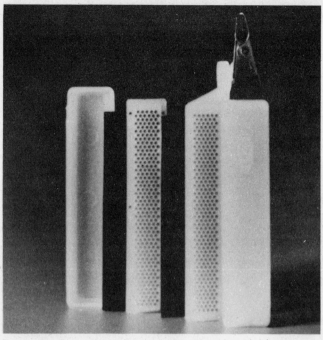

B

All is not lost, however. Many cities and states have passed "right-to-know" legislation, which requires that an employer fully inform any employee of the chemical nature of the materials and their level in the air in the workplace as well as of their potential harmful effects.

The survey in appendix A will help you to assess the quality of the indoor air and to determine whether you should seek outside assistance.

CHAPTER 9

WHERE DO WE GO FROM HERE?

You have taken the first step toward improving the health and safety conditions in the workplace by reading this book and becoming aware of other sources of information. The next step is to begin the systematic implementation of the surveys suggested throughout, using the guide in appendix A. The best way is not to try to do it alone. Recruit some of your co-workers, as well as your supervisor and employer if they are amenable. Summarize information on some problems that are relevant to your office and distribute the summary to your co-workers. They will begin to relate to the issues when they can recognize them. A little agitation won't hurt. Nothing breeds more success than initial success at achieving a solution to a problem. If you can find one readily identifiable problem and also come up with a suggestion for change, this will go a long way toward creating that change. Sound covers for typewriters, adjustable blinds for windows, relocation of video display terminals to eliminate glare, regular fire drills: these are all areas where you can begin to improve health and safety in your office.

Ideally a health and safety committee should inspect the office on a regular basis and suggest improvements, set up a timetable for changes, and keep records of accidents and health problems if they occur. Such a committee should be composed of representatives from both management and employees. But it is also a good idea for management and office workers each to have their own committees as well, since discussion and problem solving will be freer in such forums. The work of these committees can then be brought to the joint health and safety committee for consideration and action.

There is a good deal of work for the health and safety committee to do, especially in the area of inspections. A subcommittee on fire safety should be appointed to carry out the suggestions in chapter 6. Other inspections should include evaluation of the ventilating system, checking on the maintenance of equipment, the frequency of light-bulb replacement, and so on. If there is a question or concern about any product or equipment used in the office, the committee should write to the manufacturers and obtain available material safety data or product safety data sheets.

The health and safety committee should further be able to review equipment before it is purchased to make sure that user needs have been taken into consideration. It is not unreasonable to have a committee of potential VDT operators involved in choosing the VDT that will be the most comfortable to use. It is also not unreasonable to delegate a committee of workers to consider various arrangements of office furniture and lighting within a work space that will make it a pleasanter place to work in. A health and safety committee could be presented with various alternatives, and with a range of funds to be allocated for the tasks that need to be fulfilled, and be allowed to participate in the planning process.

Participation by workers in planning is not as outlandish as it may sound. In other countries, such as the Federal Republic of Germany, workers are represented on the boards of all companies and review any technological change prior to its installation in the workplace. In several provinces of Canada, health and safety committees consisting of equal representation by labor and management are mandated for all workplaces above a minimal size. These committees have the right to inspect the workplace and must meet at least monthly to discuss matters related to health and safety. In some American and Canadian offices where workers are represented by labor unions, specific rights to inspect and to recommend substitute practices have been obtained in collective-bargaining agreements. Examples of model contract language are given in appendix D.

Record keeping is extremely important. Complete records of all accidents, illnesses, and worker suggestions and complaints should be kept and reviewed regularly to see if patterns are developing. These records should also include how often fire drills are held and inspections made.

Your Rights and Resources Under the Law

Theoretically the Occupational Safety and Health Act (OSHA) passed by Congress in 1970 guarantees "insofar as practicable that no employee shall suffer diminished health, functional capacity or life expectancy as a result of his [or her] work experience." Under OSHA, which is administered by the Department of Labor, standards for workplace exposure to toxic substances and conditions are to be formulated and enforced, and workplaces are to be investigated and inspected. OSHA also has the right to penalize employers that maintain workplaces found to be in violation of the provisions of the act.

Unfortunately, the progress of OSHA has been slow and tortuous. Very few standards have been passed since its inception. OSHA is continually buffeted by the winds of political change and is clearly a political football in every major presidential race. Furthermore, even under administrations friendly to the needs of working people, the emphasis of OSHA has been almost exclusively on the health and safety hazards of heavy industry. The steel mills, the chemical factories, and the construction sites have pre-empted the limited resources of the agency. Office work has low priority.

Despite this, you should be aware of the resources that are available to you. Workers have the right to request an inspection of their workplace, and can remain anonymous if they so desire. If you feel that you have a safety or health hazard that warrants inspection, then you should avail yourself of your right to such an inspection under the law. Your local OSHA office will help you file a complaint. OSHA provides that no worker shall be discriminated against for exercising her or his rights under the act. Employers who feel they have a health or safety problem can also call the OSHA office in for consultation.

Another government agency that can assist in health and safety problems is the National Institute of Occupational Safety and Health (NIOSH), which is part of the U.S. Department of Health and Human Services. NIOSH can provide technical assistance and can also carry out health-hazard evaluations—though the waiting line for such an evaluation may be very long. NIOSH has been active in the past in investigating complaints about video display terminals and office air pollution, and has uncovered some hazardous situations in offices.

Your local health department and state health and environmental health departments may also be of assistance, although their resources are usually far more limited than the federal government's. Fire safety and sanitation standards and rules, however, may be very clearly spelled out.

The Center for Disease Control in Atlanta may be helpful in investigating an outbreak of infectious disease or—as has happened in a few locations—a suspicious incidence of birth defects, although the latter type of study is extremely difficult to carry out and usually inconclusive.

Although this may sound simplistic, political activity is really an important aspect of health and safety. If you feel strongly about the working conditions in your office, if you find it as reprehensible as we do that there are inadequate standards governing office working conditions, then you should let your local congressperson and city and state representatives know. Form a delegation with your co-workers and visit congressional representatives, informing them of your working conditions and of the urgent need to include the office in health and safety regulations since this is where the majority of Americans work. The theoretical inclusion of offices in general standards is not good enough: realistic and applicable standards are urgently needed for lighting, ventilation, machine design, noise, and all the other problems discussed throughout this book. Local communities and states have been organizing and passing "right-to-know" laws, which require full disclosure of chemical ingredients and their effects to workers and in some cases to the community. If your community does not have a right-to-know law, then contact an organization in a state that does and find out how they went about organizing and getting one passed.

While many office hazards, such as air pollution, affect everyone who works in an office in much the same way, women as a group are exposed to greater risks because they compose the vast majority of the clerical work force. The limited and repetitive patterns of clerical work expose workers more intensely to both physical and psychological hazards and to social disadvantage. Congressional testimony by 9 to 5, the National Association of Working Women, which highlights this issue, is reprinted as appendix C.

Day Care

The other great stressor for working women is the juggling act they must perform to keep all their functions at home and at work running smoothly. Evidence is mounting about the potential health effects of this burden. "After controlling for the standard risk factors, the most significant predictors of CHD [coronary heart disease] among clerical workers were suppressed hostility, having a nonsupportive boss, and decreased job mobility. The findings suggest that women working in clerical jobs are at higher risk of developing CHD than other women, and that this risk increases with family responsibilities." Drs. Suzanne Haynes and Manning Feinleib, who analyzed data on women, work, and coronary heart disease that were part of a long-range study based on the population of Framingham, Massachusetts, found that the risk for coronary heart disease was significantly increased for female clerical workers as compared with other female workers and with women who were full-time homemakers. The women clericals worked under a nonsupportive boss, had family responsibilities such as three or more children, and suppressed their hostility at this very stressful life—that is, they didn't yell back or respond outwardly but internalized all their anger.

One solution to some of this stress is to provide reliable, positive, convenient, and inexpensive child care to working parents. It is interesting to compare currently available child-care facilities with those available during World War II, when government policy encouraged all women (including mothers) to work in war-related industries. Government-sponsored research developed models for the best style of child care, and companies made this service available near the work site so that women could conveniently drop off and pick up their children and even visit them during the lunch hour and breaks.

The employees represented by the Civil Service Employees Association (CSEA), the New York State Public Employees Federation, and its parent union, the Service Employees International Union, have recently negotiated a landmark contract with the state of New York to provide day-care centers. The centers will be planned and administered by boards that include representatives of the state, the unions, community day-care specialists, and the parents themselves. The idea for these centers was first incorporated into a 1972 CSEA contract, but implementation did not begin until 1979, when they were funded by the CSEA. The centers have breast-feeding programs. They also make it possible for fathers to see their children; in fact, it was reported that more fathers than mothers visited the centers, taking their older children for walks during lunchtime. The children in the centers range from eight weeks to five years old. As Meyer S. Fruchter, state director of employee relations, put it: "From the employer's viewpoint, onsite day care gives the state an advantage in recruiting and retaining employees. All too often, competent and trained women leave the work force after childbirth because they can't locate suitable child care. Employer-sponsored child care is no longer a frill but a necessity."

A great deal of emphasis has rightfully been placed on the need for child-care facilities to assist the working mother. But many working women, particularly those in their middle years, have a different family responsibility: care of their sick or aged parents and in-laws. The facilities for senior citizens in our society are possibly even worse than those for our children, and the working woman may be particularly burdened by this caretaking role.

Turning Back the Clock

Without guns, tanks, or armaments but with keyboards, semiconductors, and microchips, a bloodless battle is being waged, changing the lives of millions of people. It is the latest episode in the two-hundred-year-old industrial revolution, and it has brought automation to the office. It would be easy to decry the automation of the office as portending the enslavement of all office workers. But as with any revolution, the overall impact of office automation for bettering lives, simplifying tasks, and improving job satisfaction will depend on the harnessing of those aspects of the technology that adversely affect people while promoting those aspects that improve the quality of their lives. The old way of entering long rows and columns of figures by hand is not necessarily superior to entering them on a machine, unless the machine is so poorly designed that it damages your health, or unless you are hooked to a computer that monitors every second of your day.

While it is not predestined that office automation will bring about more evil than good, the signs are not hopeful, especially in light of projected employment trends. The U.S. Department of Labor predicts that more than 50 percent of the 20 million new jobs in 1990 will be white-collar work on the managerial, professional, technical, sales, and clerical levels. Clerical work will grow more rapidly than any other occupation in the 1980s. It is estimated that 4.8 million jobs, dominated by women, will open in clerical areas alone.

The most troublesome possibility confronting us is the new alternative of work in the home, a strange mixture of high-technology labor and the centuries-old exploitation of workers in cottage industries.

"Home is where the office is" blares the *New York* magazine headline across a photograph of a bright, cheerful businessman seated at an antique desk on an Oriental rug in his living room. His two beautiful children are pointing at his pens and his multibuttoned telephone. He is surrounded by stacks of impressive-looking print-outs. Other vignettes of corporate home success fill this magazine issue (April 12, 1982) and describe the freedom and self-fulfillment of the entrepreneur who makes the break from the corporate rat-race to strike out successfully on his own. It is the American dream come true: free enterprise, competition, independence, initiative, creativity, self-fulfillment, while still being very much part of the action, wheeling and dealing in the world of big business. All this takes place in the comfort of one's own home, with gourmet lunches served elegantly to business guests by uniformed servants.

Is this the wave of freedom predicted by futurists and made possible by rapid telecommunications and computer links to stock markets, office staff, and inventories? Perhaps this is the path of liberation and independence for the select few, the elite of the business world who have the connections, the savvy, the money, the education—and the luck—to make it. But to the middle-management person or the small businessman, it means doing all the clerical work yourself or being stuck with paying for the services and overseeing them as well.

We believe that a more likely future portrait of homework is captured in an advertisement by a major dictating-equipment manufacturer, who assures companies that with modern word-processing equipment, valuable office staff need not be lost to family obligations.

With one eye on the computer terminal and the other on the baby in the playpen, our secretary-heroine has one foot on the dictaphone pedal, both ears hooked into a transcriber headset, and both hands on the keyboard. It appears that the most pressing problem for the futurists planning the latter half of the eighties will be to find something for our superwomen to do with that unoccupied foot.

Let us recall clearly and distinctly what cottage industries represent. They were the transitional period between full-scale industrialization of the textile, clothing, shoe, and millinery industries. Women, usually aided by children and often by aged parents—too old for fieldwork—and maiden aunts, worked long hours at piecework rates to produce goods that were brought to the manufacturer. Cottage-industry work, then and now, means piecework rates, no minimum wage, no fringe benefits like health insurance, pension, vacations, sick leave, paid religious and civic holidays. It means much lower wages and it means the absence of the benefits of work: friends on the job, a breakdown of the isolation of work, the ability to get together to improve conditions. We believe, and studies have confirmed this belief, that these are all essential aspects of maintaining mental health on the job.

In 1980 there was a move by the Reagan administration to legalize cottage industries and thereby to subvert the minimum-wage laws. This was proposed at the same time that extensive exceptions to child-labor law were also being proposed. "Putting out," the term used during the American Revolution for home weaving of cloth from yarn produced by manufacturers, and which later evolved into a sexual term applied to women, may yet be the appropriate term for homework as we near the close of the twentieth century. For homework may indeed represent the prostitution of every reform gained by working people over the last two hundred years. Activating ourselves to deal with the questions of health and safety in the workplace is one step we can take to stop these negative aspects of technology from occurring and to ensure that modern times and modern work-styles provide us with the safe and healthful conditions that are our right.

AN OFFICE
HEALTH AND SAFETY
SURVEY

The following survey is designed to provide you with an outline of the main areas of health and safety in your office that you should be aware of and survey regularly. We have divided the survey into sections and listed the pages that give more details. The questions are framed so that YES is the correct answer. Every NO and every I DON'T KNOW could mean a health or safety problem. After you complete the survey, the negatives or unknowns can be the starting point for you or a health and safety committee to begin work to improve your working conditions. Repeat this survey regularly, and keep records of the results in order to evaluate progress in health and safety improvements.

I. EVALUATING THE VENTILATION AND AIR QUALITY
  (*See pages* 129–161)

☐ 1. Does the air seem fresh, not stuffy?

☐ 2. Is the air free from unpleasant fumes and odors?

☐ 3. Does your workplace have a ventilation system?

☐ 4. Do you have a map of vents and ducts?

☐ 5. Are there both supply and exhaust vents in each work area?

☐ 6. Are the supply and exhaust vents separated enough to avoid "dead spaces"?

☐ 7. Have you evaluated the vents to see if they are:
    a. functioning (using a tissue or smoke tube)?
    b. operating continuously?
    c. unobstructed by furniture, walls, or partitions?

☐ 8. Is the building's fresh-air intake located away from smokestacks, vehicle exhaust, or other sources of pollutants?

☐ 9. Have the following measurements been made in each work area at representative times of the workday and workweek to get typical levels:
    a. temperature?
    b. humidity (with hygrometer)?

☐ 10. Do you know the standards for airflow and fresh air for your workplace?

☐ 11. Are American Society of Heating, Refrigeration, and Air-Conditioning Engineers (ASHRAE) standards met for:
    a. temperature?
    b. humidity?
    c. airflow?
    d. percentage of fresh air supplied and mixed with recirculated air?

☐ 12. Have potential sources of air pollution such as the following been identified and measured:
    a. cigarette smoke components?
    b. carbon dioxide from human breathing?
    c. chemicals generated by office machines, such as ozone (see pages 79–81)?
    d. formaldehyde from pressed board or insulation?

          e. fumes from auto exhausts (especially if workplace is near garage or road)?

          f. asbestos from insulation, ducts, or aging floor or ceiling tiles?

☐ 13. Is your work environment free from asbestos fibers?

          a. Are surfaces free of white fibrous dust settling, particularly overnight or on weekends?

          b. Have open vents, ducts, or other areas been checked for exposed or damaged white fibrous material?

          c. Have ceilings or walls been spray-coated with materials for sound reduction?

          d. If yes, have air samples and surface-material samples been tested for asbestos?

          e. If asbestos is present, has an expert been called in to determine whether to remove the asbestos or seal it in?

☐ 14. Is microorganism contamination prevented by sterilization of:

          a. humidifying system?

          b. air-conditioning system?

          c. evaporative condenser?

          d. water tower?

          e. other sources of stagnant water?

          f. old, musty files and books that are retrieved or handled?

☐ 15. Are appropriate precautions taken to prevent exposure of maintenance people or office personnel to sterilizing agents?

☐ 16. Are people removed from the area and ventilation increased during:

          a. painting?

          b. pesticide spraying?

          c. heavy cleaning?

☐ 17. Is sufficient time allowed to pass before personnel return to treated areas?

☐ 18. Is your office near manufacturing, laboratory, or other chemical-intensive facilities?

 a. Do you know what pollutants are being generated?

 b. Have appropriate tests been made in your office for their presence?

☐ 19. Is your building free of microwave pollution?

 a. If your building is located near broadcasting towers or radar installations, has a radiological expert measured levels?

 b. Has metal screening been installed in buildings with excessive microwave levels?

☐ 20. Have offices in building basements been measured for radon levels?

 a. If radon is present, have sealant paints been applied and levels remeasured?

II. EVALUATING FIRE SAFETY
 (*See pages 98–111*)

☐ 1. Does your building have a fire safety plan with the following features:

 a. automatic fire detection with building alarm and local fire department relay.

 b. automatic sprinkler system?

 c. fire communications system reaching each work area?

 d. deputy fire warden appointed for each 7,500 square feet of space?

 e. two searchers appointed for each floor?

 f. automatic return of elevators to ground floor in case of fire?

 g. exits clearly marked?

 h. written and posted evacuation plans on each floor?

 i. quarterly fire drills?

 j. flammability standards and information on each item of office equipment and furnishings?

 k. special precautions for high-hazard areas?

☐ 2. Are the fire extinguishers:
    a. within 75 feet of each person?
    b. inspected and tagged with the schedules and dates of professional inspections?

☐ 3. Are there daily inspections by deputy fire wardens to ensure that:
    a. fire extinguishers are in place?
    b. exit paths are unobstructed?
    c. hallways and emergency lights are in working order?

☐ 4. Are there monthly inspections by the appointed fire warden to ensure that:
    a. the organization chart is current and posted?
    b. there is an updated list of persons needing assistance during an emergency?
    c. extinguishers are in position, tagged, sealed, and pinned; pressure gauge full; hose and nozzle in good condition; location sign in place?
    d. standpipe is unobstructed; nozzle and hose are in good condition?
    e. fire alarm boxes are unobstructed?
    f. sprinkler heads are unobstructed and clean?
    g. corridors and aisles are clear?
    h. exit signs and lights are in place and lit?
    i. storage rooms and shelves are neat and orderly?
    j. flammable liquids are properly stored?
    k. trash and waste handling procedures are in place to contain and promptly remove waste?
    l. electrical cords are in good condition?

☐ 5. Are the following fire-safety evaluations performed yearly:
    a. review of manufacturers' affidavits ensuring fire safety of furnishings and building materials?
    b. check to ensure that fuel load is no more than 15 pounds per square foot unless special precautions have been taken?
    c. removal of flammable plastic objects such as wastebaskets or artificial plants, and replacement with noncombustible models?

☐ 6. Have the schedule and dates for professional evaluation of the following been posted:
   a. automatic fire-detection system?
   b. alarm system?
   c. automatic notification of local fire department?
   d. fire extinguishers, hoses, and valves?
   e. fire record-keeping system?
   f. any changes in building compartmentalization?

☐ 7. Is there ongoing consultation with the fire department for:
   a. automatic fire-notification system?
   b. help in planning fire evacuation procedures?
   c. visits to enable the department to gain familiarity with the building?
   d. help in fire drills?

III. EVALUATING OFFICE MACHINES AND SUPPLIES
   (See pages 78–85)

☐ 1. Do you have the following readily available:
   a. a list of all office machines?
   b. instruction booklets for all machines?
   c. product safety information?
   d. material safety data sheets (MSDs) on all chemicals used or machines operated?

☐ 2. Does the maintenance of the machines include:
   a. regular cleaning/servicing according to manufacturers' instructions?
   b. posting of maintenance schedules near machines?
   c. accessible gloves or other supplies for safe handling of chemicals needed for maintenance by office staff?

☐ 3. Are machine users adequately trained?

☐ 4. Are users aware of signs of machine malfunction?

☐ 5. Have the machines been installed:
   a. according to manufacturers' instructions?
   b. with adequate space for free movement around machines where needed?

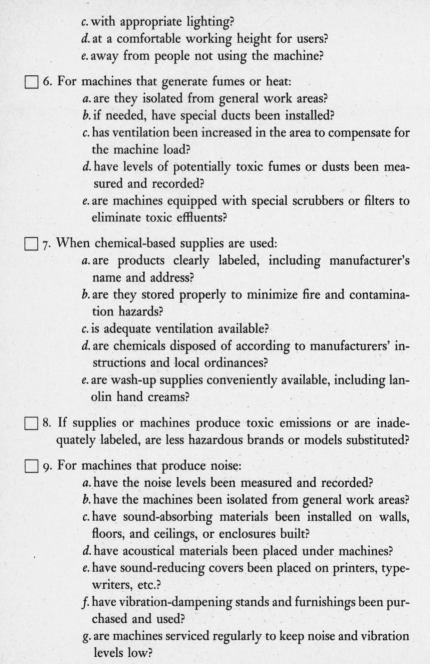

    c. with appropriate lighting?
    d. at a comfortable working height for users?
    e. away from people not using the machine?

☐ 6. For machines that generate fumes or heat:
    a. are they isolated from general work areas?
    b. if needed, have special ducts been installed?
    c. has ventilation been increased in the area to compensate for the machine load?
    d. have levels of potentially toxic fumes or dusts been measured and recorded?
    e. are machines equipped with special scrubbers or filters to eliminate toxic effluents?

☐ 7. When chemical-based supplies are used:
    a. are products clearly labeled, including manufacturer's name and address?
    b. are they stored properly to minimize fire and contamination hazards?
    c. is adequate ventilation available?
    d. are chemicals disposed of according to manufacturers' instructions and local ordinances?
    e. are wash-up supplies conveniently available, including lanolin hand creams?

☐ 8. If supplies or machines produce toxic emissions or are inadequately labeled, are less hazardous brands or models substituted?

☐ 9. For machines that produce noise:
    a. have the noise levels been measured and recorded?
    b. have the machines been isolated from general work areas?
    c. have sound-absorbing materials been installed on walls, floors, and ceilings, or enclosures built?
    d. have acoustical materials been placed under machines?
    e. have sound-reducing covers been placed on printers, typewriters, etc.?
    f. have vibration-dampening stands and furnishings been purchased and used?
    g. are machines serviced regularly to keep noise and vibration levels low?

☐ 10. Have the electrical safety factors of machine use been taken into account?

　　a. Are electrical cords recessed away from walking and work areas?

　　b. Are cords maintained and not frayed?

　　c. Are all electrical plugs grounded with three-pronged plugs and outlets?

　　d. Is each machine plugged into a separate outlet?

　　e. Do all machines meet Underwriters' Laboratory or similar safety standards?

　　f. Are all automatic electrical cutoffs functioning and not bypassed?

　　g. Are covers and other safety devices kept in place when the machine is in use?

☐ 11. Is the machine designed to prevent mechanical injury?

　　a. Are machines free from sharp or protruding edges?

　　b. Are machines guarded to prevent clothes, hair, or fingers from being caught in moving parts that are less than 7 feet above the ground?

　　c. Are "pinch points" that can pinch fingers or hands guarded (for example, in check processors)?

　　d. Are wire screens used to cover openings larger than 1/2 inch on fans?

　　e. Are there finger guards or locking devices on turning or cutting equipment, like paper cutters?

IV. EVALUATING VIDEO DISPLAY TERMINALS
(See pages 41–70)

☐ 1. Does the video display terminal have the following characteristics:

　　a. thin, detachable keyboard?

　　b. adjustable screen?

　　c. minimum flicker?

　　d. adjustable brightness and contrast?

　　e. upper-case and lower-case characters?

　　f. antiglare screen?

　　g. low heat output?

　　h. no high-frequency noise?

       i. nonglare machine surface?

       j. antistatic carpeting and machine ground?

       k. product safety data sheet, including radiation-testing information?

☐ 2. Does the VDT workstation have the following features:

       a. nonglare walls, ceilings, and work surfaces?

       b. adjustable, nonglare lighting, shielded and indirect?

       c. screen at right angles to windows?

       d. adjustable window coverings?

☐ 3. Before VDT systems are introduced and started up, is there:

       a. user participation in the equipment/system decision making?

       b. discussion between management and employees about work organization?

       c. provision for an adequate number of workstations?

       d. adequate training, including safety and health information?

       e. sufficient customer support from supplier?

       f. efficient, easily used programs to minimize worker frustration?

☐ 4. Is video display terminal work organized to:

       a. provide rotations between VDT and non-VDT work tasks?

       b. provide rest breaks away from the machine?

       c. allow a comfortable work pace?

       d. eliminate pacing and timing of keystroke and recording of error rate by machine?

☐ 5. Does management provide for regular eye examinations and corrective lenses when needed prior to introduction of VDTs and thereafter?

☐ 6. Are the video display terminals maintained by regular cleaning and servicing per manufacturers' directions?

       a. Are schedules and dates of maintenance posted?

☐ 7. In case of malfunction, is operation of VDT suspended until proper maintenance has been carried out?

V. EVALUATING OFFICE FURNITURE AND SPACE
(See pages 71–78; 112–117)

☐ 1. Is your chair designed so that:
    a. when you are seated, your hips and knees are bent at right angles and your feet flat on the floor?
    b. the seat height is 2 inches less than the distance between your knee crease and the floor?
    c. the seat is slanted slightly backward?

☐ 2. Does your chair have:
    a. adjustable seat height?
    b. a scrolled seat edge?
    c. a rough-textured wool or rayon seat cover?
    d. adjustable backrest height?
    e. a 5-pronged base for stability?
    f. rollers or casters for jobs with frequent movement while sitting?
    g. a wheel-locking mechanism to prevent slipping?
    h. a firm floor surface beneath for easy movement?
    i. the seat ends about 5 inches behind the knee crease?
    j. the backrest makes contact with the back 4 to 6 inches above the seat?
    k. the backrest is small and kidney-shaped if your arms are extended—as in typing—for most of the day?
    l. the backrest is firm and straight if your job does not require lengthy arm extension?
    m. the backrest tilts back and forth?
    n. the chair swivels easily for jobs requiring sideways motion?

☐ 3. Is your desk designed so that you can sit with hands and forearms at right angles to the body while working?

☐ 4. Does your desk have the following features:
    a. a lower surface for a VDT or typewriter?
    b. adequate knee space and legroom?
    c. a nonglare finish?
    d. adequate surface space for the tasks assigned?

      e. adequate storage, with vertical space organizers, drawers, and locked personal space?
      f. smooth, rounded corners?

☐ 5. Is there a movable footrest available where needed?

☐ 6. Are adjustable document holders available for typists and VDT operators?

☐ 7. Are stools and standing counters available in order to alternate sitting and standing tasks comfortably?

☐ 8. Does your work area provide privacy so that:
      a. you need not be constantly in the view of others?
      b. you can exercise some control over people entering directly into your workspace?
      c. you can have a conversation without being overheard?

☐ 9. Are you permitted to personalize or decorate your work area?

☐ 10. Can you rearrange your work area to be more comfortable for you?

☐ 11. Can you look out of a window while at your workstation?

VI. EVALUATING THE LIGHTING
    (See pages 88–97)

☐ 1. Do you feel comfortable with the lighting in your work area?

☐ 2. Can you distinguish fine details of visual tasks at work?

☐ 3. Do you have an adjustable lamp, preferably with a swing-arm and fitted with a refractor or lens to prevent glare?

☐ 4. Have you tested your work area for glare?
      a. Can you see comfortably without shielding your eyes from the light source?
      b. Can you place a mirror on your work surface without seeing a lighting fixture or a bright spot reflected in it?
      c. Can you read from glossy paper without experiencing "blind" spots?

☐ 5. Have these steps been taken to reduce glare, shadows, and reflections:

    a. Does two-thirds of the light come from direct sources, one-third from reflected indirect light?

    b. Are light fixtures and windows positioned at the side of or behind the work surface, not in front of or directly over it?

    c. Are light sources shielded with diffusers or baffles?

    d. Have windows adjustable shades?

    e. Do reflectances of furniture, ceilings, walls, and floors meet Illuminating Engineers' Society (IES) recommendations?

    f. Has paper that is purchased for routine use a matte rather than a glossy surface?

    g. Is there high contrast between light paper and dark, matte inks?

☐ 6. Have the lighting levels been measured with a light meter (photometer)?

    a. Do levels meet IES recommendations?

    b. Are lighting levels re-evaluated when workstation layouts, tasks, or speed of work change?

☐ 7. If lighting levels have been cut to conserve energy, have overall lighting specifications been re-evaluated and modified where necessary?

☐ 8. Are the fluorescent lights in your work area:

    a. shielded with plastic?

    b. "warm"-color types?

    c. supplemented with natural light?

    d. maintained to prevent flicker and ballast hum?

☐ 9. Does general office maintenance provide:

    a. scheduled replacement of bulbs?

    b. cleaning of fixtures?

    c. replacement of defective equipment?

VII. EVALUATING OFFICE NOISE
(See pages 117–125)

☐ 1. Have you identified and measured the sources of noise and the noise levels in your office?

☐ 2. Do you keep a record of the noise levels?

☐ 3. Is the noise level low enough to provide:
   a. minimum noise irritation?
   b. an environment where conversations on the telephone and at your workstation are easily carried out?

☐ 4. If there are noise sources in your office, have the following steps been taken:
   a. noisy machines isolated?
   b. sound-absorbing (acoustical) screens or walls installed to minimize noise from machines that cannot be isolated?
   c. acoustical coverings installed on walls, floors, and ceilings?
   d. acoustical draperies added to windows?

☐ 5. Have all telephones and other ringing equipment been modified with nonirritating rings or replaced with flashing lights where feasible?

VIII. EVALUATING OFFICE AMENITIES
(See pages 134–138)

☐ 1. Are the restrooms for the employees:
   a. conveniently located?
   b. clean and odor-free?
   c. well ventilated with window or exhaust fan and temperature-controlled?
   d. adequately private?
   e. supplied with an adequate number of comfortable, hygienic toilets?
   f. supplied with clean washbasins and hot and cold running water?
   g. supplied with enough paper towels and toilet paper?

b. stocked with tampon and sanitary-napkin dispensers in women's toilets?

i. cleaned frequently and supplied with frequently emptied refuse receptacles?

j. designed to provide a separate area with comfortable seating or a couch, away from the toilet area, if no other lounges are available?

k. designed with colors, lighting, and a general ambience in which employees can relax during breaks, or if feeling ill?

l. designed with separate smoking and nonsmoking areas and adequate ventilation to prevent smoke buildup?

☐ 2. Is the lunchroom or lounge area:

a. conveniently located?

b. separate from the work areas?

c. clean and well maintained by paid staff, or else equitably cleaned on a rotating-duty basis by all employees using the area?

d. well ventilated and temperature-controlled?

e. big enough for people to eat or rest comfortably?

f. furnished and decorated pleasantly?

g. provided with sufficient numbers of chairs and tables?

h. stocked with sufficient cutlery?

i. designed to allow you to "put your feet up" and relax?

j. provided with hot and cold running water?

k. stocked with economical, fresh, and nutritious foods?

l. provided with adequate refrigerator space for employees who bring their own food?

m. provided with an outside view?

n. available for breakfast or other break times?

o. designed with separate smoking and nonsmoking areas and adequate ventilation to avoid smoke buildup?

☐ 3. Do the coatrooms have:

a. sufficient numbers of hangers?

b. adequate storage space?

c. space and seating for changing footwear?

d. space for drying wet garments and umbrellas?

e. adequate ventilation?

f. security from theft?

☐ 4. Are the first-aid facilities:
    a. fully stocked?
    b. under the supervision of a designated person with authority to replace supplies when used up?
    c. available to all employees?

☐ 5. Are the identity of the first-aid person and the location of the facilities made known to employees?

☐ 6. Are exercise facilities available to office workers?

☐ 7. Is release time available for exercise?

IX. EVALUATING OFFICE SAFETY
(Many safety items are covered in other sections of the survey.)

☐ 1. Are adequate precautions taken against slips and falls?
    a. Is the office kept generally uncluttered with boxes or other objects?
    b. Are all electrical cords and other wires taped down and not strung across walkways?
    c. Is the floor made of nonslip material?
    d. Is the carpeting secured around the edges?
    e. Have abrupt changes in floor-surface types been avoided?

☐ 2. Has equipment been designed to prevent strains and sprains?
    a. Are dollies and hand trucks available to help in moving and lifting?
    b. Are frequently moved machines or furniture mounted on rolling bases or casters?
    c. Are self-locking footstools provided in all areas where overhead reaching is required?
    d. Has your job been designed to avoid constant repetitive flexing of the wrists or fingers?
    e. Are tools and equipment available in sizes and shapes that do not strain the hands or limbs?

☐ 3. Are all file cabinets bolted to prevent tipping if more than one drawer is opened?

X. EVALUATING THE ORGANIZATION OF WORK

☐ 1. Can you determine the speed at which you will work?

☐ 2. Does the amount of work expected from you allow you to work at a comfortable rate?

☐ 3. Can you make decisions about the ways in which you do your job?

☐ 4. Can you alternate tasks on your job if some of them are very repetitious?

☐ 5. Can you choose the work shifts you prefer?

☐ 6. Can you choose whether or not to take overtime assignments?

☐ 7. Do your supervisors or management treat you with respect and dignity?

☐ 8. Is your opinion sought on matters that directly concern your work?

☐ 9. Are you consulted before equipment or supplies are purchased for your use?

☐ 10. Are you aware of where the work you do fits into the total work in your office?

☐ 11. Is the direct line of management that you report to made clear?

☐ 12. Do you know when your work is being checked or audited?

☐ 13. Are you ever provided with feedback about your work?

☐ 14. Are you ever told you have been doing your job well?

☐ 15. Do you have adequate leeway to take time off for personal business or family obligations?

☐ 16. Does your company provide written job descriptions specifying the tasks expected of people in your job classification?

☐ 17. Is there a clear description of the benefits and conditions of employment at your job?

☐ 18. Is there a formal written procedure for pursuing grievances on the job?

☐ 19. Is there a work atmosphere free of harassment and discrimination on the basis of race, sex, age, creed, national origin, marital status, parenthood status, or physical disability?

☐ 20. Is there a formal complaint and resolution procedure for harassment and discrimination?

☐ 21. Are there skills-training and advancement opportunities for all workers?

☐ 22. Is there job security, including retraining of workers when new technologies are introduced?

☐ 23. Is there provision for child care on the work premises?

☐ 24. Have you and your co-workers developed informal co-worker support groups to deal with workplace issues?

☐ 25. Are there formal mechanisms—employee associations, unions, office-worker organizations—for dealing with grievances?

☐ 26. Is there an active health and safety committee?

☐ 27. Do employees and management meet regularly and fruitfully to recognize and resolve health and safety issues?

☐ 28. Is there an employee health and safety organization?

XI. EVALUATING HEALTH SYMPTOMS
(See pages 13–40)

In this section we summarize some of the symptoms you may wish to survey among your co-workers to determine if similar patterns of complaints are developing. This may be a useful clue to uncovering health and safety hazards in the office. In this section, unlike the others, the more NOS you have, the fewer the health and safety problems.

☐ 1. *Eyes.* If you have any of the symptoms below, you should seek the help of a professional. If corrective lenses or other medical remedies do not help, there may be a source of eyestrain or other eye hazard in the workplace. Specifically, do you experience:

a. burning or stinging sensations?
b. twitching?
c. soreness or irritation?
d. redness?
e. itching?
f. general discomfort and fatigue?
g. blurred or foggy vision?
h. difficulty focusing your eyes?
i. impaired color perception?
j. impaired ability to distinguish fine details?
k. problems with eyeglasses or contact lenses?
l. impaired distance vision?
m. headaches?
n. heaviness in the eyelids or swollen eyelids?
o. blind spots in the visual field?

☐ 2. *Lungs and Respiratory System.* Do you experience:
a. frequent colds?
b. attacks of wheezing and coughing or other allergic reactions?
c. feelings of tightness, pain, or pressure in the chest?
d. asthma-like conditions (which may be diagnosed as allergic alveolitis and hypersensitivity pneumonitis)?
e. chronic bronchitis?
f. emphysema?
g. excess phlegm production?
h. drying of mucous membranes in the nose and throat?

☐ 3. *The Skin.* Do you experience:
a. reddened skin?
b. rough and cracked skin?
c. peeling?
d. open sores that do not heal?
e. rashes?
f. swelling, inflammation, and itching?

☐ 4. Are there particular jobs or products that can produce the symptoms? Do they get better during vacations or other periods away from the job?

☐ 5. *Stress.* The following are symptoms that are often associated with stress, although they are not unique to stress-related disease. Continuing presence of these symptoms requires evaluation by a health practitioner to rule out the possibility of organic disease. Do you experience any of the following symptoms:

    a. frequent indigestion, heartburn, diarrhea, or stomach cramps?

    b. chronic fatigue or exhaustion?

    c. general feeling of malaise?

    d. increased tendency to eat excessively or not enough?

    e. increased tendency to drink or smoke excessively?

    f. trouble sleeping or waking frequently?

    g. feelings of tension, anxiety, or moodiness?

    h. increased difficulty in socializing at home or at work?

    i. aches and pains, particularly back and neck aches?

    j. menstrual-cycle irregularities?

    k. absenteeism?

    l. loss of sexual interest or normal abilities?

RESOURCE ORGANIZATIONS

I. GOVERNMENT AGENCIES

A. Environmental Protection Agency

Office of Public Affairs
401 M Street SW
Washington, DC 20460

B. National Cancer Institute

Cancer Information Clearinghouse
Office of Cancer Communications
7910 Woodmont Avenue
Bethesda, MD 20205

C. National Institute for Occupational Safety and Health (NIOSH)

NIOSH publishes technical documents, conducts research, and performs health-hazard evaluations at worksites.

NIOSH FACILITIES

National Headquarters
Parklawn Building
5600 Fishers Lane
Rockville, MD 20857
(301)443-2140

Morgantown
Appalachian Laboratory for
Occupational Safety & Health
944 Chestnut Ridge Road
Morgantown, WV 26805
(304)599-7521

Cincinnati
Robert A. Taft Laboratories
4676 Columbia Parkway
Cincinnati, OH 45226
(513)684-8326

NIOSH REGIONAL OFFICES

Region I
JFK Federal Building
Room 1401
Boston, MA 02203
(617)223-6668

Region II
26 Federal Plaza
Room 3300
New York, NY 10007
(212)264-2485

Region III
P.O. Box 13716
Philadelphia, PA 19101
(215)596-6716

Region IV
101 Marietta Tower
Suite 502B
Atlanta, GA 30323
(404)221-2396

Region V
300 South Wacker Drive
33rd Floor
Chicago, IL 60606
(312)886-3881

Region VI
1200 Main Tower Building
Dallas, TX 75202
(214)655-3916

Region VII
601 East Twelfth Street
5th Floor West
Kansas City, MO 64106
(816)374-5332

Region VIII
11037 Federal Building
Denver, CO 80294
(303)837-3979

Region IX
50 United Plaza
Room 231
San Francisco, CA 94102
(415)556-3781

Region X
1321 Second Avenue
Mail Stop 502
Seattle, WA 98101
(206)442-0530

D. Occupational Safety and Health Administration (OSHA)

Regional Offices provide technical assistance and distribution of publications. The Labor Liaison's office in these Regional Offices can tell you whom to contact for a specific problem. Use the 24-hour toll-free number (area code 800), if provided. Many states have local area offices; the Regional Office can provide you with their locations.

National Office
U.S. Department of Labor
200 Constitution Avenue NW
Washington, D.C. 20216

Region I
(Connecticut, Maine, Massachusetts, New Hampshire, Rhode Island, Vermont)
JFK Federal Building
Room 1804
Government Center
Boston, MA 02203
(617)223-6712
(800)225-6161

Region II
(New York, New Jersey, Puerto Rico, Virgin Islands, Canal Zone)
1 Astor Plaza
Room 3445
1515 Broadway
New York, NY 10036
(212)399-5754

Region III
(Delaware, District of Columbia, Maryland, Pennsylvania, Virginia, West Virginia)
Gateway Building
Suite 2100
3535 Market Street
Philadelphia, PA 19104
(215)596-1201

Region IV
(Alabama, Florida, Georgia, Kentucky, Mississippi, North Carolina, South Carolina, Tennessee)
1375 Peachtree Street, NE
Suite 587
Atlanta, GA 30309
(404)881-3573
(800)282-1048 (outside Georgia)
(800)241-8598 (South Carolina and Tennessee)

Region V
(Illinois, Indiana, Minnesota, Michigan, Ohio, Wisconsin)
230 South Dearborn Street
32nd Floor
Room 3263
Chicago, IL 60604
(312)353-2220
(800)942-3174 (IL)
(800)382-9470 (IN)
(800)482-0745 (MI)
(800)582-1708 (OH)
(800)242-9608 (WI)

Region VI
(Arkansas, Louisiana, New Mexico, Oklahoma, Texas)
555 Griffin Square
Room 602
Dallas, TX 75202
(214)767-4731

Region VII
(Iowa, Kansas, Missouri, Ne-
braska)
911 Walnut Street
Room 3000
Kansas City, MO 64106
(816)374-5861
(800)642-8463, 662-2948 (NE)
(800)892-2574, 392-7743 (MO)
(800)362-1896 (KS)

Region VIII
(Colorado, Montana, North
Dakota, South Dakota, Utah, Wy-
oming)
Federal Building
Room 1554
1961 Stout Street
Denver, CO 80294
(303)837-3883

Region IX
(California, Arizona, Nevada, Hawaii)
Box 36017
450 Golden Gate Avenue
San Francisco, CA 94102
(415)556-0584

Region X
(Alaska, Idaho, Oregon, Washing-
ton)
Federal Office Building
Room 6048
909 First Avenue
Seattle, WA 98174
(206)442-5930

STATES WITH APPROVED PLANS
Below is a list of OSHA State Plan Offices. For complaints or information about your State Plan, contact your state Federal OSHA
office.

Alaska
Commissioner
Alaska Department of Labor
Box 1149
Juneau, AK 99801
(907)465-2700

Arizona
Director
Occupational Safety & Health Di-
vision
Industrial Commission of Arizona
P.O. Box 19070
Phoenix, AZ 85005
(602)271-5795

California
Director
Department of Industrial Relations
455 Golden Gate Avenue
San Francisco, CA 94102
(916)445-1935

Colorado
Executive Director
Department of Labor & Employment
200 East Ninth Avenue
Denver, CO 80203
(303)573-6440

Hawaii
Director
Labor & Industrial Relations
825 Mililani Street
Honolulu, HI 96813
(808)548-3150

Indiana
Commissioner
Indiana Division of Labor
1013 State Office Building
Indianapolis, IN 46204
(317)633-4473

Iowa
Commissioner
Bureau of Labor
State House
East Seventh & Court Avenue
Des Moines, IA 50319
(515)281-3606

Kentucky
Commissioner
Kentucky Department of Labor
Capitol Plaza Towers
12th Floor
Frankfort, KY 40601
(502)564-3070

Maryland
Commissioner
Department of Licensing & Regulation
Division of Labor & Industry
203 E. Baltimore Street
Baltimore, MD 21202
(301)383-2251

Michigan
Director
Michigan Department of Labor
309 North Washington
Box 30015
Lansing, MI 48909
(517)373-9600

Director
Michigan Department of Public Health
3500 North Logan Street
Lansing, MI 48914
(517)373-1320

Minnesota
Commissioner
Department of Labor & Industry
Space Center Building
5th Floor
444 Lafayette Road
St. Paul, MN 55101
(612)296-2342

Nevada
Director
Department of Occupational Safety & Health
Nevada Industrial Commission
1923 North Carson Street
Carson City, NE 89701
(702)885-5240

New Mexico
Director
Environmental Improvement Division
Health & Environment Department
P.O. Box 968
Santa Fe, NM 87503
(505)827-5273

North Carolina
Commissioner
North Carolina Department of Labor
P.O. Box 27407
11 West Edenton Street
Raleigh, NC 27611
(919)733-7166

Oregon
Director
Workers Compensation Department
Labor and Industries Building
Salem, OR 97310
(503)378-3302

Puerto Rico
Secretary of Labor
Commonwealth of Puerto Rico
414 Barbosa Avenue
San Juan, PR 00917
(809)765-3030

South Carolina
Commissioner
South Carolina Department of Labor
3600 Forest Drive
P.O. Box 11329
Columbia, SC 29211
(803)758-2851

Tennessee
Commissioner
Tennessee Department of Labor
501 Union Building
Suite "A"
Second Floor
Nashville, TN 37219
(615)741-2582

Utah
Chairman
Utah Industrial Commission
350 East Fifth South
Salt Lake City, UT 84111
(801)533-4000

Vermont
Commissioner
Department of Labor & Industry
Montpelier, VT 05602
(802)828-2286

Virgin Islands
Commissioner of Labor
Government of Virgin Islands
P.O. Box 890
Christainsted
St. Croix, VI 00820
(809)773-1994

Virginia
Commissioner
Department of Labor & Industry
P.O. Box 12064
Richmond, VA 23241
(804)786-2376

Commissioner
State Department of Health
James Madison Building
109 Governor Street
Richmond, VA 23219
(703)770-3563

Washington
Director
Department of Labor & Industry
General Administration Building
Room 344
Olympia, WA 98504
(206)753-6307

Wyoming
Administrator
Occupational Health & Safety Department
200 East Eighth Avenue
P.O. Box 2186
Cheyenne, WY 82002
(307)777-7786

E. State and Local Health Departments

Some state and local health departments can help you with workplace health and safety problems. Look in the blue pages of your telephone book for their addresses and telephone numbers.

II. NATIONAL ORGANIZATIONS

Most of these organizations have fact sheets, newsletters, and other publications to help you. They can also answer your questions or find someone who has technical expertise in your area of concern.

Center for Occupational Hazards
5 Beekman Street
New York, NY 10038
(212)227-6220

Coalition of Labor Union Women
Health Project
15 Union Square
New York, NY 10038
(212)255-7800

Women's Occupational Health
Resource Center
Columbia University School of
Public Health
21 Audubon Avenue
New York, NY 10032
(212)694-3737

Working Women Education Fund
1224 Huron Road
Cleveland, OH 44115
(216)566-9308

A. 9 to 5, National Association of Working Women

NATIONAL OFFICES

Midwest Office
1224 Huron Road
Cleveland, OH 44115
(216)566-9308

East Coast Office
140 Clarendon Street
Boston, MA 02116
(617)247-4943

Washington, D.C. Office
2000 Florida Avenue NW
Washington, DC 20009
(202)797-1384

LOCAL AFFILIATES

9 to 5
140 Clarendon Street
Boston, MA 02116
(617)536-6003

Rhode Island Working Women
100 Washington Street
Providence, RI 02903
(401)331-6077

Hartford Working Women
57 Pratt Street
Hartford, CT 06103
(203)525-4793

Women Office Workers
680 Lexington Avenue
New York, NY 10022
(212)688-4160

Women Employed in Baltimore
128 W. Franklin Street
Baltimore, MD 21201
(301)837-3830

Pittsburgh Working Women
Fourth & Wood Streets
Pittsburgh, PA 15222
(412)261-3714

Cleveland Women Working
1224 Huron Road
Cleveland, OH 44115
(216)566-8511

Dayton Women Working
141 West Third Street
Dayton, OH 45402
(513)228-8587

Cincinnati Women Working
Ninth and Walnut
Cincinnati, OH 45202
(513)381-2455

Seattle Working Women
1118 Fifth Avenue
Seattle, WA 98101
(206)624-2985

Women Organized for Employment
127 Montgomery
San Francisco, CA 94104
(415)982-8963

Los Angeles Working Women
304 South Broadway
Room 534
Los Angeles, CA 90013
(213)628-8080

III. STATE AND LOCAL GROUPS

A. COSH Groups

COSH stands for "Committee/Coalition/Council on Occupational Safety and Health." Many cities and states have COSH groups formed by workers, unions, and health activists to assist unions and workers in occupational safety and health areas. Many COSH groups publish newsletters and fact sheets; sponsor conferences; and have access to trade unionists, physicians, nurses, industrial hygienists, chemists, lawyers, educators, and students to help with occupational safety and health problems.

California

Bay Area Committee on Occupational Safety & Health (BACOSH)
4135 Gilbert Street
Oakland, CA 94611

Los Angeles Committee on Occupational Safety & Health
13013 Morningside Way
Los Angeles, CA 90066
(213)824-6019

San Diego Committee for Occupational Safety & Health (SDCOSH)
P.O. Box 9901
San Diego, CA 92109
(714)459-2160
(Ruth Herfetz)

Santa Clara Committee on Occupational Safety & Health (SantaCOSH) (includes Electronics Committee for Occupational Safety & Health—ECOSH)
655 Castro Street
Mountain View, CA 94041
(415)969-7233

White Lung Association
P.O. Box 5089
San Pedro, CA 90733
(212)519-1555

Illinois

Chicago Area Committee on Occupational Safety & Health (CACOSH)
542 South Dearborn Street
Room 502
Chicago, IL 60605
(312)939-2104

Maryland

Maryland Committee for Occupational Safety & Health (MARYCOSH)
P.O. Box 3825
Baltimore, MD 21217

Massachusetts

Massachusetts Coalition for Occupational Safety & Health (MassCOSH)
120 Boylston Street
Room 206
Boston, MA 02116
(617)482-4283

Massachusetts Coalition for Occupational Safety & Health (MassCOSH)
Western Region
323 High Street
Holyoke, MA 01040

Minnesota

Minnesota Area Committee on Occupational Safety & Health (MACOSH)
1729 Nicollet Avenue South
Minneapolis, MN 55403
(612)291-1815 (Tom O'Connell)

New Jersey

New Jersey Committee for Occupational Safety & Health (NJCOSH)
701 East Elizabeth Avenue
Linden, NJ 07036
(201)925-1030

New York

New York Committee on Occupational Safety & Health (NYCOSH)
32 Union Square East
Room 404-5
New York, NY 10003
(212)599-4592

Western New York Council on Occupational Safety & Health (WNYCOSH)
343 Huntington Avenue
Buffalo, NY 14214
(716)842-4271

Rochester Council on Occupational Safety & Health (ROCOSH)
18 Wellington Avenue
Rochester, NY 14611

Allegheny Council on Occupational Safety & Health (ALCOSH)
Jamestown Labor Council
P.O. Box 184
Jamestown, NY 14701
(716)664-2590

Oneida-Herkimer Council on Occupational Safety & Health (OHCOSH)
Central New York Labor Agency
Mayro Building
Room 128
239 Genessee Street
Utica, NY 13501
(315)735-6101

Central N.Y. Council on Occupational Safety & Health (CNYCOSH)
119 Sherman Street
Watertown, NY 13601
(315)782-3771

North Carolina

North Carolina Occupational Safety & Health Project (NCOSH)
P.O. Box 2514
Durham, NC 27705
(919)286-2276

Brown Lung Association
Greensboro Chapter
P.O. Box 13296
Greensboro, NC 27405
(919)273-0464

Pennsylvania

Philadelphia Area Project on Occupational Safety & Health (PHILAPOSH)
1321 Arch Street
Room 607
Philadelphia, PA 19107
(215)568-5188

Rhode Island

Rhode Island Committee on Occupational Safety & Health (RICOSH)
371 Broadway
Providence, RI 02909
(401)751-2015

South Carolina

Brown Lung Association
Greenville Chapter
P.O. Box 334
Greenville, SC 29602
(802)235-2886

Tennessee

Jamie Cohen
Tennessee Committee for Occupational Safety & Health (TNCOSH)
705 North Broadway
Room 212
Knoxville, TN 37092

Washington

Washington Occupational Health Resource Center
Box 18371
Seattle, WA 98118
(206)762-7288 (Vicki Laden)

West Virginia

Kanawha Valley Coalition on Occupational Safety & Health (KVCOSH)
P.O. Box 3062
Charleston, WV 25331
(304)925-6664

Wisconsin

Wisconsin Committee on Occupational Safety & Health (WISCOSH)
2468 West Juneau
Milwaukee, WI 53233
(414)643-0928 (Jerry Heidtke)

B. Labor Education Programs

The following universities provide occupational safety and health programs as part of their worker extension schools. These programs provide both outreach and on-campus training.

University of Alabama in Birmingham
    Center for Labor Education & Research
    School of Business
    University Station
    Birmingham, AL 35294
    (205)934-2101

University of California–Berkeley
    Labor Occupational Health Program
    Institute of Industrial Relations
    2521 Channing Way
    Berkeley, CA 94720
    (415)642-5507

University of California–Los Angeles
    Center for Labor Research & Education
    Institute of Industrial Relations
    Los Angeles, CA 90024
    (213)825-3537

University of Connecticut
    Labor Education Center
    Storrs, CT 06268
    (203)486-3417

University of Hawaii
    Center for Labor Education & Research
    1420-A Lower Campus Road
    Building 3
    Honolulu, HI 96822
    (808)948-7145

University of Illinois
Institute of Labor & Industrial
Relations
504 East Armory
Champaign, IL 61820
(217)333-0980

Chicago Office:
Chicago Labor Education Program
1315 SEO Building
P.O. Box 4348
Chicago, IL 60680
(312)996-2623

Indiana University
Division of Labor Studies
312 North Park
Bloomington, IN 47401
(812)337-9082

University of Kentucky
Center for Labor Education &
Research
643 Maxwelton Court
Lexington, KY 40506
(606)258-4811

University of Maine at Orono
Bureau of Labor Education
128 College Avenue
Orono, ME 04473
(207)581-7032

Antioch
AFL-CIO Labor Studies Center
10000 New Hampshire Avenue
Silver Spring, MD 20903
(301)431-6400

Michigan State University
Labor Program Service
School of Labor & Industrial
Relations
South Kedzie Hall
East Lansing, MI 48824
(517)355-5070, 355-2214

University of Michigan
Institute of Labor & Industrial
Relations
401 Fourth Street
Ann Arbor, MI 48103
(313) 763-1187

University of Minnesota
Labor Education Service, IRC
447 BA Tower
271 19th Avenue South
Minneapolis, MN 55455
(612)373-3662, 4110, 5380, 5306

Rutgers University, The State
University of New Jersey
Labor Education Center
Institute of Management &
Labor Relations
University Extension Division
Ryders Lane & Clifton Avenue
New Brunswick, NJ 08903
(201) 932-9502

Cornell University
New York State School of Industrial & Labor Relations
Division of Extension & Public
Service
Ithaca, NY 14850
(607)256-3281

Metropolitan District Staff:
New York State School of Industrial & Labor Relations
7 East 43rd Street
New York, NY 10017
(212)697-2247

Western District Staff:
New York State School of Industrial & Labor Relations
120 Delaware Avenue
Room 225
Buffalo, NY 14202
(716)842-4270

The Ohio State University
Labor Education & Research Service
1810 College Road
Columbus, OH 43210
(614)422-8157

University of Oregon
Labor Education & Research Center
Eugene, OR 97403
(503)686-5054

University of Wisconsin—Extension
School for Workers
1 South Park Street
Room 701
Madison, WI 53706
(608)262-2111

NEW TECHNOLOGY IN THE AMERICAN WORKPLACE

Judith Gregory, *Research Director, Working Women Education Fund*

Testimony for 9 to 5, National Association of Working Women

Hearings by the Subcommittee on Education and Labor, U.S. House of Representatives Committee on Education and Labor

June 23, 1982

The coming of the "office of the future" and the growing use of microcomputers have become one of the most frequently discussed and debated topics in contemporary society. The use of computer technology in offices has grown explosively in recent years. In 1979, researchers at Stanford University estimated that 1.5 million of the nation's 3.5 million offices were large enough for some form of office automation (R. Uhlig et al., *Office of the Future*, Elsevier, New York, 1979). Industry experts estimate that 7 to 10 million U.S. workers now use video display terminals (VDTs or CRTs), the key units of office automation, in their jobs. These devices barely existed a decade ago. As microcomputers continue to decrease in cost and increase in power, a greater number of small- and medium-sized businesses will be able to afford automated office systems.

The growing market for automated equipment is reflected by spectacular rates of growth in the computer industry. The market for word processing, for example, is expected to grow at a rate of 500% during the five-year period from 1978 (when it was worth $780 million) to 1984 (when it is expected to yield $4.2 billion in revenues), according to *Fortune* magazine (December 3, 1979). The overall office automation market—including data processing, electronic mail, high-speed copiers, and other more exotic equipment—netted $4 billion in revenues in 1980; it is expected to increase at an annual rate of 40–45% through 1985. Office automation, as *Time* (November 23, 1981) put it, now "dwarfs almost every other sector of U.S. business."

THE DRAMATIC IMPACT ON JOBS

The widespread introduction of office automation is creating profound changes in the nature of office work. "We are on the brink of a second industrial revolution which will eliminate drudgery and boredom once and for all," business periodicals proclaim. The technological revolution "is creating more stimulating careers for office workers," a writer rejoiced in a special feature of *U.S. News & World Report* (September 18, 1978).

Examined more closely, however, American management's idea of the "office of the future" means little more than a re-creation of the factory of the past. Today's office workers find themselves threatened with many of the same processes of "job degradation" which undermined the skills and dignity of an earlier generation of industrial workers. Without conscious and concerted interventions by concerned policy makers and employers, labor unions and office workers themselves, we risk society-wide dangers, and we will lose important opportunities to use new technology to address age-old problems which plague women's work today, problems of low pay, job segregation, dead-end jobs, and discriminatory employment practices.

Office automation can and should be used to enhance jobs; provide chances for advancement for women clericals; increase productivity; provide a healthier work environment; and improve our standard of living. But, as automation is being implemented today, the opposite is occurring for the majority of women in the office.

THE CLERICAL WORK FORCE TODAY

Women office workers are on the front line of the new wave of automation. Clerical employment is the largest single category of the work force in the U.S., accounting for nearly one in five of all employed workers. The Department of Labor predicts that clerical work will be the fastest-growing major occupational group in the 1980s. And it is also an increasingly female work force—in 1950, women made up 62% of all clerical workers and by 1980, fully 80%. Of the 45.5 million women working in the U.S. today, 35% are employed in clerical jobs. The occupations especially targeted for computerization—file clerks, bookkeepers, secretaries, typists, bank tellers, and various finance and insurance industry jobs—are all at least 90% women. Despite their crucial role in the economy, the average pay for clericals hovers around $11,000 a year.

We believe that you cannot solve problems unless you face them squarely. We see the issues raised by office automation differently from the glowing images many optimistic business proponents paint, because our organization, 9 to 5, National Association of Working Women, represents clerical women. I am here to describe our concerns about computer technology from the viewpoint of those at the bottom of the office hierarchy.

> "I've been doing this job for ten years and I've been tired for ten years. It's the monotony that does it. I'd like to know what it feels like not to be tired," says a 31-year-old data-entry clerk for a Midwest utility company.

> "I feel like saying to my boss, 'What do you think I am—an extension of this machine?'" a Boston office worker cries out in frustration.

"Now they have a new setup called the 'open office' where I work," a woman who works at a terminal all day for a New York newspaper explains. "There are panels six feet high around all the operators. We're divided into work groups of four to six with a supervisor for each work group. In many cases, we don't see another person all day except for a ten-minute coffee break and lunchtime. All we see is the walls around us and sometimes the supervisor. The isolation is terrible."

These experiences are the daily reality for nearly 20% of the nation's labor force. A secretary at a Cleveland accounting firm in a prestigious downtown office told 9 to 5: "I've been here almost a year and I've got seniority among the secretaries." Emily and two of her co-workers experience almost daily headaches, nervous stomachs, and shaky hands. They're upset that another one of the secretaries, who has high blood pressure, was recently sent to the hospital for tests. They feel their employers just don't care: "The place looks gorgeous, and that's where the management's priorities lie. They're not really as interested in efficiency as they are in using people up and pushing them out the back door."

In April 1980, 9 to 5 (then Working Women, National Association of Office Workers) released *Race Against Time: Automation of the Office*, the first report in this country to discuss the problems of office computerization from the clerical worker's viewpoint. In the report, we state our contention that innovations in new office technology have a vast potential to upgrade office jobs, skills, and pay, and to provide more avenues for job satisfaction for clericals. We present a sharp critique of the rampant problems we found: deskilling, devaluing, and degrading of women office workers' jobs; a decline in promotional opportunities, potential for large-scale job loss; and increased health risks. (I will provide the committee members with copies of the report.)

Today, I will focus on five major societal problems posed by the introduction of computer and telecommunications technologies.

DANGERS OF THE COMPUTER AGE

The Computer Age confronts society with five grave dangers:

- The danger of structural unemployment in the not-so-distant future
- The danger of increased sex, race, and age discrimination in a polarized work force

- The danger of degradation of working conditions, increased job stress, and occupational health hazards in the office
- The danger of runaway offices and the dilemma of "office home-work" as a new level of "office mobility" is achieved
- The danger, in the office and services sectors, of decreased productivity, decreased efficiency, and declines in both the equality and accessibility of services for the general public

1. *The Specter of Structural Unemployment*

The dynamic of computer technology is against job creation in any sector where it is applied—it is a labor-reducing technology. It already takes fewer people to do the same or a greater volume of work. The International Federation of Clerical, Executive and Technical Employees (FIET) predicts that for white-collar employment, "there is likely to be a cumulative employment impact hitting one sector at a time but building up over a ten-year period." A 1978 study for the Organization for Economic Cooperation and Development, reported in the *New York Times*, warned: "The evidence we have is suggesting increasingly that the employment displacement effects of automation anticipated in the 1950s are now beginning to arrive."

A French study for the Ministry of Industry predicts 30% reductions among clericals employed in the finance industries by 1990 (S. Nora and A. Minc, *Computerizing Society*, MIT Press, Cambridge, 1980).

In the United States, clerical work is still expanding explosively— the U.S. Department of Labor estimates that there will be 4.6 million new jobs for clerical workers, nearly one in four of all *new* jobs created, in this decade. The continued need for clerical workers appears to be "masking" the potential job-displacing effects of automation in office industries such as insurance and banking. While employment in banking is still expanding, for example, the *rate* of job growth slowed from 4.5% annually from 1960 to 1973 to 3.2% a year from 1973 to 1976, while the volume of transactions continued to climb steadily. The finance industries are "growth" industries, while other employment sectors lack similar advantage. In fact, today there is higher unemployment among white-collar and clerical workers than any time since the years after World War II, yet another sign of the far-reaching effects of the recession. And there is an ever greater need for more jobs, not fewer. For women workers, the figures are startling. While a record 12 million women entered the work force in the 1970s, an even greater number will seek work—an additional 16.5 million women—in the 1980s (*Business Week*, March 15, 1982).

The effects of office automation on employment may occur more slowly in the U.S. than in some European countries or neighboring Canada, but a dramatic loss in jobs is very possible in the next ten to fifteen years. We must begin developing public policy on these issues now. Because computer technology affects both blue-collar and white-collar jobs, we are faced with the disturbing question: where will new jobs be created at all in our economy of the future?

2. The Danger of Increased Sex, Race, and Age Discrimination in a Polarized Work Force

There is increasing concern over the danger of "polarization" of the office employment structure, with an increased but still relatively small number of highly technical jobs at the uppermost level and a large number of deskilled jobs at the base, with a "skills gap" between them that becomes harder and harder to bridge (H. Menzies, *Women and the Chip*, Institute for Research on Public Policy, Montreal, 1981. See also J. W. Driscoll, "Office Automation: The Dynamics of a Technological Boondoggle," Sloan School of Management, MIT, March 1981). The result is a new version of the "internal dual labor market" that translates into more sex segregation for women office workers. Office automation relies on a base of data-entry and data-processing jobs which involve repetitive, standardized, fast-paced, and accurate work. By homogenizing many different clerical functions into information processing at display terminals, jobs become more interchangeable. The characteristics of secondary labor market jobs—low-wage, low-benefit, high-turnover, non-union, insecure, and semiskilled jobs—are extended further into office industries.

A manager described the changing structure of office employment quite boldly to writer Barbara Garson ("The Electronic Sweatshop: Scanning the Office of the Future," *Mother Jones*, July 1981): "We are moving from the pyramid structure of office employment to the Mae West," he said. "The employment chart of the future will still show those swellings (of good jobs) on the top, and we'll never completely get rid of those big bulges of clerks on the bottom. What we're trying to do right now is pull in that waistline (expensive middle management and skilled secretaries)."

In an assessment of word-processing vendors' claims compared to users' experiences and research findings, Dr. Leslie Schneider of the Institute for Industrial Social Research, University of Trondheim, concludes: "The possibility of 'new and more stimulating careers' with word processing will be limited to a few super secretaries at the top and not to the majority of clericals. . . . Most clericals will probably end up with the same or more routine jobs unless there is a *planned* effort to improve their work" ("Words, Words, Only Words: How Word-Processing Vendors Sell Their Wares in Norway," IFIM, Trondheim, 1982).

Sex, race, and age discrimination continue, and are not only perpetuated but are often made more intense.

The explosive growth of computer-related occupations ushered in with the office automation revolution represents an unprecedented opportunity to address the long-standing problem of sex and race segregation in the office work force. The Bureau of Labor Statistics projects that approximately 685,000 new jobs will be created in the 1980s—an increase of 47% by 1990 (BLS, USDL, *Employment Trends in the Computer Field*, 1981) in jobs which include computer operators, computer technicians, computer programmers, systems analysts, data-base managers, and other information specialists and computer specialists. Some observers estimate that the *need* for programmers is already 40% greater than the current supply (See J. Jobin, *Women's Day*, 1981).

While women have made progress in entering computer fields (women comprise 29% of computer programmers and 22% of systems analysts, according to 1980 BLS statistics), researchers find persistent disparity in placement and wages of women compared to men (S. Dubnoff, "Women in Computer Programming: Do They Get an Even Break?" Center for Survey Research, Boston, 1979, for example). Women are underrepresented in the better programming and specialists' jobs; they are concentrated overwhelmingly in the lower ranks of computer jobs. While 78% of the women in computer occupations work either as keypunchers or computer operators, only 31% of men in computer jobs are in these positions. In fact, computer operations has recently become "feminized," shifting from 44% women in 1975 to 60% women in 1980. Pay increases declined in these job categories during the same period.

The participation rate of women predictably decreases as one climbs

up the office computer-related job ladder: over 95% of keypunch operators are women; 62% of computer operators and 75% of office machine
operators are women; only 26% of the higher-paid computer specialists
are women.

Minority women are especially concentrated in "back-office" data-
entry polls, often involving shiftwork. A recent examination of trends
in job segregation by race and sex by Julianne Malveaux points out that
the clerical jobs that black women dominate—postal clerks, telephone
operators, keypunchers, duplicating machine operators—have a "behind the scenes" character to them ("Recent Trends in Occupational
Segregation by Race and Sex," paper presented at the Workshop on Job
Segregation by Sex, National Academy of Sciences, Washington, D.C.,
May 1982). Many of these jobs are the special targets of office automation.
There are about a quarter-million keypunchers today, for example, some
20% of whom are black and other minority women. Keypunchers are
typically older and have longer job tenure than the average clerical
workers. These workers are particularly vulnerable—keypunching is an
occupation expected to decline in the next ten years (according to
Department of Labor predictions), and should be targeted for meaningful job retraining efforts.

Older women clerical workers also face exacerbated problems as their
jobs undergo technological change. The notion that "older workers
don't want to learn new things" is a prevalent stereotype. In our view,
the problem is exclusion of older workers from on-the-job training
programs, as we found in our study *Vanished Dreams: Age Discrimination
and the Older Woman Worker* (Working Women Education Fund, 1980).
Some of the experiences older women office workers told us include:

"They don't want to 'waste' training on an older person."

"I told them so many times that I wanted to be trained in data-
entry when the program began," said one frustrated 59-year-old
woman. "Instead they hired two young men off the street in their
twenties, and had the nerve to ask me to train one of them to be
my supervisor after he went through the data-entry course."

A 49-year-old woman who talked to us during a lunch break from
job hunting said, "First it started out as a rumor—that half of us were
going to be replaced by new word processors and CRT machines. Well,

within a month they had laid off me and four other girls, all of us with some number of years in towards our pension. Now they have two kids right out of high school running those machines." Rather than the "two kids," the older employees could have been trained to run the new machines. Instead, they were laid off.

3. The Danger of Degradation of Working Conditions and Increased Occupational Health Risks, Especially Increased Job Stress

Let me take you into the world of the automated office by telling you just one woman's story:

> Rose re-entered the work force after twenty years away. Her excellent typing skills quickly landed her a job as one of twelve CRT operators in a downtown Cleveland publishing company. She found that office work had changed a great deal during her years away from the work force. "The chairs were good and the machines adjustable, too. But I have never been confined to one place doing key entry at such a pace." She explains, "The computer at one end of the room keeps track of the keystrokes you do. The more keystrokes, the more money you *might* get. At the end of the day, the figures are posted. You look at your speed, you look at everyone else's and you say, 'Tomorrow I'm going to do better.' They get you thinking just like they want to, you're really pushing hard."

Rose's situation may sound extreme, but not really. The underlying principles are more and more widespread. Constant computerized monitoring of individual workers' speed and volume of work is used to establish a median "quota" or "average" for the "output" required of each employee. The work load demanded is then continuously revised upward. Typically, workers in the lower third by speed or volume are pressured to meet the "average." Once they've done so, the "average" then becomes the "minimum" acceptable level, and the pressure to increase speed and work load begins again. Failure to meet the "quota" or "average" can result in disciplinary action or loss of one's job; other workers will leave "voluntarily" if the pace is unbearable. Such systems will make speed-ups a way of life in the office if unchallenged.

Problems which threaten to degrade office working conditions for the majority of clerical workers include: problems of *deskilling, devalu-*

ing of office work, and increased health risks related to poor machine design, workstation design, and job design.

Problems of deskilling. While office automation has improved jobs for some, the majority of women office workers' jobs are more closely supervised and increasingly "specialized"—meaning that each person performs ever smaller fractions of the larger task. When this happens, each job requires less training and offers less chance for advancement. When new computer systems are introduced, certain skills may be made obsolete (while new skills are belittled and unrewarded) and variety is lost from the work. The problems of deskilling can occur in a variety of ways.

> In the midwest headquarters of a multinational corporation, secretarial jobs were broken down into component parts when word-processing equipment was brought into the department. As a result, one woman does electronic filing all day, another extracts data all day, one answers phones all day, another handles correspondence all day, and so on. The company requires that each woman do a "tour of duty" of several months in each subtask in order to be considered for promotion. In other words, each woman must be promoted four times to get back where she started. This is one example of how companies use the power of new office technology to wipe the slate clean and start over with new rules.

Clerical jobs are becoming more dead-end, as career paths are disrupted, and altered for the worse more often than not. Sociologists Roslyn Feldberg and Evelyn Glenn found in a 1977 study of five large employers in New England that when computerization was introduced, the proportion of low-level clerical jobs remained the same, and that clericals were rarely upgraded to fill new skilled jobs. The study found that the automated clerical jobs were more mechanical and narrow, and that "the main avenue for clerical workers are either horizontal or downward," but not up (*Social Problems,* vol. 25, October 1977; also, work in progress, discussions with authors).

We often hear that "it's only the boring jobs" which are eliminated by automation, that new office technology "will eliminate boredom and drudgery once and for all," and the new jobs will be more interesting and stimulating. These are among the most common myths about computer technology.

A recent study of Wall Street legal secretaries' jobs shows how these highly skilled and high-prestige jobs were adversely affected, leading to demoralization, job dissatisfaction, and job insecurity among the women (Mary Murphree, "Rationalization and Satisfaction in Clerical Work: A Case Study of Wall Street Legal Secretaries," Ph.D. thesis, Columbia University, 1981). Dr. Murphree found that

> while early forms of office computerization served to upgrade and assist secretarial worklives . . . current innovations are striking at the heart of the traditional legal secretarial craft and creating a number of serious problems. . . . The most challenging and responsible tasks traditionally in the legal secretarial domain are gradually being transferred away from the secretaries to *cadres* of professional and para-professional workers such as para-legal assistants, librarians, accountants, personnel specialists and word-processing proof-readers, thereby reducing the secretarial function to one of merely "telephone gatekeeper."

A 1980 study in a Swedish insurance company found that 100% of the VDT operators felt there was *no decrease* in the number of routine tasks, the mental strain, or demand for attention since the introduction of the VDTs (G. Johansson and G. Aronsson, *Stress Reactions in Computerized Administrative Work*, Stockholm, 1980). A team of researchers from the National Institute for Occupational Safety and Health (NIOSH) conducted a field study on VDT workers in 1980. They observe that: "Clerical VDT workers' jobs are akin to machine-paced assembly lines in manufacturing plants in the sense that they involve minimal control over tasks or workplace, boring, repetitive tasks, work overload, close monitoring by supervisors, and fear of being downgraded or replaced by the VDT. . . . Computerization processes designed to simplify work in order to increase 'thru-put' without concern for human elements turn such offices into clerical assembly lines akin to industrial, mechanized, paced assembly lines." (B. G. F. Cohen, M. J. Smith, and L. W. Stammerjohn, Jr., "Psychosocial Factors Contributing to Job Stress of Clerical VDT Operators," in *Machine-Pacing and Occupational Stress*, Taylor & Francis, London, 1981).

Devaluing and *undervaluing* of office work. For the majority of women office workers, office automation means working harder and faster, for more people at once, without getting paid better. Full-time VDT operators in 1979 made only $7 more a week than conventional typists, despite claims by computer vendors that productivity soars from 50% to 500% depending on the nature of the work. In the banking and insurance industries (among the most computer-intensive) wages for clericals are 8% to 19% below already low national averages by occupation, according to the U.S. Department of Labor.

Office workers also find that their new skills are undervalued and often go unrewarded. Employers underestimate the skills of experienced word-processing operators, for example. Some experts believe that word processing may provide a natural "step" to computer programming if the relationships between the different skills are understood. According to Linda Taylor, President of the Association for Women in Computing, women doing word processing "know the conventions of programming, how to communicate with and instruct a machine, how to store and retrieve data. That is only a step away from COBOL programming—and not a major step."

An article on prospects for pay equity in federal employment gives an example of how adaptation to new technology is not carefully considered in job evaluation systems. Lyne Revo-Cohen calls the case of federal word processors "a classic example of how compensation has not kept pace with new skills required to master technological changes." She writes: "When the government re-audited jobs of clericals using word-processing equipment, the job classification was lowered. Word processors were informed that because their jobs required more than 75% typing, and because the end product of their work was a typed manuscript, the job series will top out at GS 4. This, contrary to the fact that the job had become more technical, complicated, demanding and productive. The impact on morale and turnover has been highly negative and costly. Another option might have been to take the job out of the clerk-typist category, reclassify it as 'video-text operator,' and build in a broadened career ladder" (*Federal Service Labor Relations Review*, Spring 1982, forthcoming).

Increased health risks associated with work at VDTs and related especially to the organization of work in automated offices are discussed in Working Women's report, *Warning: Health Hazards for Office Workers* (Cleveland, April 1981).

Research is beginning to uncover a virtual epidemic of stress symptoms and stress-related disease among office workers. Millions of workers are affected. And the symptoms do not disappear at the end of the workday. Millions of families may also be affected by the problems caused by office job stress.

A 1979–80 study by the National Institute of Occupational Safety and Health (NIOSH) found alarming levels of stress among video display terminal operators at Blue Shield's San Francisco offices. In fact, the study found that clerical VDT operators showed higher stress ratings than any other group of workers NIOSH has ever studied, including air traffic controllers. Eighty to 90% experienced eyestrain or muscle strain. High levels of anxiety, depression, and fatigue were reported (M. J. Smith, et al., NIOSH, *Potential Health Hazards of Video Display Terminals*, Cincinnati, June 1981).

Findings from the Framingham Heart Study released in February of 1980 showed that women clerical workers developed coronary heart disease (CHD)—clearly identified as a stress-related disease—at almost twice the rate of other women workers. Women clerical workers with children and married to blue-collar husbands developed CHD at nearly twice the rate of all *men* workers (S. Haynes and M. Feinleib, *American Journal of Public Health* vol. 70, no. 2, February 1980).

Through automation, the enjoyable aspects of clerical work—variety, contact with other people, natural rest breaks and changes in routine—are threatened with elimination. The most stressful aspects—repetitive tasks, constant sitting, dead-end jobs, isolation, a relentlessly fast work pace—are on the rise.

An estimated 5 to 10 million video display terminals (VDTs) were in use in 1977. The long-term health effects of sitting before a flickering screen for eight hours a day will take years to determine. The short-term effects, however, are already clear: eyestrain, headache, back, neck, and shoulder pain, fatigue, nausea, digestive problems, short-term loss of visual clarity, and temporary changes in color perception. (See *Warning . . .* WWEF, 1981.) While some new models of VDTs are designed for better safety, they account for only a fraction of machines in use.

Many of the health problems associated with VDTs are related to psychosocial factors. In the NIOSH study, when clerical VDT operators were compared with "conventional clericals" and professionals using VDTs, the researchers found that "the pattern emerging from the results clearly indicates that the clerical VDT operators report the highest stress level, the professional operators report the least amount and the clerical workers who do not use VDTs fall in between. This suggests VDT use is not the only contributor to job-stress elevation; job content must also be a contributor" (NIOSH, 1981). There were vast differences between the VDT clericals and VDT professionals in working conditions: the degree of decision making, control over work pace and job tasks, use of skills, and satisfaction and rewards for the work done.

This finding underscores our view that it's not the technology per se which causes these problems, but rather *how* the technology is used by management, and how workers are allowed to, or forced to, use it.

4. The Danger of Runaway Offices and the Dilemma of Office Homework

The combination of telecommunications and microprocessor technologies makes it possible for office work to be geographically dispersed and reorganized as a new level of "office mobility" is achieved.

Runaway office work. We are beginning to see more movement of office jobs, particularly by the clerical-intensive finance industries. Citibank, for example, moved its credit-card operation to South Dakota because the state has no ceilings on the maximum interest rates which can be charged for credit transactions. Delaware loosened its banking laws in 1981, thus attracting credit and lending offices of ten of the nation's biggest banks (*U.S. News & World Report*, February 2, 1982). Other states (and banks) are expected to follow suit. This can trigger a competitive chain reaction similar to that which has developed over tax incentives to business in the manufacturing sector.

The *"offshore office"* provides another parallel to the experience of runaway factory jobs. A certain amount of bulk information-processing work has been performed outside of the country for some time. In the past, this work was shipped to and from offshore location by plane but can now be done via satellite by entrepeneurs like George R. Simpson of New York-based Satellite Data Corporation, recently interviewed in *Business Week* (March 15, 1982). Mr. Simpson's company relays printed materials by satellite to Barbados, where it is done by data-entry clerks earning an average hourly wage of $1.50. In Simpson's words: "We can do the work in Barbados for less than it costs in New York to pay for floor space. . . . The economics are so compelling [that a company] could take a whole building in Hartford, Connecticut, and transfer the whole function to India or Pakistan."

"*Office homework*" poses a dilemma for policies to protect workers from unfair labor practices while allowing flexibility for workers who might not otherwise be able to work. We believe there are positive and negative aspects involved in this problematic trend.

Still in a very experimental stage, it is unclear how big a trend "telecommuting" might become for clerical workers. It is certainly a possibility which should be monitored and analyzed carefully, and an area where effective public policy needs to be developed. Experts quoted in *Business Week* recently (May 3, 1982) predict that as many as 15 million workers could be earning their primary income from so-called homework by the mid-1990s.

The implications of electronic homework will be very different for workers in different positions of power and prestige. For professionals and executives, having a computer at home is highly convenient and gives greater flexibility, whereas for clericals such as data-entry workers the work will be monitored and paid under piece rates in electronic homework situations. The history of subcontracted homework for lower-level workers is one of employers taking advantage of isolated workers through decreasing piece rates, reduced benefits, and evasion of labor laws.

A thoughtful assessment of the social questions involved in the "telecommuting" trend is provided by Professor Margrethe Olson of New York University (CAIS Working Paper no. 25, NYU, 1981).

Office homework is often touted as an easy solution for the critical shortage of child care for working parents with small children. Yet Olson found increased stress among office homeworkers with families, especially women. In fact, it is not a solution to child care at all: a woman who can afford to will have a baby-sitter in the home while she is working, or will take the child to day care if available. The notion that mothers can sit at a terminal and take care of children at the same time just doesn't match what women do or want to do for their children. Yet, given the choice of no work or working at home, virtually all the women with small children in Olson's study said they would choose to keep working.

Olson found that individuals who are successful at homework tend to be withdrawn from social and community life. If one has children, the ability to "discipline" one's family is an important factor in working at home successfully. Such observations make us uneasy—we believe they only hint at larger social problems.

In 9 to 5's opinion, Olson's findings suggest that those who could benefit most—lower-income mothers of small children—are not necessarily the workers management will consider for employment first or even at all. Work in the home is clearly not the answer to the lack of child-care facilities; women still desire and need day-care centers or baby-sitters to care for children while they work, whether they are at home or in an office, and need the wages to afford to. Further, these "office homeworkers" of the future will need government protections against exploitation by unethical employers.

5. The Danger, in the Office and Service Sectors, of Decreased Productivity and Efficiency, and Declines in the Quality and Accessibility of Services for the General Public.

Studies on stress, automation, and health show that error rates increase anywhere from 40 to 400% when the control over the pace of work is taken away from workers and given over to a machine-controlled system (B. H. Beith, Department of Psychology, North Carolina State University, "Work Repetition and Pacing as a Source of Occupational Stress," presented to International Conference on Machine Pacing and Occupational Stress, NIOSH and Purdue University, March 1981). Constant computerized monitoring of individual work performance, the use of prompter devices, and automatic call distributors are creating the electronic equivalent of the moving assembly line, which some researchers believe will have worse effects on error rates and workers' well-being than the notoriously alienating industrial assembly line (S. L. Sauter, et al., "VDT-Computer Automation of Work Practices as a Stressor in Information-Processing Jobs: Some Methodological Considerations," Department of Preventive Medicine, University of Wisconsin–Madison, March 1981).

In other words, rigidly computer-controlled office work systems are counterproductive as well as harmful to one's health. A study by NIOSH finds that both job satisfaction and performance improved when operators controlled their own work pace (B. G. Cohen, NIOSH Taft Laboratories, Stress Section, presentation at the American Public Health Association Convention, Detroit, October 1980).

An office worker told Harvard Business School Professor Shoshanah Zuboff (CISR no. 71—Sloan Working Paper no. 1224–81, MIT, June 1981):

"When a person makes a mistake with a computer, to try and get it corrected is so much red tape. So you tend to let it go. Maybe when they see how bad the information is, they'll give us back our jobs."

SUMMARY

Altogether, we must face the danger that the future could be worse than the present—and that it will only be better if we make it better through conscious efforts.

We firmly believe that each of these dangers can be turned on its head and transformed into an opportunity to address problems of today's work force and the work force of tomorrow. The flexibility and versatility of computer technology makes it uniquely possible to create better jobs, better working conditions, better uses of human resources, unprecedented chances to address and reduce discrimination by designing training programs which provide for "occupational bridging," the ability to provide improved services and more widely available services, and to provide increased employment by implementing new technologies with social criteria in mind.

We believe there is a critical role for public policy, for the development of interventions which will prevent the problems posed by computer technology in the American workplace, and help release its potential benefits for all office workers. 9 to 5's recommendations represent first steps in this process (see attached *Recommendations*).

Action by the Congress is urgently needed for several reasons: (1) Employers do not willingly take actions needed to protect office workers' jobs, health, or well-being; (2) More than 90% of all U.S. private-sector women clerical workers, and more than 80% of public-sector clericals, lack union representation and therefore do not have access to collective bargaining as an avenue to improve working conditions and challenge unfair management practices; and (3) Office automation is being introduced so rapidly that action must be taken *now* before irreparable harm is done to office workers' jobs, health, and quality of working life.

We must recognize the magnitude and urgency of the dangers we face. Computer consultants predict that in two to five years we may have a "frozen technology"—adverse effects will be frozen into place.

We as a society are in a critical era in the 1980s to influence office automation while the technology is still in flux. We are in a race against time to avoid these dangers, and the clock is ticking.

Thank you very much.

RECOMMENDATIONS FOR ACTION ON OFFICE TECHNOLOGY
9 TO 5, NATIONAL ASSOCIATION OF WORKING WOMEN

1. *Ensure all U.S. workers certain basic rights in relation to new technologies,* to include:

- *The right to advance information* about plans for new computer systems before decisions are made
- *The right to relevant training and education* during working hours, with employers providing "release time" with pay
- *The right to participate in systems design,* and the right to funding support to choose technical consultants of their own
- *The right to have "technology representatives,"* chosen by workers, who receive special training needed to represent workers' interests and concerns about new systems
- *A protected right to refuse to work with new computer-based systems if they have not been consulted,* if workers' concerns have not been met, and if employers are abusing new technology in ways which devalue, deskill, or degrade jobs, adversely affect health, or otherwise undermine working conditions

2. *Act to protect the occupational health and well-being of office workers* by adopting proposed Norwegian regulations limiting work at video display terminals (VDTs) to 50 percent of the working day, in order to promote good job design.

3. *Adopt the following measures for all public-sector clerical workers using VDTs (CRTs), to serve as a model for private-sector employers:*

- the proposed Norwegian regulations on work organization in VDT work
- the National Institute for Occupational Safety and Health (NIOSH) general recommendations to reduce potential health risks of VDT work, including provisions for rest breaks (15 minutes per 2 hours of

moderately demanding VDT work; 15 minutes per hour of visually intense, high workload and/or highly repetitive VDT work)
· guidelines for VDT machine design features, adopted by the state of Wisconsin for purchase bids of new equipment

4. *Restrict computerized monitoring of individual work performance, or other methods of computer-controlled pacing and measurement of work, as an invasion of workers' right to privacy.*

5. *Provide funding support for training initiatives on new technology, targeting funds for programs which will benefit those most in need,* such as:

· Women and minority workers
· Older displaced workers and re-entry workers
· Unemployed youth
· The technologically unemployed

Funds should be targeted for industries where computer technology is being introduced rapidly.

6. *Conduct studies to assess the impact of computer technology in key industries such as insurance and banking* with special attention to such issues as:

· The effects of automation on pay scale, job descriptions, and promotional opportunities for women and minority workers already concentrated at the low end of the pay scale
· Particular impacts on long-term and older employees
· Impact on turnover rates
· Impact on incidence of involuntary part-time, shiftwork, and piece-rate work
· Potential employment displacement effects
· Effects of centralization, monitoring, and machine-pacing of work

7. *Conduct a study to assess the practices and responsibilities of the computer industry.*

8. *Review the state educational system*, its programs and capabilities, in light of the impacts of computer technology.

9. *Survey labor organizations to identify problems of their members, their concerns, and suggestions for solutions to problems of new technology.*

MODEL
CONTRACT LANGUAGE

If you are in a union, you may develop specific contract language covering office health and safety. Of particular importance is language establishing a joint labor-management health and safety committee that meets regularly to resolve problems. The following language is adapted from the British Columbia Government Employees Union contract. It illustrates the range of provisions you may want to bargain for.

I. JOINT OCCUPATIONAL HEALTH AND SAFETY COMMITTEES
The Parties agree that the intent of this agreement is to ensure that all employees shall have the maximum possible access to the Committee.
  (a) The Committee will:
     (1) Have Union representatives that are employees at the workplace appointed by the Union, and Employer representatives shall be appointed by the Employer.
     (2) Participate in developing a program to reduce risk of occupational injury and illness. All minutes of the meetings of the commit-

tees shall be recorded on a mutually agreed-to form and shall be sent to the Union and the Employer.

(3) Monitor and assess results of ongoing health and safety training programs agreed to by the principals. (These training programs will inform members of Occupational Health and Safety Committees about the objectives and duties of such committees.)

(4) Review reports on office health and safety and make recommendations to the principals regarding occupational health and safety matters.

(b) Employees who are representatives of the committee shall not suffer any loss of basic pay for the time spent attending a Committee meeting.

(c) Committee meetings shall be scheduled during normal working hours whenever practicable. Time spent by designated Committee members attendings meetings held on their days of rest or outside their regularly scheduled hours of work shall not be considered time worked, but such Committee members shall receive equivalent time off at straight time.

2. POLLUTION CONTROL

The Employer and the Union agree to limit all forms of environmental pollution.

3. INVESTIGATION OF ACCIDENTS

(a) All accidents shall be investigated jointly by at least one (1) representative designated by the Union and one (1) management representative.

4. EMPLOYEE FITNESS

The Union and the Employer acknowledge that a program of employee physical fitness is a positive contribution to the health of the employees. The parties therefore agree to establish a joint committee to investigate the feasibility of expanding the fitness program.

5. VIDEO DISPLAY TERMINALS

When employees are required to monitor video display terminals that use cathode ray tubes, then:

(a) When a majority of an employee's daily work time requires monitoring such video display terminals, such employees shall have their eyes examined by an ophthalmologist of the employee's choice at the nearest community where medical facilities are available prior to initial assignment to VDT equipment and after six (6) months, a further test and annually thereafter if requested. The examination shall be at the Employer's expense where costs are not covered by insurance. Where requested, the Employer shall grant leave of absence with pay.

(b) Employees who are required to operate VDTs on a continuous basis shall be entitled to two (2) additional ten (10) minute rest breaks per workday to be scheduled by agreement at the local level.

(c)

(1) Pregnant employees shall have the option not to continue monitoring video display terminals that use cathode ray tubes.

(2) When a pregnant employee chooses not to monitor such video display terminals, if other work at the same or lower level is available within the office, she shall be reassigned to such work and paid at her regular rate of pay.

(3) Where work reassignment in (2) above is not available, a pregnant regular employee may choose to go on leave of absence without pay until she qualifies for maternity leave.

(d) The Employer shall ensure that new equipment shall:

(1) Have adjustable keyboards and screens.

(2) Meet established radiation emission standards.

The Permanent Joint Occupational Health and Safety Committee shall review and make recommendations to ensure that the lighting and equipment meet recommended standards.

6. TECHNOLOGICAL CHANGE

The procedures to be followed by the Employer and the Union concerning technological change shall include worker retraining and job security.

7. CONTRACTING OUT

The Employer agrees not to contract out any work presently performed by employees covered by this Agreement which would result in the laying off of such employees.

BIBLIOGRAPHY ON OCCUPATIONAL HEALTH AND OFFICE SAFETY HAZARDS

These references will help you explore topics of particular interest to you. Although this is not a comprehensive listing of all publications in each area, the books and articles themselves will provide you with further references to technical materials. The organizations listed in appendix B can also help you locate information on specific subjects.

I. GENERAL INFORMATION

Ashford, Nicholas. *Crisis in the Workplace: Occupational Disease and Injury.* Cambridge, Mass.: MIT Press, 1976.

Berman, Daniel. *Death on the Job.* New York: Monthly Review Press, 1978.

Craig, Marianne. *Office Workers' Survival Handbook.* London: British Society for Social Responsibility in Science, 1981.

Hricko, Andrea, with Melanie Brunt. *Working for Your Life: A Woman's Guide to Job Health Hazards.* Berkeley, Calif.: Labor Occupational Health Program/Health Research Group, 1977.

Makower, Joel. *Office Hazards and New Technology: How Your Job Can Make You Sick.* Washington, D.C.: Tilden Press, 1981.

National Institute for Occupational Safety and Health. *The Industrial Environment—Its Evaluation and Control.* Washington, D.C.: U.S. Department of Health, Education, and Welfare, 1973.

9 to 5, National Association of Working Women. *Health Hazards to Office Workers: An Overview of Problems and Solutions in Occupational Health in the Office.* Cleveland, Ohio: Working Women Education Fund, 1981.

Page, J., and Mary-Win O'Brien. *Bitter Wages: The Ralph Nader Study Group on Occupational Accidents and Disease.* New York: Grossman Publishers, 1973.

Stellman, Jeanne. *Women's Work, Women's Health: Myths and Realities.* New York: Pantheon Books, 1977.

Stellman, Jeanne, and Susan Daum. *Work Is Dangerous to Your Health.* New York: Vintage Books, 1973.

Women's Occupational Health Resource Center News. A bimonthly newsletter available from WOHRC, Columbia University, School of Public Health, 21 Audubon Avenue, New York, N.Y. 10032

II. THE BIOLOGY OF OFFICE WORK

A. General

Adams, Robert M. *Occupational Contact Dermatitis,* Philadelphia: J. B. Lippincott Co., 1969.

Doull, John, Curtis Klaassen, and Mary Amdur, eds. *Casarett and Doull's Toxicology.* New York: Macmillan Publishing Co., 1980.

Proctor, Nick H., and James P. Hughes. *Chemical Hazards of the Workplace.* Philadelphia: J. B. Lippincott Co., 1978.

Zenz, Carl, ed. *Occupational Medicine.* Chicago: Yearbook Medical Publishers, 1975.

B. Biomechanical

Calliet, René. *Low Back Pain Syndrome.* 2nd ed. Philadelphia: F. A. Davis Co., 1978.

Calliet, René. *Neck and Arm Pain.* Philadelphia: F. A. Davis Co., 1981.

National Institute for Occupational Safety and Health. *A Guide to the Work-Relatedness of Disease.* DHHS–NIOSH Publication no. 79–116. Washington, D.C.: U.S. Department of Health and Human Services, 1980.

Tischauer, Erwin. *The Biomechanical Basis of Ergonomics: Anatomy Applied to the Design of Work Situations.* New York: John Wiley & Sons, 1978.

C. Stress

Beehr, T. A., and J. E. Newman. "Job Stress, Employee Health, and Organizational Effectiveness: A Facet Analysis, Model and Literature Review," *Personnel Psychology*, 31 (1978): 665–699.

Caplan, R. D., et al. *Job Demands and Worker Health.* DHEW–NIOSH Publication no. 75–170. Washington, D.C.: U.S. Department of Health, Education, and Welfare, 1975.

Cooper, C. L., and J. Marshall, "Occupational Sources of Stress: A Review of the Literature Relating to Coronary Heart Disease and Mental Ill Health. *Journal of Occupational Psychology* 49 (1976): 11–28.

Garfield, J. "Alienated Labor, Stress, and Coronary Disease." *International Journal of Health Services* 10 (1980): 551–561.

Haynes, S. G., and M. Feinleib. "Women, Work, and Coronary Heart Disease: Prospective Findings from the Framingham Heart Study." *American Journal of Public Health* 70 (1980): 133–141.

"Job Stress: Causes and Solutions." *Occupational Health and Safety,* April 1979, pp. 46–47.

Newman, J. E., and T. A. Beehr. "Personal and Organizational Strategies for Handling Job Stress: A Review of Research and Opinion." *Personnel Psychology* 31 (1979): 1–43.

III. VIDEO DISPLAY TERMINALS

Bureau of Radiological Health, Food and Drug Administration. *An Evaluation of Radiation Emission from Video Display Terminals.* DHHS-FDA Publication no. 81-8153. Rockville, Md.: U.S. Department of Health and Human Services, February 1981.

Cakir, A., D. K. Hart, and T. F. M. Stewart. *The VDT Manual.* New York: John Wiley & Sons, 1979.

Chamot, Dennis, and Michael D. Dymnel. *Cooperation or Conflict: European Experiences with Technological Change at the Workplace.* Washington, D.C.: Department for Professional Employees, AFL-CIO, 1982.

DeMatteo, R. *Hazards of VDTs.* Toronto: Ontario Public Service Employees Union, 1982.

Grandjean, E., and E. Vigliani. *Ergonomic Aspects of Visual Display Terminals.* London: Taylor & Francis, 1981.

Health and Safety Contract Language for Operators of VDTs/CRTs. Boston, Mass.: MassCOSH (120 Boylston St., Rm. 206, 02116), 1982.

Matula, R. "Effects of Visual Display Units on the Eyes: A Bibliography (1972–1980)." *Human Factors* 23 (1981): 581–586.

Murray, W. E., et al. *Potential Health Hazards of Video Display Terminals.* DHHS–NIOSH Publication no. 81–129. Washington, D.C.: U.S. Department of Health and Human Services, 1981.

9 to 5, National Association of Working Women. *The Human Factor: 9 to 5's Consumer Guide to Word Processors.* Cleveland, Ohio: Working Women Education Fund, 1982.

9 to 5, National Association of Working Women. *Race Against Time: Automation of the Office.* Cleveland, Ohio: Working Women Education Fund, 1980.

Scientific American, vol. 247, no. 3 (September 1982). Special issue on the mechanization of work.

The VDT Newsletter. Labour Council of Metropolitan Toronto, Rm. 407, 15 Gervais Drive, Don Mills, Ontario.

The VDT Workplace Manual. Washington, D.C.: The Newspaper Guild (Research Department, 1125 15th St. NW, Rm. 835, 20005), 1982.

IV. FURNITURE AND OFFICE EQUIPMENT

Allen, David G., et al. "Keyboard Design and Operation: A Review of the Major Issues." *Human Factors* 14, no. 4 (1972): 273–293.

Duncan, Joan, and D. Ferguson. "Keyboard Operating Posture and Symptoms in Operating." *Ergonomics* 17, no. 5 (1974): 651–662.

Ferguson, D., and Joan Duncan. "Keyboard Design and Operating Posture." *Ergonomics* 17, no. 6 (1974): 631–674.

Grandjean, E. *Fitting the Task to the Man.* London: Taylor & Francis, 1969.

MacLeod, Dan. *Strains and Sprains: A Workers Guide to Job Design.* Detroit: United Automobile Workers Health and Safety Department (8000 E. Jefferson, 48214), 1982.

Tischauer, E. *The Biomechanical Basis of Ergonomics: Anatomy Applied to the Design of Work Situations.* New York: John Wiley & Sons, 1978.

V. LIGHTING

General Electric Corporation. *Office Lighting.* Nela Park, Cleveland, Ohio, 1976.

Illuminating Engineering Society. *Illuminating Engineering Society Lighting Handbook: 1981 Reference Volume and 1981 Application Volume.* New York, 1981.

Jensen, J. "Planning for Safe Workplace Lighting." *Occupational Health and Safety,* October 1979, pp. 50–53.

Lighting Design and Application Journal, January 1979. Issue on task/ambient lighting. Published by Illuminating Engineering Society, New York.

VI. FIRE, OFFICE ENVIRONMENTS, AND ARCHITECTURE

American Conference of Governmental Industrial Hygienists, Committee on Industrial Ventilation. *Industrial Ventilation: A Manual of Recommended Practice.* 12th ed. Lansing, Mich., 1972.

American Society of Heating, Refrigeration, and Air Conditioning Engineers. *ASHRAE Handbook: Fundamentals.* New York, 1977.

Dalmer, Alvin E., and Susan M. Lewis. *Planning the Office Landscape.* New York: McGraw-Hill Book Co., 1977.

Harris, David, et al. *Planning and Designing the Office Environment.* New York: Van Nostrand Reinhold Co., 1981.

Howell, R. H., and H. J. Saver. *Environmental Control Principles: An Educational Supplement to*

ASHRAE Handbook 1977 Fundamentals. New York: ASHRAE, 1977.

Kramer, Sieverts, and Partners. *Open Plan Offices.* Maidenhead, England: McGraw-Hill Book Co. (UK), 1975.

National Fire Protection Association. *Fire Protection Handbook,* 14th ed. Boston, Mass., 1976.

Occupational Safety and Health Administration. *Noise Control: A Guide for Workers and Employers.* Washington, D.C.: U.S. Department of Labor, 1980.

Pike, John. *Open Office Planning.* New York: Watson-Guptil Publications, 1978.

Sommer, Robert. *Tight Spaces: Hard Architecture and How to Humanize It.* Englewood Cliffs, N.J.: Prentice-Hall, 1974.

VII. INDOOR AIR POLLUTION

Annals of the New York Academy of Sciences, vol. 353, 1980. Special issue on airborne contagion.

Arnow, Paul M., et al. "Early Detection of Hypersensitivity Pneumonitis in Office Workers." *American Journal of Medicine* 64 (1978): 236–242.

Bulletin of the New York Academy of Medicine, vol. 57, no. 10, 1981. Special issue on health aspects of indoor air pollution.

Indoor Pollutants. Washington, D.C.: National Academy of Sciences, 1981.

Indoor Air Pollution: An Emerging Problem. Publication no. CED-80–III. Washington, D.C.: U.S. General Accounting Office, September 24, 1980.

Repace, James L., and Alfred H. Lowry. "Indoor Air Pollution, Tobacco Smoke, and Public Health." *Science* 208 (1980): 464–472.

INDEX

anti-inflammatory drugs, 17
appetite, loss of, 39
aquatic nematodes, 151
arbitrary zero, 120
arms, movement of, 15–16
Aronsson, G., 212
arthritis, 128
Arthur D. Little Corporation, 41
artificial light, 46, 91, 93
asbestos, 6, 30, 108, 158
    cancer and, 104, 141, 143
    as insulation, 141–44
asbestosis, 141, 142
A-scale readings, 121
ASHRAE (American Society of
    Heating, Refrigeration, and Air
    Conditioning Engineers), 9
Association of Scientific, Techni-
    cal and Managerial Staffs
    (ASTMS), 69
asthma, 79
astigmatism, 46
ASTMS (Association of Scientific,
    Technical and Managerial
    Staffs), 69
atopic individuals, 30, 31
automation, of offices, 11–12, 67–
    70, 167–68, 203, 206, 207, 217
autonomic nervous system, 14, 39

back injuries, 20–23, 37, 42, 48,
    73
backrests, 73, 75
baffles, 92
ballast hum, 95–96
banking, employment in, 206
Basic Building Code, 116, 129
Beith, B. H., 217
benzo(a)pyrene, 145
bifocal glasses, 47–48
Binghamton, N.Y., transformer
    explosion at, 104–5
birth defects, 43, 104
    radiation exposure and, 54, 55,
    57, 63, 66
bladder infections, 75
"blind spots," 86
blood pressure, 37, 40, 118, 137
blue-collar workers, 1, 6, 8, 67–70,
    137, 140, 207
blueprint machines, 84, 134
BOCA (Building Officials and
    Code Administrators Interna-
    tional), 116, 129

bones, injuries to, 15–20
brain, function of, 24, 38, 39
broadcasting towers, 156
bronchi, 27
bronchioles, 27
bronchitis, 28, 29, 146
Brookes, Malcolm, 117, 118
building codes, 91, 106, 116, 129
    for fire safety, 98–99, 108–10
Building Officials and Code Ad-
    ministrators   International
    (BOCA), 116, 129
"bullpen" office design, 115
Bureau of Labor Statistics, 208
Bureau of Radiological Health, 57
Bürolandschaft, 113
Business Week, 207, 215, 216
"buttoning up" of buildings, 140

cadmium, 83
cafeterias, 136
California, occupational studies in,
    1, 15
call-forwarding systems, 125
cancer:
    asbestos and, 104, 141, 143
    as chronic disease, 5–6, 7, 12,
    14, 86
    lung, 5–6, 143, 155
    possible causes of, 79, 80, 81–
    82, 85, 87, 94, 145, 152,
    155
    radiation and, 55, 57, 94
carbon black powder, 81–82
carbon dioxide, 108, 140, 158
carbonless copy paper, 85, 87
carbon monoxide, 101, 104, 140,
    157, 158, 159
Carey, Max L., 4
carpal tunnel, 17
casters, on chairs, 73–74
cataracts, 24, 27, 54
cathode ray tubes (CRTs), 41, 44,
    57
Center for Disease Control (CDC),
    U.S., 150, 165
chairs:
    casters on, 73–74
    design of, 7, 71–75
    height of, 22, 72, 74, 76
"cheaters," electrical safety and, 84
cheese washers' disease, 30
Chemical Institute of Toxicology,
    145

About the Authors

Jeanne Stellman, the author of *Work Is Dangerous to Your Health* (with Susan M. Daum, M.D.) and *Women's Work, Women's Health,* has a Ph.D. in physical chemistry and is an associate professor at Columbia University. She is also the founder and executive director of the Women's Occupational Health Resource Center at Columbia.

Mary Sue Henifin, a graduate of Harvard and Columbia with an M.P.H. in environmental science, is the editor of both *Women Look at Biology Looking at Women* and *Biological Woman: The Convenient Myth* and is also the author of numerous articles on occupational health.